THE LETTERS OF WILLIAM BLAKE

The LETTERS of
WILLIAM BLAKE

EDITED BY

Geoffrey Keynes

W. Blake

HARVARD UNIVERSITY PRESS

Cambridge, Massachusetts

1968

CONTENTS

LIST OF ILLUSTRATIONS

7

LIST OF LETTERS AND OTHER DOCUMENTS

The documents are arranged chronologically, so that page references are not given

LETTERS FROM BLAKE

9

To Hayley, William (*contd.*)
27 November 1805
11 December 1805

To Humphry, Ozias
18 January 1808 (two
drafts)
18 February 1808 (third
draft)
[1809]

To Linnell, John
11 October 1819
Wednesday [1825]
10 November 1825
1 February 1826
[? 1826]
31 March 1826
19 May 1826
2 July 1826
5 July 1826
14 July 1826
16 July 1826
29 July 1826
1 August 1826
27 January 1827

February 1827
[? February 1827]
15 March 1827
[1827]
25 April 1827
3 July 1827

To Linnell, Mrs.
11 October 1825
[? February] 1826

To Phillips, Richard
June 1806
14 October 1807

To Reveley, Willey
October 1791

To Trusler, Rev. John
16 August 1799
23 August 1799

To Turner, Dawson
9 June 1818

To Wedgwood, Josiah
8 September 1815

LETTERS TO BLAKE
From Butts, Thomas September 1800

From Cromek, R. H.
May 1807

From Cumberland, George
18 December 1808

From Flaxman, John
7 October 1801

From Hayley, William
17 April 1800
July 1800

From Reveley, Willey
October 1791

From Wedgwood, Josiah
29 July 1815

ACCOUNTS AND RECEIPTS

To Aders, Mrs.
29 July 1826

To Butts, Thomas
8 July–20 August 1803
22 January 1805
12 May–25 December 1805

5 July 1805
7 September 1805
3 March 1806
30 June 1806
9 September 1806
15 October 1806
29 January 1807

DOCUMENTS RELATING TO THE TRIAL FOR SEDITION

INDEX TO THE SONGS OF INNOCENCE & OF EXPERIENCE

DOCUMENTS RELATING TO THE ILLUSTRATIONS OF THE BOOK OF JOB

LETTER FROM RICHMOND TO PALMER

PREFACE

The Letters of William Blake were first collected by the late A. G. B.
Russell and published, together with Frederick Tatham's memoir of
Blake, in 1906. Further letters were printed in various contexts after
that date, but no separate edition was attempted until 1956, when
the present collection, now amplified, was first published. I had felt
for a long time that a new edition was called for, and first announced
my intention of editing this at the end of my *Blake Studies* published
in 1949. The book was delayed until 1956 because a number of
Blake's letters were still missing in spite of prolonged efforts to locate
them. A small number have come to light since that time and can
now be incorporated in the collection, the first edition being out of
print.

THE MISSING LETTERS

Nearly all the missing letters were addressed to William Hayley
and were among thirty-five dispersed in an auction sale at Sotheby's
in 1878, fetching no more than three or four pounds each. Eleven
were bought by Bernard Quaritch, who disposed of them soon afterwards to Alexander Macmillan, an eager Blake collector and the
publisher of Gilchrist's *Life*. Others were acquired by Frederick
Locker-Lampson for the Rowfant Library. Most of the letters sold in
1878 were seen by Mrs. Gilchrist, and she incorporated a selection
of them in the second edition of her husband's *Life*, but nearly half
the original documents have been lost to sight. Of the eleven
acquired by Macmillan ten are missing. Present members of the
Macmillan family have kindly answered my enquiries, but no clue
as to the fate of these letters since 1880 has been found. Enquiries
addressed to a large number of libraries and other institutions in the
United States have uncovered a few missing documents, and five
which were in the Rowfant Library were acquired by Harvard
University for the Houghton Library in 1953, but altogether fifteen
letters have still not been recovered and five of these have never been
printed at all except for brief extracts. Slight consolation for the
partial failure of my search may be drawn from the fact that some
of the unprinted letters must have been considered by Mrs. Gilchrist
and so are unlikely to include any of great importance. Even the
text, however, of the ten letters known only from the edition of 1880

cannot be relied upon for accuracy, since Mrs. Gilchrist's transcriptions do not conform to the standard of accuracy demanded by modern scholarship.[1]

THE TEXT OF THE LETTERS

With these exceptions all the letters from Blake known to have survived in their original form have been newly transcribed for this edition, either from the actual documents or from photostatic reproductions, and it is believed that texts as accurate as is humanly possible are now presented. Blake usually wrote a good and legible hand, and his peculiarities of spelling and use of capitals have been preserved. Although it is not always possible to be quite certain of his intention, his use of capitals was, in general, so free that, when there is doubt, a capital is more likely to have been intended than not. The habit is, moreover, so characteristic, both in manuscripts and in printed texts, that it is undoubtedly right to preserve them whenever possible. In 1906 Russell did not think so; he usually ignored this peculiarity, and corrected Blake's consistently eccentric spelling of certain words. Blake did not observe the usual custom of writing "i before e except after c", and very frequently omitted the final "e" in past participles. More often than not he used an ampersand. These and other minor oddities have been reproduced in this edition, though I have followed Russell in supplying punctuation where it seems to help the sense, even though Blake so frequently omitted it. To humour him in this respect seemed to place an unnecessary obstacle in the way of his readers, in spite of his insistence on the importance of "minute particulars" in art, if not in letters.

The printing of a separate edition of an author's letters gives a great advantage over their inclusion only in collected writings—the opportunity it affords of adding letters addressed to him, as well as other documents which are not strictly speaking letters and so would not usually find a place among them. Not many letters from Blake's correspondents have survived, but all that can be found have been included here. More numerous are the extraneous documents, such as Blake's accounts with Thomas Butts, his receipts for payments made by Butts and other patrons, documents connected with the trial for sedition in 1804, his manuscript index for the *Songs of Innocence and of Experience*, agreements and accounts kept by John

---

[1] *Five letters still unprinted:* 18 Feb. 1800; 19 Sept. 1803; 7 Aug. 1804; 9 Aug. 1804; 17 May 1805. *Ten letters known only in the Gilchrist text:* 26 Nov. 1800; 26 Oct. 1803; 2 April 1804; 4 May 1804; 28 May 1804; 23 Oct. 1804; 18 Dec. 1804; 22 Jan. 1805; 4 June 1805; with one to Flaxman,? 1800. Letters not checked from the original documents are here marked by an asterisk.

Linnell in connexion with the engraving and marketing of the *Illustrations of the Book of Job*, and finally a letter written by George Richmond to Samuel Palmer about Blake's last hours. All these shed light on Blake's life and activities and are not easily available anywhere else, so that no apology is needed for their inclusion.

A separate edition of letters can easily be overweighted with annotations, but it is hoped that the footnotes in this volume will not incur this charge. Some lightening of the burden has been achieved by adding an appendix in the form of a Register of Documents, where information is given concerning their physical form, their history and provenance, and the source of the text as printed.

BLAKE'S CORRESPONDENTS

Blake's friendship must unquestionably have been a precious possession, but his feelings were hypersensitive when they touched his integrity as an artist, and he was too ready in consequence to take offence. Friendship was thus easily upset, and it may well be that some of his correspondents, who had started by keeping his letters, ended by destroying them when relations became clouded by disagreements. This may possibly explain the absence of letters to so close a friend as Thomas Stothard, draughtsman and book illustrator, who had known Blake from his boyhood; to Joseph Johnson, the bookseller and publisher, who employed Blake as book illustrator over many years; and to Henry Fuseli, Blake's fellow-artist and admirer. We know from some of the letters that have been preserved how intimate and self-revealing Blake could be when writing to a friend of whose affection and understanding he felt secure. The best of Blake's letters are, indeed, among the most beautiful things he ever penned and could take an honoured place in any anthology of letters by men of genius.

The one friend who retained Blake's affection unclouded over more than thirty years was George Cumberland, with whose name the series of letters printed here both begins and ends. Cumberland, born three years before Blake, belonged to a middle-class family, whose chief distinction was the production of Richard Cumberland, the dramatist, a cousin of George. Richard Denison Cumberland, George's elder brother, took holy orders not long before George obtained employment in the office of the Royal Exchange Assurance Company in 1775. It is not known when George Cumberland and Blake first met; Blake's first extant letter to him, dated 1795, suggests that they had been friends for some time before this, and evidence contained in Blake's satire known as *An Island in the Moon*, probably written about 1787, indicates that they were then already

15

acquainted. It is even possible that the first suggestion of Blake's method of copper-plate etching for his Illuminated Books came from Cumberland. In 1795 Cumberland was living near Egham in Surrey. He was much interested in science and the arts, and, with Blake's help, himself dabbled in drawing, etching and engraving. At a later date he was concerned in the project for the foundation of the National Gallery. He bought copies of the Illuminated Books and in 1827 tried to interest his friends in Bristol, where he was then living, in the *Illustrations of the Book of Job*. Blake's last engraved plate, done shortly before his death, was for a small card bearing Cumberland's name surrounded by a delicate allegorical design. A print from this plate was inserted by Cumberland in a scrap-book[1] containing a series of prints from his own plates. One of these is a poem etched on metal; this may be a relic of his early interest in the method of "writing on copper", which he described in a letter to Maty's *New Review* in 1784.

Blake owed to Cumberland an introduction to another early correspondent, the Rev. Dr. Trusler (1735–1820), who also lived near Egham at Englefield Green. This attempt to help Blake proved abortive, but it stimulated him to write two admirable and provocative letters, which Dr. Trusler must have passed on to Cumberland, since they have been preserved among the Cumberland papers in the British Museum. Trusler was an eccentric clergyman who studied medicine under John Hunter, established a business as a bookseller with the object of abolishing publishers, and cultivated art. He is best known as the compiler of *Hogarth Moralized* (1768), but was also author of numerous other writings, such as *The Way to be Rich and Respectable* and *A Sure Way to Lengthen Life*. Trusler's mind was wholly antipathetic to Blake's, and they could never have come to terms. His unpublished memoirs are in the Municipal Library at Bath, but the Deputy Librarian informs me that they contain no reference to Blake.

John Flaxman (1755–1826), well known as a sculptor and author of several series of outline drawings illustrating the works of Homer, Aeschylus, Hesiod and Dante, was introduced to Blake by Stothard and became a close friend. Their relations were strained for a time, when Blake suspected him of professional jealousy, but there is no doubt that he was a sincere admirer of Blake, and did all that he could to help him professionally on many occasions. It was Flaxman who brought about contact between Blake and Hayley and so was responsible for one of the most important events in Blake's life—his transference for three years to Felpham on the coast of Sussex.

William Hayley (1745–1820), esteemed by some of his contem-

[1] Now in my collection.

II. MALEVOLENCE

water colour 1799

poraries as "a true poet", survives in our minds today solely as the friend and well-meaning patron of Blake. His character and feeble achievements have been recorded in every book on Blake, but only in Morchard Bishop's *Blake's Hayley* (1951) does the quality of this remarkable but unhappy man really emerge. Though sentimental, vain, and often silly, he possessed a streak of nobility shown by his extraordinary generosity to his friends. He intended nothing but good toward Blake, but his insensitive patronage so offended Blake's self-respect that an explosion was inevitable. Blake left Felpham in 1803 with immense relief and still full of resentment, but the help given by Hayley at the trial for sedition at Chichester assizes in 1804 quite softened his heart and changed his feelings to an overpowering gratitude. For the next two years, as his letters testify, no trouble was too great for him to undertake in helping Hayley with his *Life of Romney*, and his expressions of solicitude for Hayley's welfare and for that of his friend, Miss Harriet Poole, are obviously genuine. The missing letters, already mentioned, would have filled in further details of Blake's efforts to make amends for his ill-temper and their loss is the more to be regretted. It was certainly Hayley who briefed and paid a young barrister, Samuel Rose, to defend Blake at the trial. Rose, whose speech in court is printed here, was related to Cowper's nephew, John Johnson of Norfolk, and some record of his affairs is preserved in the Johnson family papers. Miss Barham Johnson, who is engaged on a study of her ancestor, tells me that Rose, although connected with the law, was somewhat unreliable in money matters, though his lapses were perhaps due to serious ill health, for he died of tuberculosis in December 1804, eleven months after the trial.

Thomas Butts (d. 1845), another friend whose relations with Blake remained untroubled over a long period, had first met Blake about 1793, through what connexions is not known. He was so consistent a buyer of Blake's works that he was referred to as "my employer", and the Butts collection became so large that it was, throughout the nineteenth century, the chief repository of Blake's artistic output. To Butts Blake was always able to open his heart, and it was Butts's regular payments, as will be seen from the accounts and receipts printed here, that kept the wolf from his door. Butts lived in Fitzroy Square, near enough to Blake for him sometimes to take his payment in the form of coals, and he even sought to increase Blake's income by engaging him to instruct himself and his son, young Tommy, in drawing and engraving. Both Blake and posterity owe a debt to Thomas Butts which cannot be computed, though the only letter from Butts to Blake which has been preserved suggests that Butts was a dumb admirer of genius, which he could

17

see but did not quite understand. Butts has often been referred to as "Muster-master General", and indeed his family seems to have led Gilchrist to believe that he enjoyed this title, but Professor G. E. Bentley jr. has found by reading the Muster-master General's papers in the Public Record Office that he was no more than chief clerk in the office and wrote the letters concerned with the enlistment of soldiers, sharing this work with his two sons. His salary for this employment was very modest and it is difficult to see how he could afford the generous patronage he gave to Blake unless he had other sources of income. He did, in fact, die a wealthy man and it seems probable that he was a judicious investor in commodities and real estate.[1]

John Linnell (1792–1882), the friend and benefactor of Blake's later years, first visited him in 1818 in the company of George Cumberland junior, whose father was then living in Bristol. Although Linnell was himself only a young and struggling painter, ne encouraged Blake with an understanding solicitude, and ensured that he did not suffer want during the last nine years of his life by setting him to work on his two greatest achievements—the *Illustrations to the Book of Job* and to Dante's *Divine Comedy*.

Blake's letters to Linnell do not rise to the poetic heights of some of those to Butts; they illustrate rather the day-to-day dealings of an older man with a young, but tactful, admirer. Linnell's generosity and foresight are too well known to need further emphasis.

Blake's remaining letters were addressed to casual correspondents. These were Willey Reveley, for whom Blake made some engravings in 1791; James Blake, his elder brother, who kept a hosier's shop; Sir Richard Phillips (1767–1840), publisher, and editor of *The Monthly Magazine*; Ozias Humphry (1742–1810), miniaturist, for whom he described in three versions, now first recorded and accurately transcribed, his painting of "The Last Judgment"; Josiah Wedgwood the younger (1769–1843), for whom he engraved plates for a catalogue of pottery; Maria Denman, sister of Mrs. Flaxman; Dawson Turner (1775–1858) of Yarmouth, banker, botanist, and antiquary, whose momentary interest in Blake had been aroused by Humphry; and lastly Mrs. Charles Aders, hostess to artists and men of letters.

SPURIOUS BLAKE LETTERS

My first enquiries for Blake's letters made many years ago at the Wedgwood Museum attached to the Etruria works in Staffordshire were greeted with the reply that the firm possessed a number.

[1] See Bentley's article, "Thomas Butts, White Collar Maecenas" *Publ. Mod. Langu. Assoc. of Amer.* (1956), LXXI, 1052–1066.

Unfortunately only one of these proved on examination to have been written by the Blake in whom I was interested. All the others were from the pen of a namesake whose writing and signature closely resembled those of his more famous contemporary. This William Blake is probably to be identified with the attorney whose name misled Miss Ruth Lowery into believing that the other Blake had at one time been indebted to Flaxman to the tune of £100.[1] A number of other irrelevant documents have come at various times into the American auction rooms with attributions to Blake, sometimes on the strength only of the initials W. B. There was even another engraver, once employed by Cumberland, who bore the same name,[2] and it is necessary to exercise some caution in accepting any newly discovered document as coming from the pen of the artist.

THE ILLUSTRATIONS

Any book concerning Blake lends itself particularly well to illustration owing to the wealth of material available. Considerations of expense, however, set a limit to the number that can be included, and the thirteen in this volume have therefore been chosen primarily for their close relation to the text.

The frontispiece is a little-known portrait of Blake in his old age painted on ivory by John Linnell. Although it was copied as an engraving by Jeens for Gilchrist's *Life of Blake*, 1863 and 1880, it may still be regarded as little-known, the copy being so unlike the original. It is a delicate and attractive miniature in pale colours and is a much more convincing image of Blake than Jeens's version. It is reproduced by permission of the Syndics of the Fitzwilliam Museum, Cambridge.

A later portrait of Blake is reproduced from a drawing in my collection made for Schiavonetti's etching used as frontispiece for Blair's *Grave*, 1808. The drawing, done by pen and tinted with water colours, was presumably made by the engraver himself from the portrait by Thomas Phillips now in the National Portrait Gallery. This has not been reproduced before.

Blake's two letters to the Reverend Dr. Trusler are concerned with his failure to meet his customer's views on the composition of pictures. It seems that Blake was required to produce a series of "Moral Paintings", but his first attempt, representing "Malevolence", did not meet with approval. Blake defended his ideas with some asperity, and told Cumberland that he had painted a picture

---

[1] See Miss Lowery's *Windows of the Morning*, 1940, p. 50, and my *Blake Studies*, 1949, p. 24.
[2] See *Blake Studies*, p. 54.

"in his best manner", though it can now be seen to be by no means so good as he claimed. The water colour has never been reproduced before, but is of interest as evidence of the disastrous effect of outside interference on Blake's powers of invention. When I first saw it, it was in the possession of Mrs. Gilchrist's daughter, Mrs. Frend, and is now in the United States. A photograph was kindly supplied by Dr. Jacob Schwartz, who had obtained the picture from Mrs. Frend's nephew.

The Felpham period is illustrated by a portrait of Hayley from a mezzotint by J. Jacobe, 1779, after Romney; by Herbert H. Gilchrist's attractive drawing of Blake's cottage done for his father's *Life*, 1880; and by the broadside ballad, *Little Tom the Sailor*, from an original impression in my collection. Blake's work for Hayley's *Life of Romney* is represented by his sepia drawing after Romney's picture "The Shipwreck", which was the only subject from his hand included in the volume. The drawing is in the British Museum.

The long description of his elaborate water-colour drawing of "The Last Judgment", written by Blake for Ozias Humphry, is necessarily accompanied by a reproduction of the picture which is still at Petworth House, Sussex. It is included by the courtesy of Lord Egremont.

R. H. Cromek's ill-natured letter to Blake, sent with the rejected design for the dedication "To The Queen" in Blair's *Grave*, 1808, is well known. The design itself, however, is unfamiliar and is therefore included here, though its delicate beauty cannot be fully seen in a reproduction. The colours are pale, and it has suffered from soiling before finding its final resting place in the British Museum. The Trustees of the British Museum have also allowed the inclusion of Blake's miniature of Butts with those of his wife and son.

Blake's final years are illustrated by the engraved card done for Cumberland, and his last painting in tempera, "Ugolino in Prison", from the original in my collection. This subject is represented in the series of drawings for Dante's *Divine Comedy* only by a rough pencil sketch, but Blake chose it for a highly finished painting on a panel, one of the three he is known to have made at this time.[1] He told Linnell that his "Wife alone was answerable for its having existed in any finished state", and it is a remarkable performance for a sick man of nearly seventy, done within a few months of his death. The beauty of the colouring is lost in the reproduction, but the composition can be seen to be similar to that of a number of designs made at various times after 1793, when it was among the engravings for *The Gates of Paradise*. The subject seems almost to have obsessed

---

[1] The other two are *Cain and Abel*, and *Satan Smiting Job with Boils*, both now in the Tate Gallery.

Blake's mind, but this final version is unique in showing two angels floating over the grim figures on the floor of the prison cell. These symbolise for Blake the ultimate forgiveness of sins even for so guilty a man as Ugolino, Blake differing entirely in this attitude from the author of the *Inferno*. He seldom illustrated literally, preferring to add his own glosses to the ideas of other authors.

Lastly, an example of Blake's handwriting is given by a facsimile of a short letter written to Hayley during his joyous anticipation of the pleasures to be enjoyed at Felpham. This letter is reproduced by permission of the H. E. Huntington Library, San Marino, California.

During the past forty years I have been under obligations to the curators of numerous libraries and institutions, chiefly in the United States of America, for their patient replies to my enquiries. I am indebted also to the private owners and institutions who have provided me with photostats of manuscripts in their keeping. Their names will be found in the Register of Documents at the end of the book, and I wish to record here my gratitude. Without their co-operation the printing of an accurate text could not have been achieved.

GEOFFREY KEYNES

THE LETTERS

1. WILLEY REVELEY TO BLAKE

Mr Reveley's Comp^{ts} to Mr Blake; if he wishes to engrave any of Mr Pars's drawings for the Antiquities of Athens,[1] & can do them by the end of January Mr Reveley will be glad to [send] some to him.

Great Titchfield St.

Oct. 18

2. BLAKE TO WILLEY REVELEY

OCTOBER 1791

Mr Blake's Comp^{ts} to Mr Reveley: tho full of work [as M^r R said he should be by then the plates were put in hand *del.*] he is glad to embrace the offer of engraving such beautiful things & will do what he can by the end of January.[2]

3. TO GEORGE CUMBERLAND   6 DECEMBER 1795

Lambeth

6 *Decemb^r* 1795

Dear Sir,

I congratulate you, not on any atchievement, because I know that the Genius that produces these Designs can execute them in any

[1] Reveley was engaged in editing vol. III of James Stuart's and Nicholas Revett's *The Antiquities of Athens*, published in 1794. The first volume had appeared in 1762, James Basire being the chief engraver. The second volume was edited by William Newton for Stuart's widow and is dated 1787; one engraver was Jas. Newton. Some of the drawings in the third volume were by William Pars, younger brother of Henry Pars, to whose drawing school Blake went in 1767 for five years. William Pars had been in 1764 with Dr. Richard Chandler and Nicholas Revett to Asia Minor, returning by Athens, on an antiquarian expedition financed by the Dilettanti Society.

[2] Four plates, nos. XXI–XXIV, in vol. III of *The Antiquities of Athens*, were engraved by Blake after drawings by William Pars from the sculptures on the frieze of the porticus of the Temple of Theseus; they represent the battle of the Centaurs and Lapithæ. The engravings are dated April 3, 1792.

manner, notwithstanding the pretended Philosophy which teaches that Execution is the power of One & Invention of Another[1]— Locke says it [is the] same faculty that Invents Judges, & I say he who [can] Invent can Execute.

As to laying on the Wax, it is as follows:[2]

Take a cake of Virgin's Wax[3] (I don't know what animal produces it) & stroke it regularly over the surface of a warm Plate (the Plate must be warm enough to melt the Wax as it passes over), then immediately draw a feather over it & you will get an even surface which, when cold, will recieve any impression minutely.

Note: The danger is in not covering the Plate *all over*.

Now You will, I hope, shew all the family of Antique Borers that Peace & Plenty & Domestic Happiness is the Source of Sublime Art, & prove to the Abstract Philosophers that Enjoyment & not Abstinence[4] is the food of Intellect.

Yours sincerely,
Will Blake

Health to Mrs Cumberland & family.

The pressure necessary to roll off the lines is the same as when you print, or not quite so great. I have not been able to send a proof of the bath[5] tho' I have done the corrections, my paper not being in order.

4. TO GEORGE CUMBERLAND

23 DECEMBER 1796

Dear Cumberland,

I have lately had some pricks of conscience on account of not acknowledging your friendship to me [before *del.*] immediately on

---

[1] cp. "Execution is only the result of Invention." (Public Address, *Complete Writings*, 1966, p. 596) and other similar opinions of Blake.

[2] These instructions refer to the process of transferring a drawing to a metal plate for engraving. Blake had engraved eight plates after Cumberland's designs for his *Thoughts on Outline*. The plates are dated 1794–5; the book was published in 1796, and contained sixteen other plates engraved by Cumberland from his own designs.

[3] i.e. purified bees' wax or candle wax.

[4] cp. Blake's lines:

> Abstinence sows sand all over
> The ruddy limbs & flaming hair.
> *Complete Writings*, 1966, p. 178.

[5] Blake's engraving of "the bath", illustrating Anacreon, Ode LII, is plate 23 in *Thoughts on Outline*. It is dated Jan. 1, 1795, though it should be dated 1796 to agree with the date of Blake's letter.

the receit of your beautiful book.[1] I have likewise had by me all the summer 6 Plates which you desired me to get made for you; they have laid on my shelf, without speaking to tell me whose they were or that they were [there *del.*] at all & it was some time (when I found them) before I could divine whence they came or whither they were bound or whether they were to lie there to eternity. I have now sent them to you to be transmuted, thou real Alchymist![2]

Go on. Go on. Such works as yours Nature & Providence, the Eternal Parents, demand from their children: how few produce them in such perfection: how Nature smiles on them: how Providence rewards them. How all your Brethren say, 'The sound of his harp & his flute heard from his secret forest chears us to the labours of life, & we plow & reap forgetting our labour'.

Let us see you sometimes as well as sometimes hear from you & let us often See your Works.

Compliments to Mrs Cumberland & Family.

Yours in head & heart,
Will Blake

Lambeth
23 Decemb^r 1796
a Merry Christmas

5. TO DR. TRUSLER   16 AUGUST 1799

To the Revd Dr Trusler

Revd Sir,

I find more & more that my Style of Designing is a Species by itself, & in this which I send you have been compell'd by my Genius or Angel to follow where he led; if I were to act otherwise it would not fulfill the purpose for which alone I live, which is, in conjunction with such men as my friend Cumberland, to renew the lost Art of the Greeks.[3]

---

[1] Cumberland's *Thoughts on Outline*, London, 1796.

[2] There is no clue as to the identity of these six plates.

[3] Blake had learnt during his apprenticeship to value Greek art, probably through reading Winkelmann's *Reflections on the Painting and Sculpture of the Greeks*, London, 1765 (see Keynes, *Blake Studies*, 1949, p. 47). In 1809 he had included Greek art among the things that "are the extent of the human mind" (*Descriptive Catalogue, Complete Writings*, 1966, p. 579). Later, from a different point of view, he condemned Greek art as "Mathematic Form", whereas Gothic was "Living Form" (On Virgil, *Complete Writings*, p. 778). This was associated with the idea of the opposition between Reason and Imagination, Greece being additionally evil because, with Rome, it was a Warlike State, which "never can produce Art" (ibid. See also the sentences on the Laocoön group, *Complete Writings*, p. 775).

I attempted every morning for a fortnight together to follow your Dictate, but when I found my attempts were in vain, resolv'd to shew an independence which I know will please an Author better than slavishly following the track of another, however admirable that track may be. At any rate, my Excuse must be: I could not do otherwise; it was out of my power!

I know I begged of you to give me your Ideas, & promised to build on them; here I counted without my host. I now find my mistake.[1]

The Design I have Sent Is:

A Father, taking leave of his Wife & Child, Is watch'd by Two Fiends incarnate, with intention that when his back is turned they will murder the mother & her infant.[2] If this is not Malevolence with a vengeance, I have never seen it on Earth; & if you approve of this, I have no doubt of giving you Benevolence with Equal Vigor, as also Pride & Humility, but cannot previously describe in words what I mean to Design, for fear I should Evaporate the Spirit of my Invention. But I hope that none of my Designs will be destitute of Infinite Particulars[3] which will present themselves to the Contemplator. And tho' I call them Mine, I know that they are not Mine, being of the same opinion with Milton when he says[4] That the Muse visits his Slumbers & awakes & governs his Song when Morn purples the East, & being also in the predicament of that prophet who says: I cannot go beyond the command of the Lord, to speak good or bad.[5]

If you approve of my Manner, & it is agreeable to you, I would rather Paint Pictures in oil[6] of the same dimensions than make Drawings, & on the same terms; by this means you will have a number of Cabinet pictures, which I flatter myself will not be un-

[1] It was this attempted interference by Trusler and others of his friends with his integrity as an artist that drove Blake's mind in upon itself and was responsible to a great extent for his isolation. This was symbolised by the "Comforters", or false friends, of Job.

[2] This water-colour drawing formerly the property of Mrs. Alexander Gilchrist and later of her daughter, Mrs. Gilchrist Frend, is now in the United States. It shows two assassins crouching behind a rock at the mouth of a cave and about to murder a young traveller, who, staff in hand, is parting from his wife and child. Blake used the same theme in the design for plate 2 of *Europe*.

[3] Blake frequently in his writings drew attention to the importance of "minute particulars" in all forms of art, e.g. "Labour well the Minute Particulars" (Jerusalem, pl. 55, *Complete Writings*, 1966, p. 687).

[4] *Paradise Lost*, book vii, ll. 29, 30.

[5] *Numbers*, xxiv. 13.

[6] Blake, in fact, never used an oily medium, discarding it in favour of tempera painting or "fresco", as he called them. For his opinions see "The Invention of a Portable Fresco", *Complete Writings*, 1966, p. 560.

worthy of a Scholar of Rembrandt[1] & Teniers, whom I have Studied no less than Rafael & Michael angelo. Please to send me your orders respecting this, & In my next Effort I promise more Expedition.

I am, Revd Sir,
Your very humble serv^t
Willm Blake

Hercules Build^{gs}
Lambeth
Augst 16 1799

6. TO DR. TRUSLER[2]

23 AUGUST 1799

Revd Sir,

I really am sorry that you are fall'n out with the Spiritual World, Especially if I should have to answer for it. I feel very sorry that your Ideas & Mine on Moral Painting differ so much as to have made you angry with my method of Study. If I am wrong, I am wrong in good company. I had hoped your plan comprehended All Species of this Art, & Especially that you would not regret that Species which gives Existence to Every other, namely, Visions of Eternity. You say that I want somebody to Elucidate my Ideas. But you ought to know that What is Grand is necessarily obscure to Weak men. That which can be made Explicit to the Idiot is not worth my care. The wisest of the Ancients consider'd what is not too Explicit as the fittest for Instruction, because it rouzes the faculties to act. I name Moses, Solomon, Esop, Homer, Plato.

But as you have favor'd me with your remarks on my Design, permit me in return to defend it against a mistaken one, which is, That I have supposed Malevolence without a Cause. Is not Merit in one a Cause of Envy in another, & Serenity & Happiness & Beauty a Cause of Malevolence? But Want of Money & the Distress of A Thief can never be alledged as the Cause of his Thieving, for many honest people endure greater hardships with Fortitude. We must therefore seek the Cause elsewhere than in want of Money, for that is the Miser's passion, not the Thief's.

I have therefore proved your Reasonings Ill proportion'd, which

[1] Ten years later in *A Descriptive Catalogue* and elsewhere Blake condemned the art of Rembrandt, together with that of Titian, Corregio, and Rubens, in favour of that of Rafael, Dürer, and Michelangelo (see *Complete Writings*, 1966, p. 563).

[2] This letter is marked by Cumberland: "Blake, dim'd with superstition." Cumberland regarded Blake as "a great man, but with some queer religious views".

you can never prove my figures to be; they are those of Michael Angelo, Rafael & the Antique, & of the best living Models. I percieve that your Eye is perverted by Caricature Prints, which ought not to abound so much as they do. Fun I love, but too much Fun is of all things the most loathsom. Mirth is better than Fun, & Happiness is better than Mirth. I feel that a Man may be happy in This World. And I know that This World Is a World of imagination & Vision. I see Every thing I paint In This World, but Every body does not see alike. To the Eyes of a Miser a Guinea is more beautiful than the Sun, & a bag worn with the use of Money has more beautiful proportions than a Vine filled with Grapes. The tree which moves some to tears of joy is in the Eyes of others only a Green thing that stands in the way.[1] Some See Nature all Ridicule & Deformity, & by these I shall not regulate my proportions; & Some Scarce see Nature at all. But to the Eyes of the Man of Imagination, Nature is Imagination itself. As a man is, So he Sees. As the Eye is formed, such are its Powers. You certainly Mistake, when you say that the Visions of Fancy are not to be found in This World. To Me This World is all One continued Vision of Fancy or Imagination, & I feel Flatter'd when I am told so. What is it sets Homer, Virgil & Milton in so high a rank of Art? Why is the Bible more Entertaining & Instructive than any other book? Is it not because they are addressed to the Imagination, which is Spiritual Sensation, & but mediately to the Understanding or Reason? Such is True Painting, and such was alone valued by the Greeks & the best modern Artists. Consider what Lord Bacon says: "Sense sends over to Imagination before Reason have judged, & Reason sends over to Imagination before the Decree can be acted." See Advancem^t of Learning, Part 2, P. 47 of first Edition.[2]

But I am happy to find a Great Majority of Fellow Mortals who can Elucidate My Visions, & Particularly they have been Elucidated by Children, who have taken a greater delight in contemplating my Pictures than I even hoped. Neither Youth nor Childhood is Folly or Incapacity. Some Children are Fools & so are some Old Men. But There is a vast Majority on the side of Imagination or Spiritual Sensation.

To Engrave after another Painter is infinitely more laborious than to Engrave one's own Inventions. And of the size you require my price has been Thirty Guineas, & I cannot afford to do it for less. I

---

[1] cp. "A fool sees not the same tree that a wise man sees" (Proverbs of Hell, *Complete Writings* 1966, p. 151.

[2] Blake here seems to quote Bacon with approval, though he had annotated the *Essays* in an edition dated 1798 with disagreement and abuse (see *Complete Writings*, 1966, p. 396).

had Twelve for the Head I sent you as a Specimen;[1] but after my own designs I could do at least Six times the quantity of labour in the same time, which will account for the difference of price as also that Chalk Engraving is at least six times as laborious as Aqua tinta. I have no objection to Engraving after another Artist. Engraving is the profession I was apprenticed to, & should never have attempted to live by any thing else, If orders had not come in for my Designs & Paintings, which I have the pleasure to tell you are Increasing Every Day. Thus If I am a Painter it is not to be attributed to Seeking after. But I am contented whether I live by Painting or Engraving.

I am, Rev[d] Sir, your very obedient servant,

William Blake

13 Hercules Buildings
    Lambeth
August 23. 1799

7. TO GEORGE CUMBERLAND

26 AUGUST 1799

Dear Cumberland,

I ought long ago to have written to you to thank you for your kind recommendation to D[r] Trusler, which, tho' it has fail'd of success, is not the less to be remember'd by me with Gratitude.

I have made him a Drawing in my best manner; he had sent it back with a Letter full of Criticisms, in which he says It accords not with his Intentions, which are to Reject all Fancy from his Work. How far he Expects to please, I cannot tell. But as I cannot paint Dirty rags & old shoes where I ought to place Naked Beauty[2] or simple ornament, I despair of Ever pleasing one Class of Men. Unfortunately our authors of books are among this Class; how soon we Shall have a change for the better I cannot Prophecy. D[r] Trusler says: "*Your Fancy*, from what I have seen of it, & I have seen variety at M[r] Cumberland's, seems to be in the other world, or the World of Spirits, which accords not with my Intentions, which, whilst living in This World, Wish to follow *the Nature of it*." I could not help Smiling at the difference between the doctrines of D[r] Trusler & those of Christ. But, however, for his own sake I am sorry that a Man should be so enamour'd of Rowlandson's caricatures as to call them copies from life & manners, or fit Things for a Clergyman to write upon.

---

[1] Perhaps the head of Euler, engraved for his *Elements of Algebra*, 1797, or of Wright of Derby in *The Monthly Magazine*, vol. IV, 1798.

[2] cp. "Art can never exist without Naked Beauty displayed" (Laocoön Group, *Complete Writings*, 1966, p. 776).

31

Pray let me intreat you to persevere in your Designing; it is the only source of Pleasure. All your other pleasures depend upon it. It is the Tree; your Pleasures are the Fruit. Your Inventions of Intellectual Visions are the Stamina of every thing you value. Go on, if not for your own sake, yet for ours, who love & admire your works; but, above all, For the Sake of the Arts. Do not throw aside for any long time the honour intended you by Nature to revive the Greek workmanship. I study your outlines[1] as usual, just as if they were antiques.

As to Myself, about whom you are so kindly Interested, I live by Miracle. I am Painting small Pictures from the Bible. For as to Engraving, in which art I cannot reproach myself with any neglect, yet I am laid by in a corner as if I did not Exist, & Since my Young's Night Thoughts[2] have been publish'd, Even Johnson & Fuseli have discarded my Graver. But as I know that He who Works & has his health cannot starve, I laugh at Fortune & Go on & on. I think I foresee better Things than I have ever seen. My Work pleases my employer,[3] & I have an order for Fifty small Pictures at One Guinea each, which is Something better than mere copying after another artist. But above all, I feel myself happy & contented let what will come; having passed now near twenty years in ups & downs, I am used to them, & perhaps a little practise in them may turn out to benefit. It is now Exactly Twenty years since I was upon the ocean of business,[4] & Tho' I laugh at Fortune, I am perswaded that She Alone is the Governor of Worldly Riches, & when it is Fit She will call on me; till then I wait with Patience, in hopes that She is busied among my Friends.

With Mine & My Wife's best compliments to Mr⁵ Cumberland, I remain,

Yours sincerely,
Willm Blake

Hercules Buildings
Lambeth
Aug^st 26. 1799

[1] *Thoughts on Outline*, London, 1796.

[2] *The Complaint and the Consolation; or, Night Thoughts*, by Edward Young. London: R. Edwards, 1797: folio, with 43 marginal illustrations designed and engraved by Blake. The publisher, Richard Edwards, had commissioned Blake to illustrate the poem and 537 water-colour drawings had been made. Only the first instalment of the book was issued, since there was not enough demand to justify its continuation, and the engravings were, indeed, by no means Blake's best work. The drawings are now in the Print Room at the British Museum (see Keynes, *Blake Studies*, 1949, p. 56).

[3] Thomas Butts.

[4] Blake had completed his apprenticeship to the engraver, James Basire, in July 1779, and had been working independently since that date.

III. WILLIAM HAYLEY

mezzotint by Jacobe after Romney 1779

8. TO JOHN FLAXMAN

14 DECEMBER 1799

Recievd Decr 14 1799 of Mr Flaxman the Sum of Eight pounds Eight shillings for Engraving Three Plates For the Statue of Britannia[1] & Twelve Shillings & Eight pence for Copper

p. Willm Blake

```
 8.  8.  0
 0. 12.  8
£9.  0.  8
```

9. TO WILLIAM HAYLEY*

18 FEBRUARY 1800

[Extract from a letter to Hayley, to whom he submitted an impression of the plate[2] of "The Death of Demosthenes" which] "has been approved by Mr Flaxman". [He hopes that the young sculptor] "will soon be well enough to make hundreds of designs both for the engraver and the sculptor".

10. TO WILLIAM HAYLEY

1 APRIL 1800

Dear Sir,

With all possible Expedition I send you a proof of my attempt to Express your & our Much Beloved's Countenance.[3] Mr Flaxman

---

[1] These plates were engraved for Flaxman's *A Letter to the Committee for raising The Naval Pillar, or Monument*, London, 1799, 4°. The frontispiece depicts "A Colossal Statue 230 feet high, proposed to be erected on Greenwich Hill". The second plate shows various forms of monument erected in ancient times, and the third "A View of Greenwich Hospital with the Statue of Britannia on the Hill".

[2] This plate was engraved for Hayley's *An Essay on Sculpture*, London, 4°, 1800. Flaxman writing to Hayley on 29 January 1800 says: "I have delivered the drawing of Demosthenes to Mr Blake with the right orthography of the Dedication to Neptune". The letter is in the Fairfax Murray Collection, Fitzwilliam Museum, Cambridge. In my collection is Hayley's own copy of the *Essay* and inserted in it is his son's pencil sketch for "The Death of Demosthenes"; the base of the statue at which Demosthenes is lying is marked ΠΟΣΕΙΔΑΩΝΙ, this having presumably been written in by Flaxman.

[3] An engraving from a drawing of a medallion portrait by Flaxman of Hayley's illegitimate son, Thomas Alphonso. Flaxman wrote to Hayley on 26 March 1800: "It is equally surprising & unaccountable that you have had no further news of the engravings, for Mr Howard finished a beautiful drawing from the Medallion of

has seen it & approved of my now sending it to you for your remarks. Your Sorrows and your dear son's May Jesus and his Angels assuage & if it is consistent with his divine providence restore him to us & to his labours of Art & Science in this world. So prays a fellow sufferer & Your humble servant,

Willm Blake

Hercules Buildings, Lambeth
1 April 1800

11. WILLIAM HAYLEY TO BLAKE

17 APRIL 1800

Thursday April 17 1800

My dear Blake,

You are very good to take such pains to produce a Resemblance of our dear disabled artist—you have improved yr first plate a little, & I believe with a little more alteration it may be more like than the second outline.

The great & radical defect I conceive to be this—the engraving is a Head 3 years older than the medallion—the Features by being made *longer* & *more sedate* have lost the *lively juvenility* of *16*—our dear Flaxman's medallion is *very faithful* to that *time of Life*, & certainly *like* tho I cannot say I ever thought it a *very very strong* similitude of the *Individual*.

Truth, precision, & Force of character is that exquisite & subtle essence of art, which is so apt to escape from the firmest & ablest Hand in the formation of Portraits, of whatever materials they are formed.

Romney, who was so marvellously happy in *several*, yet has failed egregiously in *many*; & so, I apprehend, has *every* modern artist from the Revival of Art to the present Hour—perhaps we should think so also of the antients if we saw all their portraits & the originals, altho yr great Connoisseurs presume to say, These said antients were far superior to the moderns in seizing this subtle Truth of character, particularly on their Gems & Medals.

But to speak of still farther alterations in yr first plate—would it not give a little younger appearance to shorten the space between

---

my Friend Thomas I think four weeks ago, since which time it has been in the hands of Mr Blake & the copper plate from it is most likely done by this time, as well as that of the head of Pericles but perhaps you are not acquainted with Mr Blake's direction? it is No. 13 Hercules Buildings near the Asylum, Surrey side of Westminster Bridge" (Fairfax Murray Collection). The engraving was published n Hayley's *Essay on Sculpture*.

the nose & the upper lip a little more by representing the mouth rather more open, in the act of speaking, which appears to me the Expression of the medallion? I submit the point to you & our dear Flaxman with *proper deference* to yr *superior judgement*; as I do the following Question whether the making the Dot at the corner of the mouth a little deeper, & adding a darker Touch also at the Bottom of the Eye would add a little gay juvenility to the Features without producing (what I by all means wish to avoid) a *Grin* or a *Smirk*—In short I wish the character of the engraving to *harmonise* a *little more*, than *it does at present*, with the following verses towards the conclusion of the Poem, which as *you* are a *kind-hearted Brother of Parnassus*, you will forgive my inserting in this letter to *explain my meaning to you*—

> "That youth of fairest Promise, fair as May,
> Pensively tender, and benignly gay,
> On thy Medallion still retains a Form
> In Health exulting, & with pleasure warm.
> Teach Thou my Hand, with mutual love, to trace
> His Mind, as perfect, as thy lines his Face!
> For Nature in that Mind" &c

You will have the goodness not to shew these verses to any one, except to our dear Flaxman, who will, I know, kindly assist you in yr endeavours to catch the exact cast of character, that I wish you to seize—I have to thank Heaven (as I do with my whole Heart) for having been able to *gratify this dear departing angel* with a sight of his *own Portrait united* to the *completion* of a *long, & severely interrupted work*; which *He* most tenderly pressed me to *complete* & which nothing I believe but *his wishes* could have enabled my wounded spirit to pursue under the Heart-rending affliction of seeing a child so justly beloved *perishing by slow Tortures*. His Life may probably not last many days—accept our united Benedictions & believe me dear Blake

your very sincere Friend

W. H.

12. TO WILLIAM HAYLEY

6 MAY 1800

Dear Sir,

I am very sorry for your immense loss,[1] which is a repetition of what all feel in this valley of misery & happiness mixed. I send the Shadow of the departed Angel:[2] hope the likeness is improved. The lip I have again lessened as you advised & done a good many other softenings to the whole. I know that our deceased friends are more

[1] The death of Thomas Alphonso Hayley on 2 May 1800.

[2] The engraving already mentioned.

35

really with us than when they were apparent to our mortal part. Thirteen years ago I lost a brother[1] & with his spirit I converse daily & hourly in the Spirit & See him in my remembrance in the regions of my Imagination. I hear his advice & even now write from his Dictate. Forgive me for Expressing to you my Enthusiasm which I wish all to partake of Since it is to me a Source of Immortal Joy: even in this world by it I am the companion of Angels. May you continue to be so more & more & to be more & more perswaded that every Mortal loss is an Immortal Gain. The Ruins of Time builds Mansions in Eternity.—I have also sent A Proof of Pericles[2] for your Remarks, thanking you for the Kindness with which you Express them & feeling heartily your Grief with a brother's Sympathy.

I remain, Dear Sir, Your humble Servant

William Blake

Lambeth.   May 6. 1800

13. WILLIAM HAYLEY TO BLAKE   JULY 1800

From Thomas Hayley to Wm Blake[3]

Accept my gentle visionary Blake,
    Sublimely fanciful & kindly mild,
Accept and fondly keep for Friendship's sake
    This favoured vision, my poetic Child.

Rich in more Grace than Fancy ever won
    To thy most tender mind this Book will be
For it belonged to my departed son.
    Thus from an Angel it descends to Thee.

14. TO GEORGE CUMBERLAND

2 JULY 1800

Dear Cumberland,

I have to congratulate you on your plan for a National Gallery[4]

[1] His younger brother, Robert, who died in February 1787 (see Keynes, *Blake Studies*, 1949, p. 3).

[2] An engraving of "Pericles", from a bust, was used as frontispiece to Hayley's *An Essay on Sculpture*, London, 1800.

[3] Written to accompany a copy of the tenth edition of Hayley's *Triumphs of Temper* sent by Hayley to Blake. This copy was seen by J. R. Smith, who printed the verses in a slightly different form in his *Nollekens and his Times*, 1828, vol. II, pp. 465–6. In this version the lines are signed: W. H. July, 1800.

[4] Cumberland was among those who were active in promoting the foundation of a National Gallery, but it was not until 1824 that the nucleus of the Gallery was formed by the purchase of the Angerstein collection of thirty-eight pictures.

being put into Execution. All your wishes shall in due time be fulfilled; the immense flood of Grecian light & glory which is coming
on Europe will more than realize our warmest wishes. Your honours
will be unbounded when your plan shall be carried into Execution
as it must be if England continues a Nation. I hear that it is now in
the hands of Ministers, That the King shews it great Countenance &
Encouragement, that it will soon be before Parliament, & that it
must be extended & enlarged to take in Originals both of Painting
& Sculpture by considering every valuable original that is brought
into England or can be purchas'd Abroad as its objects of Acquisition. Such is the Plan as I am told & such must be the plan if England
wishes to continue at all worth notice; as you have yourself observ'd
only now, we must possess Originals as well as France or be Nothing.

Excuse, I intreat you, my not returning Thanks at the proper
moment for your kind present. No perswasion could make my stupid
head believe that it was proper for me to trouble you with a letter of
meer compliment & Expression of thanks. I begin to Emerge from a
Deep pit of Melancholy, Melancholy without any real reason for it,
a Disease which God keep you from & all good men. Our artists of
all ranks praise your outlines & wish for more. Flaxman is very warm
in your commendation & more and more of A Grecian. M r Hayley
has lately mentioned your Work on outline in Notes to [Epistles on
Sculpture *del.*] an Essay on Sculpture in Six Epistles to John Flaxman. I have been too little among friends which I fear they will not
Excuse & I know not how to apologize for. Poor Fuseli, sore from
the lash of Envious tongues, praises you & dispraises with the same
breath; he is not naturally good natured, but he is artificially very
ill natured, yet even from him I learn the Estimation you are held
in among artists & connoisseurs.

I am still Employ'd in making Designs & little Pictures with now
& then an Engraving & find that in future to live will not be so
difficult as it has been. It is very Extraordinary that London in so
few years from a City of meer Necessaries or at l[e]ast a commerce
of the lowest order of luxuries should have become a City of Elegance
in some degree & that its once stupid inhabitants should enter into
an Emulation of Grecian manners. There are now, I believe, as
many Booksellers as there are Butchers & as many Printshops as of
any other trade. We remember when a Print shop was a rare bird in
London & I myself remember when I thought my pursuits of Art a
kind of criminal dissipation & neglect of the main chance, which I
hid my face for not being able to abandon as a Passion which is for-
bidden by Law & Religion, but now it appears to be Law & Gospel
too, at least I hear so from the few friends I have dared to visit in
my stupid Melancholy. Excuse this communication of sentiments

37

which I felt necessary to my repose at this time. I feel very strongly that I neglect my Duty to my Friends, but It is not want of Gratitude or Friendship but perhaps an Excess of both.

Let me hear of your welfare. Remember My & My Wife's Respectful Compliments to Mrs Cumberland & Family.

& believe me to be for Ever
Yours
William Blake

13 Hercules Buildings
Lambeth
2 July 1800

15. TO JOHN FLAXMAN

12 SEPTEMBER 1800

My Dearest Friend,

It is to you I owe All my present Happiness. It is to you I owe perhaps the Principal Happiness of my life. I have presum'd on your friendship in staying so long away & not calling to know of your welfare, but hope now every thing is nearly completed for our removal to Felpham, that I shall see you on Sunday, as we have appointed Sunday afternoon to call on Mrs. Flaxman at Hampstead. I send you a few lines, which I hope you will Excuse. And As the time is now arriv'd when Men shall again converse in Heaven & walk with Angels, I know you will be pleased with the Intention, & hope you will forgive the Poetry.

To My Dearest Friend, John Flaxman, these lines:

I bless thee, O Father of Heaven & Earth, that ever I saw Flaxman's face.
Angels stand round my Spirit in Heaven, the blessed of Heaven are
my friends upon Earth.
When Flaxman was taken to Italy, Fuseli was given to me for a
season,
And now Flaxman hath given me Hayley his friend to be mine,
such my lot upon Earth.
Now my lot in the Heavens is this, Milton lov'd me in childhood &
shew'd me his face.
Ezra came with Isaiah the Prophet, but Shakespeare in riper years
gave me his hand;
Paracelsus & Behmen[1] appear'd to me, terrors appear'd in the
Heavens above

[1] cp. "Any man of mechanical talents may, from the writings of Paracelsus or Jacob Behmen, produce ten thousand volumes of equal value with Swedenborg's, and from those of Dante or Shakespear an infinite number" (Marriage of Heaven and Hell, *Complete Writings*, 1966, p. 158).

38

And in Hell beneath, & a mighty & awful change threatened the Earth.

The American War[1] began. All its dark horrors passed before my face

Across the Atlantic to France. Then the French Revolution[2] commenc'd in thick clouds,

And My Angels have told me that seeing such visions I could not subsist on the Earth,

But by my conjunction with Flaxman, who knows to forgive Nervous Fear.

I remain, for Ever Yours,

William Blake

Be so kind as to Read & then seal the Inclosed & send it on its much beloved Mission.

16. MRS. BLAKE TO MRS. FLAXMAN

14 SEPTEMBER 1800

My Dearest Friend,

I hope you will not think we could forget your Services to us, or any way neglect to love & remember with affection even the hem of your garment; we indeed presume on your kindness in neglecting to have call'd on you since my Husband's first return from Felpham.[3] We have been incessantly busy in our great removal; but can never think of going without first paying our proper duty to you & M[r] Flaxman. We intend to call on Sunday afternoon in Hampstead, to take farewell, All things being now nearly completed for our setting forth on Tuesday Morning; it is only Sixty Miles, & Lambeth was On[e] Hundred,[4] for the terrible desart of London was between. My husband has been obliged to finish several things necessary to be finish'd before our migration; the Swallows call us, fleeting past our window at this moment. O how we delight in talking of the pleasure we shall have in preparing you a summer bower at Felpham, & we not only talk, but behold! the Angels of our journey have inspired a song to you:

---

[1] The subject of Blake's *America—a Prophecy,* 1793.

[2] cp. "The dead brood over Europe, the cloud and vision descends over chearful France", the first line of Blake's poem, *The French Revolution,* 1791 (*Complete Writings,* 1966, p. 134).

[3] Blake first visited Hayley at Felpham in order to perfect his engraved medallion of Thomas Alphonso in July 1800, and went there again in August. He moved to his cottage in Felpham on 18 September (see Mona Wilson's *Life of Blake,* 1948, p. 132).

[4] i.e. from Hampstead.

To my dear Friend, Mrs Anna Flaxman.

This Song to the flower of Flaxman's joy,
To the blossom of hope, for a sweet decoy:
Do all that you can or all that you may,
To entice him to Felpham & far away:

Away to Sweet Felpham, for Heaven is there;
The Ladder of Angels descends thro' the air;[1]
On the Turret[2] its spiral does softly descend,
Thro' the village then winds, at My Cot it does end.

You stand in the village & look up to heaven;
The precious stones glitter on flights seventy seven;
And My Brother is there, & My Friend & Thine
Descend & Ascend with the Bread & the Wine.

The Bread of sweet Thought & the Wine of Delight
Feeds the Village of Felpham by day & by night;
And at his own door the bless'd Hermit[3] does stand,
Dispensing Unceasing to all the whole Land.

W. Blake

Recieve my & my husband's love & affection, & believe me to be
Yours affectionately,

Catherine Blake

H B Lambeth
14 Sepr 1800

17. TO WILLIAM HAYLEY

16 SEPTEMBER 1800

Leader of My Angels,

My Dear & too careful & over joyous Woman has Exhausted her
strength to such a degree with expectation & gladness added to
labour in our removal that I fear it will be Thursday before we can
get away from this —— City. I shall not be able to avail myself of
the assistance of Bruno's fairies.[4] But I Invoke the Good Genii that
Surround Miss Poole's Villa to shine upon my journey thro' the
Petworth road which by your fortunate advice I mean to take; but
whether I come on Wednesday or Thursday That Day shall be
marked on my calendar with a Star of the first magnitude.

[1] Probably an allusion to the water-colour drawing of "Jacob's Ladder", which
was made about this time.
[2] The Turret of Hayley's house in Felpham.
[3] The Hermit of Eartham had been Hayley's nickname for himself.
[4] Could this be a reference to the writings of Giordano Bruno (1548–1600),
Italian heretic? There was also a pony named Bruno, which Blake afterwards rode.

Eartham will be my first temple & altar. My wife is like a flame
of many colours of precious jewels whenever she hears it named.
Excuse my haste & recieve my hearty Love & Respect.

I am, dear Sir,

Your Sincere

William Blake

H. B. Lambeth
Sept 16. 1800

My fingers Emit sparks of fire with Expectation of my future
labours.

18. TO JOHN FLAXMAN

21 SEPTEMBER 1800

Dear Sculptor of Eternity,

We are safe arrived at our Cottage, which is more beautiful than
I thought it, & more convenient. It is a perfect Model for Cottages
&, I think, for Palaces of Magnificence, only Enlarging, not alter-
ing its proportions, & adding ornaments & not principals. Nothing
can be more Grand than its Simplicity & Usefulness. Simple without
Intricacy, it seems to be the Spontaneous Effusion of Humanity,
congenial to the wants of Man. No other formed House can ever
please me so well; nor shall I ever be perswaded, I believe, that it
can be improved either in Beauty or Use.

Mr. Hayley reciev'd us with his usual brotherly affection. I have
begun to work. Felpham is a sweet place for Study, because it is
more Spiritual than London. Heaven opens here on all sides her
golden Gates; her windows are not obstructed by vapours; voices
of Celestial inhabitants are more distinctly heard, & their forms
more distinctly seen, & my Cottage is also a Shadow of their
houses. My Wife & Sister[1] are both well, courting Neptune for an
Embrace.

Our Journey was very pleasant; & tho we had a great deal of
Luggage, No Grumbling, All was Chearfulness & Good Humour
on the Road, & yet we could not arrive at our Cottage before half
past Eleven at night, owing to the necessary shifting of our Luggage
from one Chaise to another; for we had Seven Different Chaises, &
as many different drivers. We set out between Six & Seven in the
Morning of Thursday, with Sixteen heavy boxes & portfolios full of
prints. And Now Begins a New life, because another covering of
Earth is shaken off. I am more famed in Heaven for my works than

[1] Catherine Blake, the youngest member of the family.

41

I could well concieve. In my Brain are studies & Chambers fill'd with books & pictures of old, which I wrote & painted in ages of Eternity before my mortal life; & those works are the delight & Study of Archangels. Why, then, should I be anxious about the riches or fame of mortality. The Lord our father will do for us & with us according to his Divine will for our Good.

You, O Dear Flaxman, are a Sublime Archangel, My Friend & Companion from Eternity; in the Divine bosom is our Dwelling place. I look back into the regions of Reminiscence & behold our ancient days before this Earth appear'd in its vegetated mortality to my mortal vegetated Eyes.[1] I see our houses of Eternity, which can never be separated, tho' our Mortal vehicles should stand at the remotest corners of heaven from each other.

Farewell, My Best Friend. Remember Me & My Wife in Love & Friendship to our Dear Mrs. Flaxman, whom we ardently desire to Entertain beneath our thatched roof of rusted gold, & believe me for ever to remain

Your Grateful & Affectionate,

William Blake

Felpham
Septr 21, 1800
   Sunday Morning

19. TO THOMAS BUTTS

23 SEPTEMBER 1800

Dear Friend of My Angels,

   We are safe arrived at our Cottage without accident or hindrance, tho' it was between Eleven & Twelve O'Clock at night before we could get home, owing to the necessary shifting of our boxes & port-folios from one Chaise to another. We had Seven different Chaises & as many different drivers. All upon the road was chearfulness & welcome; tho' our luggage was very heavy there was no grumbling at all. We travel'd thro' a most beautiful country on a most glorious day. Our Cottage is more beautiful than I thought it, & also more convenient, for tho' small it is well proportion'd, & if I should ever build a Palace it would be only My Cottage Enlarged. Please to tell Mrs Butts that we have dedicated a Chamber [to] her service, & that it has a very fine view of the Sea. Mr Hayley reciev'd me with his usual brotherly affection. My Wife & Sister are both very well,

---

[1] cp. *Jerusalem*, pl. 77: Imagination, the real & eternal World of which this Vegetable Universe is but a faint shadow, & in which we shall live in our Eternal or Imaginative Bodies, when these Vegetable Mortal Bodies are no more.

& courting Neptune for an Embrace, whose terrors this morning made them afraid, but whose mildness is often Equal to his terrors. The Villagers of Felpham are not meer Rustics; they are polite & modest. Meat is cheaper than in London, but the sweet air & the voices of winds, trees & birds, & the odours of the happy ground, makes it a dwelling for immortals. Work will go on here with God speed.—A roller & two harrows lie before my window. I met a plow[1] on my first going out at my gate the first morning after my arrival, & the Plowboy said to the Plowman, "Father, The Gate is Open."—I have begun to Work, & find that I can work with greater pleasure than ever. Hope soon to give you a proof that Felpham is propitious to the Arts.

God bless you! I shall wish for you on Tuesday Evening as usual. Pray give My & My wife & sister's love & respects to Mrs Butts; accept them yourself, & believe me for ever

Your affectionate & obliged Friend,

William Blake

My Sister will be in town in a week, & bring with her your account & whatever else I can finish.

Direct to Me:

Blake, Felpham, near Chichester, Sussex.

20. THOMAS BUTTS TO BLAKE

SEPTEMBER 1800

Marlborough Street

Dear Sir,

I cannot immediately determine whether or no I am dignified by the Title you have graciously conferred on me—you cannot but re-collect the difficulties that have unceasingly arisen to prevent my discerning clearly whether your Angels are black, white, or grey, and that of the three on the whole I have rather inclined to the former opinion and considered you more immediately under the protection of the black-guard; however, at any rate I should thank you for an introduction to his Highness's Court, that, when refused admittance into other Mansions, I may not be received as a Stranger in this.

---

[1] The instruments of agriculture had naturally assumed for Blake a symbolical significance relating them to the arts of life in contrast to those of war and they were so used throughout the symbolical poems (see *The Prophetic Writings of W. B.*, ed. Sloss & Wallis, ii, 214, and Russell, *Letters*, p. 78).

I am well pleased with your pleasures, feeling no small interest in your Happiness, and it cannot fail to be highly gratifying to me and my affectionate Partner to know that a Corner of your Mansion of Peace is asylumed to Her, & when invalided & rendered unfit for service who shall say she may not be quarter'd on your Cot—but for the present she is for active Duty and satisfied with requesting that if there is a Snug Berth unoccupied in any Chamber of your warm Heart, that her Portrait may be suspended there, at the same time well aware that you, like me, prefer the Original to the Copy. Your good Wife will permit, & I hope may benefit from, the Embraces of Neptune, but she will presently distinguish betwixt the warmth of his Embraces & yours, & court the former with caution. I suppose you do not admit of a third in that concern, or I would offer her mine even at this distance. Allow me before I draw a Veil over this interesting Subject to lament the frailty of the fairest Sex, for who alas! of us, my good Friend, could have thought that so good a Woman would ever have exchanged Hercules Buildings for Neptune's Bed,

> So Virtuous a Woman would ever have fled
> from Hercules Buildings to Neptune's Bed?

Whether you will be a better Painter or a better Poet from your change of ways & means I know not; but this I predict, that you will be a better Man—excuse me, as you have been accustomed from friendship to do, but certain opinions imbibed from reading, nourish'd by indulgence, and rivetted by a confined Conversation, and which have been equally prejudicial to your Interest & Happiness, will now, I trust, disperse as a Day-break Vapour, and you will henceforth become a Member of that Community of which you are at present, in the opinion of the Archbishop of Canterbury, but a Sign to mark the residence of dim incredulity, haggard suspicion, & bloated philosophy—whatever can be effected by sterling sense, by opinions which harmonize society and beautify creation, will in future be exemplified in you, & the time I trust is not distant, and that because I truly regard you, when you will be a more valorous Champion of Revelation & Humiliation than any of those who now wield the Sword of the Spirit; with your natural & acquired Powers nothing is wanting but a proper direction of them, & altho' the way is both straight & narrow I know you too well to fear your want of resolution to persevere & to pursue it—you have the Plough & the Harrow in full view & the Gate you have been prophetically told is Open, can you then hesitate joyfully to enter into it?

I have much to congratulate you on—Meat cheap, Music for nothing, a command of the Sea, and brotherly affection fluttering around ye—The Arts have promised to be propitious and the Graces will courtesy to your wishes—

> Happy, happy, happy Pair,
> On Earth, in Sea, or eke in Air,
> In morn, at noon, & thro' the Night
> From Visions fair receiving light,
> Long may ye live, your Guardians' Care,
> And when ye die may not a Hair
> Fall to the lot of Demons black,
> Be singed by Fire, or heard to crack,
> But may your faithful Spirit upward bear
> Your gentle Souls to Him whose care
> Is ever sure and ever nigh
> Those who on Providence rely,
> And in his Paradise above
> Where all is Beauty, Truth & Love,
> O May ye be allowed to chuse
> For your firm Friend a Heaven-born Muse,
> From purest Fountains sip delight,
> Be cloathed in Glory burning bright,
> For ever blest, for ever free,
> The loveliest Blossoms on Life's Tree.

I have no more Nonsense for you just now, but must assure you that I shall always sincerely devote myself to your service when my humble endeavours may be useful. Mrs. Butts greets your Wife & charming Sister with a holy Kiss and I, with old Neptune, bestow my Embraces there also—for yourself I commend you to the protection of your Guard & am,

Dear Sir,
Yours most cordially
& faithfully[1]

21. TO THOMAS BUTTS

Friend of Religion & Order,

I thank you for your very beautiful & encouraging Verses, which I account a Crown of Laurels, & I also thank you for your reprehension of follies by me foster'd. Your prediction will, I hope, be fulfilled in me, & in future I am the determined advocate of Religion

---

[1] There is no signature, this letter being a rough draft which Butts kept with his letters from Blake. The fair copy sent to Blake has not survived.

& Humility, the two bands of Society. Having been so full of the Business of Settling the sticks & feathers of my nest, I have not got any forwarder with "the three Marys" or with any other of your commissions; but I hope, now I have commenced a new life of industry to do credit to that new life by Improved Works. Recieve from me a return of verses, such as Felpham produces by me, tho' not such as she produces by her Eldest Son;[1] however, such as they are, I cannot resist the temptation to send them to you.

To my Friend Butts I write
My first Vision of Light,
On the yellow sands sitting.
The Sun was Emitting
His Glorious beams
From Heaven's high Streams.
Over Sea, over Land
My Eyes did Expand
Into regions of air
Away from all Care,
Into regions of fire
Remote from Desire;
The Light of the Morning
Heaven's Mountains adorning:
In particles bright
The jewels of Light
Dinstinct shone & clear.
Amaz'd & in fear
I each particle gazed,
Astonish'd, Amazed;
For each was a Man
Human-form'd. Swift I ran,
For they beckon'd to me
Remote by the Sea,
Saying: Each grain of Sand,[2]
Every Stone on the Land,
Each rock & each hill,
Each fountain & rill,
Each herb & each tree,
Mountain, hill, earth & sea,

[1] William Hayley.

[2] The grain of sand is an instance of the "minute particulars", which in Blake's mind were the vision-apprehended realities and therefore illusions. cp. "To see a World in a Grain of Sand" (Auguries of Innocence, *Complete Writings*, 1966, p. 431), and many other examples (see *The Prophetic Writings of W. B.*, ed. Sloss & Wallis, 1926, ii, 201).

46

Cloud, Meteor & Star,
Are Men Seen Afar.
I stood in the Streams
Of Heaven's bright beams,
And Saw Felpham sweet
Beneath my bright feet
In soft Female charms;
And in her fair arms
My Shadow[1] I knew
And my wife's shadow too,
And My Sister & Friend.
We like Infants descend
In our Shadows on Earth,
Like a weak mortal birth.
My Eyes more & more
Like a Sea without shore
Continue Expanding,
The Heavens commanding,
Till the Jewels of Light,
Heavenly Men beaming bright,
Appear'd as One Man[2]
Who Complacent began
My limbs to infold
In his beams of bright gold;
Like dross purg'd away
All my mire & my clay.
Soft consum'd in delight
In his bosom Sun bright
I remain'd. Soft he smil'd,
And I heard his voice Mild
Saying: This is My Fold,
O Thou Ram horn'd with gold,
Who wakest from Sleep
On the Sides of the Deep.
On the Mountains around
The roarings resound
Of the lion & wolf,
The loud Sea & deep gulf.
These are guards of My Fold,
O Thou Ram horn'd with gold!
And the voice faded mild.

[1] The "Shadow" is the body, corporeal objects being the shadows of realities in the spiritual world (see Sloss & Wallis, ii, 222).

[2] The single Man is Los, the Spirit of Prophecy (see Sloss & Wallis, ii, 188).

I remain'd as a Child;
All I ever had known
Before me bright Shone.
I saw you & your wife
By the fountains of Life.
Such the Vision to me
Appear'd on the Sea.

Mrs Butts will, I hope, Excuse my not having finish'd the Portrait.[1] I wait for less hurried moments. Our Cottage looks more & more beautiful. And tho' the weather is wet, the Air is Mild, much Milder than it was in London when we came away. Chichester is a very handsome City, Seven miles from us; we can get most Conveniences there. The Country is not so destitute of accomodations to our wants as I expected it would be. We have had but little time for viewing the Country, but what we have seen is Most Beautiful, & the People are Genuine Saxons, handsomer than the people about London. Mrs Butts will Excuse the following lines:

To Mrs Butts.

Wife of the Friend of those I most revere,
Recieve this tribute from a Harp sincere;
Go on in Virtuous Seed sowing on Mold
Of Human Vegetation, & Behold
Your Harvest Springing to Eternal life,
Parent of Youthful Minds, & Happy Wife!

W. B.

I am for Ever Yours,
William Blake

Felpham
Octr 2^d 1800

22. TO WILLIAM HAYLEY*

26 NOVEMBER 1800

Dear Sir,

Absorbed by the poets[2] Milton, Homer, Camoens, Ercilla, Ariosto, and Spenser, whose physiognomies have been my delightful study,

---

[1] A miniature of Thomas Butts.

[2] Blake was at work upon a series of heads of the poets to be used as a frieze in Hayley's new library at Felpham. Twenty heads with appropriate attributes were painted in tempera on separate canvases. The heads of Ercilla and Ariosto have disappeared, but the remaining eighteen are now in the Manchester Art Gallery, and include one of Hayley's son, Thomas Alphonso. Reproductions were published by Thomas Wright for the Blake Society, Olney, 1925.

48

Little Tom[1] has been of late unattended to, and my wife's illness not being quite gone off, she has not printed any more since you went to London. But we can muster a few in colours and some in black, which I hope will be no less favour'd, tho' they are rough like rough sailors. We mean to begin printing again to-morrow. Time flies very fast and very merrily. I sometimes try to be miserable that I may do more work, but find it is a foolish experiment. Happinesses have wings and wheels; miseries are leaden legged, and their whole employment is to clip the wings and to take off the wheels of our chariots. We determine, therefore, to be happy and do all that we can, tho' not all that we would. Our dear friend Flaxman is the theme of my emulation in this of industry, as well as in other virtues and merits. Gladly I hear of his full health and spirits. Happy son of the immortal Phidias, his lot is truly glorious, and mine no less happy in his friendship and in that of his friends. Our cottage is surrounded by the same guardians you left with us; they keep off every wind. We hear the west howl at a distance, the south bounds on high over our thatch, and smiling on our cottage says: "You lay too low for my anger to injure." As to the east and north, I believe they cannot get past the Turret.

My wife joins with me in duty and affection to you. Please to remember us both in love to Mr. and Mrs. Flaxman, and

believe me to be your affectionate,

Enthusiastic, hope-fostered visionary,

William Blake

Felpham
26th November 1800

23. TO WILLIAM HAYLEY [?]*

c. 1800

I have sent all the sketches of this subject that I ever have produced. The others of the Presentation[2] I have studied, but not yet put on paper. You shall have that in a shorter time than I have taken about this, as I have nearly got rid of engraving, and feel

---

[1] *Little Tom the Sailor*, a broadside ballad by Hayley with head- and tail-pieces etched on soft metal by Blake. The sheet was "Printed for & Sold by the Widow Spicer of Folkestone for the benefit of her Orphans: October 5, 1800". Very few copies have survived. They were printed in dark brown ink and touched up with sepia washes. One, now in the British Museum, has been coloured by Blake or his wife.

[2] This perhaps refers to the water colour painting of "The Presentation of Christ in the Temple", now in the Fogg Art Museum, Cambridge, Mass., formerly in the Butts collection.

49

myself perfectly happy. I am full of business thank God, and you and Mr. Flaxman. [*Extract from sale catalogue.*]

24. TO THOMAS BUTTS

10 MAY 1801

My Dear Sir,

The necessary application to my Duty, as well to my old as new friends, has prevented me from that respect I owe in particular to you. And your accustomed forgiveness of my want of dexterity in certain points Emboldens me to hope that Forgiveness to be continued to me a little longer, When I shall be Enabled to throw off all obstructions to success.

Mr Hayley acts like a Prince. I am at complete Ease, but I wish to do my duty, especially to you, who were the precursor of my present Fortune. I never will send you a picture unworthy of my present proficiency. I soon shall send you several; my present engagements are in Miniature Painting.[1] Miniature is become a Goddess in my Eyes, & my Friends in Sussex say that I Excel in the pursuit. I have a great many orders, & they Multiply.

Now—let me intreat you to give me orders to furnish every accomodation in my power to recieve you & Mrs Butts. I know my Cottage is too narrow for your Ease & comfort; we have one room in which we could make a bed to lodge you both, & if this is sufficient, it is at your service; but as beds & rooms & accomodations are easily procur'd by one on the spot, permit me to offer my service in either way, either in my cottage, or in a lod[g]ing in the village, as is most agreeable to you, if you & Mrs Butts should think Bognor a pleasant relief from business in the Summer. It will give me the utmost delight to do my best.

Sussex is certainly a happy place, & Felpham in particular is the sweetest spot on Earth, at least it is so to me & My Good Wife, who desires her kindest Love to Mrs Butts & yourself; accept mine also, & believe me to remain,

Your devoted,

Felpham   Will Blake
May 10, 1801

[1] Blake completed miniatures of Thomas Butts, his wife and son, which are now in the British Museum Print Room. He also made others of William Cowper after Romney (in the possession of Mrs. Cowper Johnson) and of Cowper's cousin, the Rev. John Johnson (in the possession of Miss Barham Johnson). He also painted one of Mrs. Hayley, now lost, and there must have been others, but they have not been identified (see Geoffrey Keynes, "Blake's miniatures", *Times Lit. Sup.*, 1960, p. 72). In the sedition trial at Chichester in 1804 Blake described himself as "miniature Painter", rendered by Scofield as "Military Painter" (see p. 76).

25. TO THOMAS BUTTS

11 SEPTEMBER 1801

My Dear Sir,

I hope you will continue to excuse my want of steady perseverance, by which want I am still so much your debtor & you so much my Credit-er; but such as I can be, I will. I can be grateful, & I can soon Send you some of your designs which I have nearly completed. In the mean time by my Sister's hands I transmit to Mrs Butts an attempt at your likeness,[1] which I hope She, who is the best judge, will think like. Time flies faster (as seems to me) here than in London. I labour incessantly & accomplish not one half of what I intend, because my Abstract folly hurries me often away while I am at work, carrying me over Mountains & Valleys, which are not Real, in a Land of Abstraction where Spectres of the Dead[2] wander. This I endeavour to prevent & with my whole might chain my feet to the world of Duty & Reality; but in vain! the faster I bind, the better is the Ballast, for I, so far from being bound down, take the world with me in my flights, & often it seems lighter than a ball of wool rolled by the wind. Bacon & Newton[3] would prescribe ways of making the world heavier to me, & Pitt[4] would prescribe distress for a medicinal potion; but as none on Earth can give me Mental Distress, & I know that all Distress inflicted by Heaven is a Mercy, a Fig for all Corporeal! Such Distress is My mock & scorn. Alas! wretched, happy, ineffectual labourer of time's moments that I am! who shall deliver me from this Spirit of Abstraction & Improvidence? Such, my Dear Sir, Is the truth of my state, & I tell it you in palliation of my seeming neglect of your most pleasant orders; but I have not neglected them, & yet a Year is rolled over, & only now I approach the prospect of sending you some, which you may expect soon. I should have sent them by My Sister, but, as the Coach goes three times a week to London & they [shall *del.*] will arrive as safe as with her, I shall have an opportunity of inclosing several together which are not yet completed. I thank you again & again for your generous forbearance, of which I have need—& now I must express my wishes to see you at Felpham & to shew you Mr Hayley's Library, which is still unfinish'd, but is in a finishing way & looks well. I ought also to mention my Extreme disappointment

---

[1] The miniature already mentioned.

[2] "The spectres of the dead" are used by Blake in more than one sense. Here he seems to mean "the abstract idea for which the artist cannot, save by inspiration, find the living form, the eternally right expression" (see Sloss & Wallis, ii, 226–8).

[3] Bacon and Newton are the symbols of science and materialism, the enemies of imagination and art.

[4] Pitt's name is the symbol of the promoter of War. cp. Blake's tempera painting of "The Spiritual Form of Pitt guiding Behemoth", now in the Tate Gallery.

51

at Mr Johnson's[1] forgetfulness, who appointed to call on you but did Not. He is also a happy Abstract, known by all his Friends as the most innocent forgetter of his own Interests. He is a nephew to the late Mr Cowper the Poet; you would like him much. I continue painting Miniatures & Improve more & more, as all my friends tell me; but my Principal labour at this time is Engraving Plates for Cowper's Life,[2] a Work of Magnitude, which Mr Hayley is now Labouring with all his matchless industry, & which will be a most valuable acquisition to Literature, not only on account of Mr Hayley's composition, but also as it will contain Letters of Cowper to his friends, Perhaps, or rather Certainly, the very best letters that ever were published.

My wife joins with me in Love to you & Mrs Butts, hoping that her joy is now increased, & yours also, in an increase of family & of health & happiness.

I remain, Dear Sir,
Ever Yours Sincerely,
William Blake

Felpham Cottage
  of Cottages the prettiest
September 11. 1801

Next time I have the happiness to see you, I am determined to paint another Portrait of you from Life in my best manner,[3] for Memory will not do in such minute operations; for I have now discover'd that without Nature before the painter's Eye, he can never produce any thing in the walks of Natural Painting. Historical Designing is one thing & Portrait Painting another, & they are as Distinct as any two Arts can be. Happy would that Man be who could unite them!

P.S. Please to Remember our best respects to Mr Birch,[4] & tell him that Felpham Men are the mildest of the human race; if it is the will of Providence, they shall be the wisest. We hope that he will, next summer, joke us face to face.—God bless you all!

---

[1] The Rev. John Johnson, Cowper's cousin, whom Blake had met when Johnson was on a visit to Hayley.

[2] *The Life and Posthumous Writings of William Cowper by William Hayley*, Chichester, 3 vols., 4°, 1803–4, containing five engravings by Blake, one of which is an excellent stippled plate of a bust of Cowper in a night-cap after Lawrence.

[3] No portrait of Butts by Blake other than the miniature is known to exist.

[4] John Birch (1745–1815), surgeon, who attended Blake and his wife. See also pp. 66 and 110. He was also a believer in the efficacy of electrical treatment for rheumatism and other disorders, and published a *Letter to the author on medical electricity* in George Adams' *Essay on Electricity*, London, 1792, 8°.

26. JOHN FLAXMAN TO BLAKE

[This letter is written on the second leaf of a letter from Flaxman to Hayley. Flaxman, writing from Buckingham Street, Fitzroy Square, Oct. 7, 1801, concludes his message to Hayley with the words, "I shall beg your permission to address the other side to M͏ʳ Blake".]

Dear Blake,.

I rejoice in your happiness & contentment under the kind & affectionate auspices of our Friend. M͏ʳˢ Flaxman & myself would feel no small gratification in a visit of participation in the domestic Innocence & satisfaction of your rural retreat; but the same Providence that has given retirement to you, has placed me in a great City where my employments continually exact an attention neither to be remitted or delayed, & thus the All bestowing Hand deals out happiness to his creatures when they are sensible of His Goodness; the little commissions I troubled you with in my last are such as one friend offers unwillingly to another on account of the scanty recompence, but I know you relieve yourself from more tedious labours by Composition & Design, when they are done let me have them & I will take care to get the money for you.

My Wife unites in love to you & M͏ʳˢ Blake

with your affectionate

J Flaxman

27. TO JOHN FLAXMAN

Dear Flaxman,

I rejoice to hear that your Great Work is accomplish'd. Peace[1] opens the way to greater still. The Kingdoms of this World are now become the Kingdoms of God & his Christ, & we shall reign with him for ever & ever. The Reign of Literature & the Arts Commences. Blessed are those who are found studious of Literature & Humane & polite accomplishments. Such have their lamps burning & such shall shine as the stars.

M͏ʳ Thomas, your friend to whom you was so kind as to make honourable mention of me, has been at Felpham & did me the favor to call on me. I have promis'd him to send my designs for Comus[2] when I have done them, directed to you.

[1] Peace with Napoleon Buonaparte. Negotiations were opened this year and concluded in March 1802.

[2] Blake completed two sets of eight illustrations each for *Comus* in watercolours. Both are now in America, one in the Boston Museum of Fine Arts and the other in the H. E. Huntington Library, California. The set sent to "Mr. Thomas" is probably the latter.

Now I hope to see the Great Works of Art, as they are so near to Felpham, Paris being scarce further off than London. But I hope that France & England will henceforth be as One Country and their Arts One, & that you will Ere long be erecting Monuments In Paris—Emblems of Peace.

My Wife joins with me in love to You & Mrs Flaxman.

I remain, Yours Sincerely

Oct 19 1801 William Blake

[Postscript in Hayley's hand]

I have just seen Weller[1]—all yr Friends in the south are willing to await yr Leisure for Works of Marble, but Weller says it would soothe & comfort the good sister of the upright Mr. D.[2] to see a little sketch from yr Hand.

adio.

28. TO THOMAS BUTTS 10 JANUARY 1802

Felpham Jany 10. 1802

Dear Sir,

Your very kind & affectionate Letter & the many kind things you have said in it, call'd upon me for an immediate answer; but it found My Wife & Myself so Ill, & My wife so very ill, that till now I have not been able to do this duty. The Ague & Rheumatism have been almost her constant Enemies, which she has combated in vain ever since we have been here; & her sickness is always my sorrow, of course. But what you tell me about your sight afflicted me not a little, & that about your health, in another part of your letter, makes me intreat you to take due care of both; it is a part of our duty to God & man to take due care of his Gifts; & tho' we ought not [to] think *more* highly of ourselves, yet we ought to think *As* highly of ourselves as immortals ought to think.

When I came down here, I was more sanguine than I am at present; but it was because I was ignorant of many things which have since occurred, & chiefly the unhealthiness of the place. Yet I do not repent of coming on a thousand accounts; & Mr H., I doubt not, will do ultimately all that both he & I wish—that is, to lift me out of difficulty; but this is no easy matter to a man who, having Spiritual Enemies of such formidable magnitude, cannot expect to want natural hidden ones.

[1] Mr. Weller, wood carver, of Chichester, to whom Blake afterwards gave a copy of Hayley's *Ballads*, 1805 (see Keynes, *Bibliography of Blake*, 1921, pp. 419–20).

[2] "Mr. D." is "M^r. Dear, a man of great integrity" mentioned in the accompanying letter (with no. 26) from Flaxman to Hayley. Francis Dear, citizen and Alderman of Chichester, died in 1801 and is commemorated in the Cathedral by a monument done by Flaxman.

Your approbation of my pictures is a Multitude to Me, & I doubt not that all your kind wishes in my behalf shall in due time be fulfilled. Your kind offer of pecuniary assistance I can only thank you for at present, because I have enough to serve my present purpose here; our expenses are small, & our income, from our incessant labour, fully adequate to [it *del*.] them at present. I am now engaged in Engraving 6 small plates for a New Edition of Mr Hayley's Triumphs of Temper,[1] from drawings by Maria Flaxman, sister to my friend the Sculptor, and it seems that other things will follow in course, if I do but Copy these well; but Patience! if Great things do not turn out, it is because such things depend on the Spiritual & not on the Natural World; & if it was fit for me, I doubt not that I should be Employ'd in Greater things; & when it is proper, my Talents shall be properly exercised in Public, as I hope they are now in private; for, till then, I leave no stone unturn'd & no path unexplor'd that tends to improvement in my beloved Arts. One thing of real consequence I have accomplish'd by coming into the country, which is to me consolation enough: namely, I have recollected all my scatter'd thoughts on Art & resumed my primitive & original ways of Execution in both painting & engraving, which in the confusion of London I had very much lost & obliterated from my mind. But whatever becomes of my labours, I would rather that they should be preserv'd in your Green House (not, as you mistakenly call it, dung hill) than in the cold gallery of fashion.—The Sun may yet shine, & then they will be brought into open air.

But you have so generously & openly desired that I will divide my griefs with you, that I cannot hide what it is now become my duty to explain.—My unhappiness has arisen from a source which, if explor'd too narrowly, might hurt my pecuniary circumstances, As my dependence is on Engraving at present, & particularly on the Engravings I have in hand for Mr H.: & I find on all hands great objections to my doing any thing but the meer drudgery of business, & intimations that if I do not confine myself to this, I shall not live; this has always pursu'd me. You will understand by this the source of all my uneasiness. This from Johnson[2] & Fuseli brought me down here, & this from Mr H. will bring me back again; for that I cannot live without doing my duty to lay up treasures in heaven is Certain

---

[1] *The Triumphs of Temper. A Poem: In Six Cantos.* By William Hayley Esq. The Twelfth Edition corrected. With New Original Designs by Maria Flaxman. London, 1803, 8°. With six plates engraved by Blake, which appeared also in the thirteenth edition, 1807.

[2] Joseph Johnson, bookseller and publisher, who had employed Blake in engraving many illustrations for books.

& Determined, & to this I have long made up my mind, & why this should be made an objection to Me, while Drunkenness, Lewdness, Gluttony & even Idleness itself, does not hurt other men, let Satan himself Explain. The Thing I have most at Heart—more than life, or all that seems to make life comfortable without—Is the Interest of True Religion & Science,[1] & whenever any thing appears to affect that Interest (Especially if I myself omit any duty to my [self *de.*] Station as a Soldier of Christ), It gives me the greatest of torments. I am not ashamed, afraid, or averse to tell you what Ought to be Told: That I am under the direction of Messengers from Heaven, Daily & Nightly; but the nature of such things is not, as some suppose, without trouble or care. Temptations are on the right hand & left; behind, the sea of time & space[2] roars & follows swiftly; he who keeps not right onward is lost, & if our footsteps slide in clay, how can we do otherwise than fear & tremble? but I should not have troubled You with this account of my spiritual state, unless it had been necessary in explaining the actual cause of my uneasiness, into which you are so kind as to Enquire; for I never obtrude such things on others unless question'd, & then I never disguise the truth. —But if we fear to do the dictates of our Angels, & tremble at the Tasks set before us; if we refuse to do Spiritual Acts because of Natural Fears or Natural Desires! Who can describe the dismal torments of such a state!—I too well remember the Threats I heard!—If you, who are organised by Divine Providence for Spiritual communion, Refuse, & bury your Talent in the Earth, even tho' you should want Natural Bread, Sorrow & Desperation pursues you thro' life, & after death Shame & confusion of face to eternity. Every one in Eternity will leave you, aghast at the Man who was crown'd with glory & honour by his brethren, & betray'd their cause to their enemies. You will be call'd the base Judas who betray'd his Friend!—Such words would make any stout man tremble, & how then could I be at ease? But I am now no longer in That State, & now go on again with my Task, Fearless, and tho' my path is difficult, I have no fear of stumbling while I keep it.

My wife desires her kindest Love to Mrs Butts, & I have permitted her to send it to you also; we often wish that we could unite again in Society, & hope that the time is not distant when we shall do so, being determin'd not to remain another winter here, but to return to London.

---

[1] That is of Art, which to Blake was almost synonymous with Christianity: "Science" is here used in the special sense of spiritual knowledge (see Sloss & Wallis, ii, 216).

[2] "The sea of time and space" signifies experiences in the material world, which interfere with the exercise of vision and imagination.

I hear a voice you cannot hear, that says I must not stay,
I see a hand you cannot see, that beckons me away.[1]

Naked we came here, naked of Natural things, & naked we shall return; but while cloth'd with the Divine Mercy, we are richly cloth'd in Spiritual & suffer all the rest gladly. Pray give my Love to Mrs Butts & your family, I am, Yours Sincerely,

William Blake

P.S. Your Obliging proposal of Exhibiting my two Pictures likewise calls for my thanks; I will finish the other, & then we shall judge of the matter with certainty.

29. TO THOMAS BUTTS

22 NOVEMBER 1802

Felpham, Novr 22: 1802.

Dear Sir,

My Brother[2] tells me that he fears you are offended with me. I fear so too, because there appears some reason why you might be so. But when you have heard me out, you will not be so.

I have now given two years to the intense study of those parts of the art which relate to light & shade & colour, & am Convinc'd that either my understanding is incapable of comprehending the beauties of Colouring, or the Pictures which I painted for you Are Equal in Every part of the Art, & superior in One, to any thing that has been done since the age of Rafael.—All Sr J. Reynolds's discourses to the Royal Academy will shew that the Venetian finesse in Art can never be united with the Majesty of Colouring necessary to Historical beauty; & in a letter to the Revd Mr Gilpin, author of a work on Picturesque Scenery, he says Thus:[3] "It may be worth "consideration whether the epithet Picturesque is not applicable" "to the excellencies of the inferior Schools rather than to the higher." "The works of Michael Angelo, Rafael, &c appear to me to have" "nothing of it: whereas Rubens & the Venetian Painters may almost" "be said to have Nothing Else.—Perhaps Picturesque is somewhat" "synonymous to the word Taste, which we should think improperly" "applied to Homer or Milton, but very well to Prior or Pope. I" "suspect that the application of these words are to Excellencies of" "an inferior order, & which are incompatible with the Grand Style."

---

[1] These four lines, written by Blake as two, are from Thomas Tickell's "Lucy and Colin", included in Percy's *Reliques of Ancient English Poetry*, London, 1765, vol. III, p. 308.

[2] His elder brother, James, the hosier.

[3] *Three Essays on Picturesque Beauty*, by William Gilpin, 1792, p. 35.

"You are certainly right in saying that variety of Tints & Forms is"
"Picturesque; but it must be remember'd, on the other hand, that"
"the reverse of this (*uniformity of Colour* & a *long continuation of lines*)"
"produces Grandeur."—So Says S ir Joshua, and So say I; for I
have now proved that the parts of the art which I neglected to dis-
play in those little pictures & drawings which I had the pleasure &
profit to do for you, are incompatible with the designs.—There is
nothing in the Art which our Painters do that I can confess myself
ignorant of. I also Know & Understand & can assuredly affirm,
that the works I have done for You are Equal to Carrache or Rafael
(and I am now Seven years older than Rafael was when he died),
I say they are Equal to Carrache or Rafael, or Else I am Blind,
Stupid, Ignorant and Incapable in two years' Study to understand
those things which a Boarding School Miss can comprehend in a
fortnight. Be assured, My dear Friend, that there is not one touch
in those Drawings & Pictures but what came from my Head & my
Heart in Unison; That I am Proud of being their Author and
Grateful to you my Employer; & that I look upon you as the Chief
of my Friends, whom I would endeavour to please, because you,
among all men, have enabled me to produce these things. I would
not send you a Drawing or a Picture till I had again reconsider'd
my notions of Art, & had put myself back as if I was a learner. I
have proved that I am Right, & shall now Go on with the Vigor
I was in my Childhood famous for.

But I do not pretend to be Perfect: but, if my Works have faults,
Carrache, Corregio, & Rafael's have faults also; let me observe that
the yellow leather flesh of old men, the ill drawn & ugly young
women, &, above all, the dawbed black & yellow shadows that are
found in most fine, ay, & the finest pictures, I altogether reject as
ruinous to Effect, tho' Connoisseurs may think otherwise.

Let me also notice that Carrache's Pictures are not like Correggio's, nor Correggio's like Rafael's; &, if neither of them was to
be encouraged till he did like any of the others, he must die without
Encouragement. My Pictures are unlike any of these Painters, & I
would have them to be so. I think the manner I adopt More Perfect
than any other; no doubt They thought the same of theirs.

You will be tempted to think that, as I improve, The Pictures,
& c., that I did for you are not what I would now wish them to be.
On this I beg to say That they are what I intended them, & that
I know I never shall do better; for, if I was to do them over again,
they would lose as much as they gain'd, because they were done in
the heat of My Spirits.

But You will Justly enquire why I have not written all this time
to you? I answer I have been very Unhappy, & could not think of

troubling you about it, or any of my real Friends. (I have written many letters to you which I burn'd & did not send) & why I have not before now finish'd the Miniature I promiss'd to Mrs Butts? I answer I have not, till now, in any degree pleased myself, & now I must intreat you to Excuse faults, for Portrait Painting is the direct contrary to Designing & Historical Painting in every respect. If you have not Nature before you for Every Touch, you cannot Paint Portrait; & if you have Nature before you at all, you cannot Paint History; it was Michael Angelo's opinion & is Mine. Pray Give My Wife's love with mine to Mrs Butts; assure her that it cannot be long before I have the pleasure of Painting from you in Person, & then that She may Expect a likeness, but now I have done All I could, & know she will forgive any failure in consideration of the Endeavour.

And now let me finish with assuring you that, Tho' I have been very unhappy, I am so no longer. I am again Emerged into the light of Day; I still & shall to Eternity Embrace Christianity and Adore him who is the Express image of God; but I have travel'd thro' Perils & Darkness not unlike a Champion. I have Conquer'd, and shall still Go on Conquering. Nothing can withstand the fury of my Course among the Stars of God & in the Abysses of the Accuser. My Enthusiasm is still what it was, only Enlarged and confirm'd.

I now Send Two Pictures & hope you will approve of them. I have inclosed the Account of Money reciev'd & Work done, which I ought long ago to have sent you; pray forgive Errors in omissions of this kind. I am incapable of many attentions which it is my Duty to observe towards you, thro' multitude of employment & thro' hope of soon seeing you again. I often omit to Enquire of you. But pray let me now hear how you do & of the welfare of your family.

Accept my Sincere love & respect.

I remain Yours Sincerely,
Willm Blake

A Piece of Sea Weed serves for a Barometer; at [it] gets wet & dry as the weather gets so.

30. TO THOMAS BUTTS

22 NOVEMBER 1802

Dear Sir,

After I had finish'd my Letter, I found that I had not said half what I intended to say, & in particular I wish to ask you what subject you choose to be painted on the remaining Canvas which I brought down with me (for there were three), and to tell you that several of the Drawings were in great forwardness; you will see by the Inclosed Account that the remaining Number of Drawings which you gave me orders for is Eighteen. I will finish these with all possible Expedition, if indeed I have not tired you, or, as it is politely call'd, Bored you too much already; or, if you would rather cry out Enough, Off, Off!, tell me in a Letter of forgiveness if you were offended, & of accustom'd friendship if you were not. But I will bore you more with some Verses which My Wife desires me to Copy out & send you with her kind love & Respect; they were Composed above a twelve-month ago, while walking from Felpham to Lavant to meet my Sister:

> With happiness stretch'd across the hills
> In a cloud that dewy sweetness distills,
> With a blue sky spread over with wings
> And a mild sun that mounts & sings,
> With trees & fields full of Fairy elves
> And little devils who fight for themselves—
> Rememb'ring the Verses that Hayley sung
> When my heart knock'd against the root of my tongue—[1]
> With Angels planted in Hawthorn bowers
> And God himself in the passing hours,
> With Silver Angels across my way
> And Golden Demons that none can stay,
> With my Father hovering upon the wind
> And my Brother Robert[2] just behind
> And my Brother John[3] the evil one
> In a black cloud making his mone;
> Tho' dead, they appear upon my path,
> Notwithstanding my terrible wrath:

[1] The two lines beginning "Rememb'ring the Verses", are written in the margin and marked: "These 2 lines were omitted in transcribing & ought to come in at X". The "Verses that Hayley sung" are probably to be identified with a MS entitled *Genesis, the Seven Days of the Created World*. This consists of about 200 lines of blank verse written in Blake's hand, recently identified by Mr. Kenneth Povey as a close translation of the opening lines of Tasso's *Le Sette Giornate del Mondo Creato* (see *Times Literary Supplement*, 3 November 1952). The MS is now in private hands in America and was printed in a limited edition by the Cummington Press, Cummington, Mass. [1952].

[2] Robert, the youngest of the family, died at the age of 25 in 1787. He had been William's special favourite (see Keynes, *Blake Studies*. 1948, p. 3).

[3] John, the third son in the family, was said by Frederick Tatham to have "lived a few reckless days, enlisted as a soldier, and died". He had been apprenticed to a ginger-bread maker, but afterwards begged at William's door (see *Letters of W. B.*, ed. Russell, p. 2).

They beg, they intreat, they drop their tears,
Fill'd full of hopes, fill'd full of fears—
With a thousand Angels upon the Wind
Pouring disconsolate from behind
To drive them off, & before my way
A frowning Thistle implores my stay.
What to others a trifle appears
Fills me full of smiles or tears;
For double the vision my Eyes do see,[1]
And a double vision is always with me.
With my inward Eye 'tis an old Man grey;
With my outward, a Thistle across my way.
"If thou goest back," the thistle said,
"Thou art to endless woe betray'd;
For here does Theotormon[2] lower
And here is Enitharmon's bower
And Los the terrible thus hath sworn,
Because thou backward dost return,
Poverty, Envy, old age & fear
Shall bring thy Wife upon a bier;
And Butts shall give what Fuseli gave,
A dark black Rock & a gloomy Cave."

I struck the Thistle with my foot,
And broke him up from his delving root:
"Must the duties of life each other cross?"
"Must every joy be dung & dross?"
"Must my dear Butts feel cold neglect"
"Because I give Hayley his due respect?"
"Must Flaxman look upon me as wild,"
"And all my friends be with doubts beguil'd?"
"Must my Wife live in my Sister's bane,"
"Or my Sister survive on my Love's pain?"
"The curses of Los the terrible shade"
"And his dismal terrors make me afraid."

So I spoke & struck in my wrath
The old man weltering upon my path.

[1] Single vision is purely material perception; in double vision intellect has made its contribution; threefold vision is emotional, and fourfold spiritual. This is all expressed in the last lines of the poem.

[2] Theotormon is one of the four sons of Los and Enitharmon, that is of the Spirit of Prophecy. These sons remained in the spiritual world of Blake's mythology and were the guardians of the spiritual life (see Sloss & Wallis, ii, 194, and Russell, *Letters*, 1906, p. 109).

Then Los appear'd in all his power:
In the Sun he appear'd, descending before
My face in fierce flames; in my double sight
'Twas outward a Sun: inward Los in his might.

"My hands are labour'd day & night,"
"And Ease comes never in my sight."
"My Wife has no indulgence given"
"Except what comes to her from heaven."
"We eat little, we drink less;"
"This Earth breeds not our happiness."
"Another Sun feeds our life's streams."
"We are not warmed with thy beams;"
"Thou measurest not the Time to me,"
"Nor yet the Space that I do see;"
"My Mind is not with thy light array'd."
"Thy terrors shall not make me afraid."

When I had my Defiance given,
The Sun stood trembling in heaven;
The Moon that glow'd remote below,
Became leprous & white as snow;
And every soul of men on the Earth
Felt affliction & sorrow & sickness & dearth.
Los flam'd in my path, & the Sun was hot
With the bows of my Mind & the Arrows of Thought[1]—
My bowstring fierce with Ardour breathes,
My arrows glow in their golden sheaves;
My brothers & father march before;
The heavens drop with human gore.

Now I a fourfold vision see,
And a fourfold vision is given to me;
'Tis fourfold in my supreme delight
And threefold in soft Beulah's night
And twofold Always. May God us keep
From Single vision & Newton's sleep!

I also inclose you some Ballads by Mr Hayley,[2] with prints to

---

[1] cp. *Milton*, Preface:

> Bring me my Bow of burning gold:
> Bring me my Arrows of desire:

[2] *Designs to a Series of Ballads written by William Hayley*, Chichester, 1802, 4⁰, in four parts with fourteen engravings by Blake.

them by Your H^{ble.} Servt. I should have sent them before now, but could not get any thing done for You to please myself; for I do assure you that I have truly studied the two little pictures I now send, & do not repent of the time I have spent upon them.

God bless you.

Yours,
W. B.

P.S. I have taken the liberty to trouble you with a letter to my Brother, which you will be so kind as to send or give him, & oblige yours,   W.B.

31. TO JAMES BLAKE

30 JANUARY 1803

Felpham,
Jan^{y.}, 30, 1803.

Dear Brother,

Your Letter mentioning Mr Butts' account of my Ague surprized me because I have no Ague, but have had a Cold this Winter. You know that it is my way to make the best of every thing. I never make myself nor my friends uneasy if I can help it. My Wife has had Agues & Rheumatisms almost ever since she has been here, but our time is almost out that we took the Cottage for. I did not mention our Sickness to you & should not to Mr Butts but for a determination which we have lately made, namely To leave This Place, because I am now certain of what I have long doubted, Viz that H. is jealous as Stothard was & will be no further My friend than he is compell'd by circumstances. The truth is, As a Poet he is frighten'd at me & as a Painter his views & mine are opposite; he thinks to turn me into a Portrait Painter as he did Poor Romney, but this he nor all the devils in hell will never do. I must own that seeing H. like S., Envious (& that he is I am now certain) made me very uneasy, but it is over & I now defy the worst & fear not while I am true to myself which I will be. This is the uneasiness I spoke of to Mr Butts, but I did not tell him so plain & wish you to keep it a secret & to burn this letter because it speaks so plain. I told Mr Butts that I did not wish to Explore too much the cause of our determination to leave Felpham because of pecuniary connexions between H. & me—Be not then uneasy on any account & tell my Sister not to be uneasy, for I am fully Employ'd & Well Paid. I have made it so much H's interest to employ me that he can no longer treat me with indifference & now it is in my power to stay or return or remove to

63

any other place that I choose, because I am getting before hand in money matters. The Profits arising from Publications are immense, & I now have it in my power to commence publication with many very formidable works, which I have finish'd & ready. A Book price half a guinea may be got out at the Expense of Ten pounds & its almost certain profits are 500 G. I am only sorry that I did not know the methods of publishing years ago, & this is one of the numerous benefits I have obtain'd by coming here, for I should never have known the nature of Publication unless I had known H. & his connexions & his method of managing. It now would be folly not to venture publishing. I am now Engraving Six little plates for a little work[1] of M^r H's, for which I am to have 10 Guineas each, & the certain profits of that work are a fortune such as would make me independent, supposing that I could substantiate such a one of my own & I mean to try many. But I again say as I said before, We are very Happy sitting at tea by a wood fire in our Cottage, the wind singing above our roof & the sea roaring at a distance, but if sickness comes all is unpleasant.

But my letter to Mr Butts appears to me not to be so explicit as that to you, for I told you that I should come to London in the Spring to commence Publisher & he has offer'd me every assistance in his power without knowing my intention. But since I wrote yours we had made the resolution of which we inform'd him, viz to leave Felpham entirely. I also told you what I was about & that I was not ignorant of what was doing in London in works of art. But I did not mention Illness because I hoped to get better (for I was really very ill when I wrote to him the last time) & was not then perswaded as I am now that the air tho' warm is unhealthy.

However, this I know will set you at Ease. I am now so full of work that I have had no time to go on with the Ballads, & my prospects of more & more work continually are certain. My Heads of Cowper for M^r H's life of Cowper have pleas'd his Relations exceedingly & in Particular Lady Hesketh & Lord Cowper—to please Lady H. was a doubtful chance who almost ador'd her Cousin the poet & thought him all perfection, & she writes that she is quite satisfied with the portraits & charm'd by the great Head in particular, tho' she never could bear the original Picture.

But I ought to mention to you that our present idea is: To take a house in some village further from the Sea, Perhaps Lavant, & in or near the road to London for the sake of convenience. I also ought to inform you that I read your letter to Mr H. & that he is very afraid of losing me & also very afraid that my Friends in London should have a bad opinion of the reception he has given to me. But

[1] Hayley's *Triumphs of Temper*, 1803.

My Wife has undertaken to Print the whole number of the Plates for Cowper's work, which She does to admiration, & being under my own eye the prints are as fine as the French prints & please every one: in short I have Got every thing so under my thumb that it is more profitable that things should be as they are than any other way, tho' not so agreeable, because we wish naturally for friendship in preference to interest.—The Publishers[1] are already indebted to My Wife Twenty Guineas for work deliver'd; this is a small specimen of how we go on: then fear nothing & let my Sister fear nothing because it appears to me that I am now too old & have had too much experience to be any longer imposed upon, only illness makes all uncomfortable & this we must prevent by every means in our power.

I send with this 5 Copies of N4 of the Ballads for Mrs Flaxman & Five more, two of which you will be so good as to give to Mrs Chetwynd[2] if she should call or send for them. These Ballads are likely to be Profitable, for we have Sold all that we have had time to print. Evans the Bookseller in Pallmall says they go off very well, & why should we repent of having done them? it is doing Nothing that is to be repented of & not doing such things as these.

Pray remember us both to Mr Hall when you see him.

I write in great haste & with a head full of botheration about various projected works & particularly a work now Proposed to the Public at the End of Cowper's Life, which will very likely be of great consequence; it is Cowper's Milton, the same that Fuseli's Milton Gallery was painted for, & if we succeed in our intentions the prints to this work will be very profitable to me & not only profitable, but honourable at any rate.[3] The Project pleases Lord Cowper's family, & I am now labouring in my thoughts Designs for this & other works equally creditable. These are works to be boasted of, & therefore I cannot feel depress'd, tho' I know that as far as Designing & Poetry are concern'd I am Envied in many Quarters, but I will cram the dogs, for I know that the Public are my friends & love my works & will embrace them whenever they see them. My only Difficulty is to produce fast enough.

I go on Merrily with my Greek & Latin; am very sorry that I did not begin to learn languages early in life as I find it very Easy; am now learning my Hebrew אבּג.[4] I read Greek as fluently as an

---

[1] Joseph Seagrave of Chichester.

[2] Among Romney's sitters was a Mr. Chetwynd.

[3] These plates were not engraved.

[4] That is, ABC. Several times after this date Blake introduced Hebrew characters in his designs, as in the lithograph of *Enoch*, 1807, the engraving of the *Laocoön*, c. 1817, and the title-page and plate 2 of *Illustrations of the Book of Job*, 1826. He also made, perhaps in 1803, a series of trial sketches of Hebrew characters, using

65

Oxford scholar & the Testament is my chief master: astonishing indeed is the English Translation, it is almost word for word, & if the Hebrew Bible is as well translated, which I do not doubt it is, we need not doubt of its having been translated as well as written by the Holy Ghost.

. .   my wife joins me in Love to you both.

I am, Sincerely yours,

W. Blake

32. TO THOMAS BUTTS

25 APRIL 1803

My Dear Sir,

I write in haste, having reciev'd a pressing Letter from my Brother. I intended to have sent the Picture of the Riposo,[1] which is nearly finish'd much to my satisfaction, but not quite; you shall have it soon. I now send the 4 Numbers for Mr Birch, with best Respects to him. The Reason the Ballads have been suspended is the pressure of other business, but they will go on again soon.[2]

Accept of my thanks for your kind & heartening Letter. You have Faith in the Endeavours of Me, your weak brother & fellow Disciple; how great must be your faith in our Divine Master! You are to me a Lesson of Humility, while you Exalt me by such distinguishing commendations. I know that you see certain merits in me, which, by God's Grace, shall be made fully apparent & perfect in Eternity; in the mean time I must not bury the Talents in the Earth, but do my endeavour to live to the Glory of our Lord & Saviour; & I am also grateful to the kind hand that endeavours to lift me out of despondency, even if it lifts me too high.

And now, My Dear Sir, Congratulate me on my return to London, with the full approbation of Mr Hayley & with Promise— But, Alas!

Now I may say to you, what perhaps I should not dare to say to any one else: That I can alone carry on my visionary studies in London unannoy'd, & that I may converse with my friends in

---

human figures for the component parts; this drawing is now in the Whitworth Institute Gallery, Manchester, and is reproduced in *Pencil Drawings*, ed. Keynes, 1927, pl. 27.

[1] There is a water-colour painting of this subject formerly in the Graham Robertson collection, and now in the Print Room at the British Museum, but the allusion seems to be to a tempera, now destroyed. It is described by Rossetti (Gilchrist, *Life*, 1880, ii, 238) as: "Tempera. The Holy Family are within a tent; an angel at its entrance; the donkey outside. Very dark by decay of the surface, and otherwise injured."

[2] No further numbers were in fact published.

Eternity, See Visions, Dream Dreams & prophecy & speak Parables
unobserv'd & at liberty from the Doubts of other Mortals; perhaps
Doubts proceeding from Kindness, but Doubts are always per-
nicious, Especially when we Doubt our Friends. Christ is very
decided on this Point: "He who is Not With Me is Against Me."
There is no Medium or Middle state; & if a Man is the Enemy of
my Spiritual Life while he pretends to be the Friend of my Corporeal, he is a Real Enemy—but the Man may be the friend of my
Spiritual Life while he seems the Enemy of my Corporeal, but Not
Vice Versa.

What is very pleasant, Every one who hears of my going to
London again Applauds it as the only course for the interest of all
concern'd in My Works, Observing that I ought not to be away
from the opportunities London affords of seeing fine Pictures, and
the various improvements in Works of Art going on in London.

But none can know the Spiritual Acts of my three years' Slumber
on the banks of the Ocean, unless he has seen them in the Spirit, or
unless he should read My long Poem[1] descriptive of those Acts; for
I have in these three years composed an immense number of verses
on One Grand Theme, Similar to Homer's Iliad or Milton's
Paradise Lost, the Persons & Machinery intirely new to the Inhabitants of Earth (some of the Persons Excepted). I have written
this Poem from immediate Dictation, twelve or sometimes twenty
or thirty lines at a time, without Premeditation & even against my
Will; the Time it has taken in writing was thus render'd Non
Existent, & an immense Poem Exists which seems to be the Labour
of a long Life, all produc'd without Labour or Study. I mention
this to shew you what I think the Grand Reason of my being
brought down here.

I have a thousand & ten thousand things to say to you. My heart
is full of futurity. I percieve that the sore travel which has been given
me these three years leads to Glory & Honour. I rejoice & I tremble:
"I am fearfully & wonderfully made." I had been reading the
cxxxix Psalm a little before your Letter arrived. I take your advice.
I see the face of my Heavenly Father; he lays his Hand upon my
Head & gives a blessing to all my works; why should I be troubled?
why should my heart & flesh cry out? I will go on in the Strength
of the Lord; through Hell will I sing forth his Praises, that the
Dragons of the Deep may praise him, & that those who dwell in
darkness & in the Sea coasts may be gather'd into his Kingdom.

[1] This no doubt refers to the long symbolic poem entitled *Milton*. The title-page
of this, dated 1804, indicates that there were to be twelve books, though only two
were finished about 1808. The rest of the material seems to have been transferred
to the longer poem, *Jerusalem*, finished about 1818.

Excuse my, perhaps, too great Enthusiasm. Please to accept of & give our Loves to Mrs Butts & your amiable Family, & believe me to be,

Ever Yours Affectionately,
Will Blake

Felpham
April 25. 1803

33. TO THOMAS BUTTS

6 JULY 1803

Dear Sir,

I send you the Riposo, which I hope you will think my best Picture in many respects. It represents the Holy Family in Egypt, Guarded in their Repose from those Fiends, the Egyptian Gods,[1] and tho' not directly taken from a Poem of Milton's (for till I had design'd it Milton's Poem did not come into my Thoughts), Yet it is very similar to his Hymn on the Nativity,[2] which you will find among his smaller Poems, & will read with great delight. I have given, in the background, a building, which may be supposed the ruin of a Part of Nimrod's tower,[3] which I conjecture to have spread over many Countries; for he ought to be reckon'd of the Giant brood.

I have now on the Stocks the following drawings[4] for you: 1. Jephthah sacrificing his Daughter; 2. Ruth & her mother in Law & Sister; 3. The three Maries at the Sepulcher; 4. The Death of Joseph; 5. The Death of the Virgin Mary; 6. St Paul Preaching; & 7. The Angel of the Divine Presence clothing Adam & Eve with Coats of Skins.

These are all in great forwardness, & I am satisfied that I improve very much & shall continue to do so while I live, which is a blessing I can never be too thankful for both to God & Man.

[1] cp. the sentences on the Laocoön print, c. 1820: "The Gods of Greece & Egypt were Mathematical Diagrams". "Egypt . . . Whose Gods are the Powers of this World, Goddess Nature, Who first spoil & then destroy Imaginative Art; For their Glory is War and Dominion." (*Complete Writings*, 1966, p. 776).

[2] Six years later, in 1809, Blake made a series of water-colour designs for this poem, which are now in the Whitworth Institute Gallery, Manchester.

[3] That is, the Tower of Babel, traditionally supposed to have been built by Nimrod, the huntsman and slayer, symbol of violence and cruelty, and therefore one of the brutal Giant Brood.

[4] All these water-colour drawings were afterwards in the Graham Robertson collection except no. 6. No. 1 is now in the British Museum Print Room, no. 2 in the Southampton Art Gallery, no. 5 in the Tate Gallery, nos. 3 and 7 in the Fitzwilliam Museum, Cambridge, and no. 6 in the Rhode Island School of Design, U.S.A.

We look forward every day with pleasure toward our meeting again in London with those whom we have learn'd to value by absence no less perhaps than we did by presence; for recollection often surpasses every thing, indeed, the prospect of returning to our friends is supremely delightful—Then, I am determin'd that Mrs Butts shall have a good likeness of You, if I have hands & eyes left; for I am become a likeness taker & succeed admirably well; but this is not to be atchiev'd without the original sitting before you for Every touch, all likenesses from memory being necessarily very very defective; but Nature & Fancy are Two Things & can Never be joined; neither ought any one to attempt it, for it is Idolatry & destroys the Soul.

I ought to tell you that Mr H. is quite agreeable to our return, & that there is all the appearance in the world of our being fully employ'd in Engraving for his projected Works, Particularly Cowper's Milton, a Work now on foot by Subscription, & I understand that the Subscription goes on briskly. This work is to be a very Elegant one & to consist of All Milton's Poems, with Cowper's Notes and translations by Cowper from Milton's Latin & Italian Poems.[1] These works will be ornamented with Engravings from Designs from Romney, Flaxman & Y^r hble Servt, & to be Engrav'd also by the last mention'd. The Profits of the work are intended to be appropriated to Erect a Monument to the Memory of Cowper in St Paul's or Westminster Abbey. Such is the Project—& Mr Addington & Mr Pitt are both among the Subscribers, which are already numerous & of the first rank; the price of the Work is Six Guineas— Thus I hope that all our three years' trouble Ends in Good Luck at last & shall be forgot by my affections & only remember'd by my Understanding; to be a Memento in time to come, & to speak to future generations by a Sublime Allegory, which is now perfectly completed into a Grand Poem. I may praise it, since I dare not pretend to be any other than the Secretary; the Authors are in Eternity. I consider it as the Grandest Poem that this World Contains. Allegory address'd to the Intellectual powers, while it is altogether hidden from the Corporeal Understanding, is My Definition of the Most Sublime Poetry; it is also somewhat in the same manner defin'd by Plato. This Poem shall, by Divine Assistance be progressively Printed & Ornamented with Prints & given to the Public. But of this work I take care to say little to Mr H., since he is as much averse to my poetry as he is to a Chapter in the Bible. He knows that I have writ it, for I have shewn it to him, & he has

---

[1] *Latin and Italian Poems of Milton translated into English verse . . . by the late William Cowper.* Edited by William Hayley, 1808. The book contains two plates engraved by Raimbach after Flaxman, but none by Blake.

read Part by his own desire & has looked with sufficient contempt to inhance my opinion of it. But I do not wish to irritate by seeming too obstinate in Poetic pursuits. But if all the World should set their faces against This, I have Orders to set my face like a flint (Ezekiel iiiC, 9v)[1] against their faces, & my forehead against their foreheads.

As to Mr H., I feel myself at liberty to say as follows upon this ticklish subject: I regard Fashion in Poetry as little as I do in Painting; so, if both Poets & Painters should alternately dislike (but I know the majority of them will not), I am not to regard it at all, but Mr H. approves of My Designs as little as he does of my Poems, and I have been forced to insist on his leaving me in both to my own Self Will; for I am determin'd to be no longer Pester'd with his Genteel Ignorance & Polite Disapprobation. I know myself both Poet & Painter, & it is not his affected Contempt that can move me to any thing but a more assiduous pursuit of both Arts. Indeed, by my late Firmness I have brought down his affected Loftiness, & he begins to think I have some Genius: as if Genius & Assurance were the same thing! but his imbecile attempts to depress Me only deserve laughter. I say thus much to you, knowing that you will not make a bad use of it. But it is a Fact too true That, if I had only depended on Mortal Things, both myself & my Wife must have been Lost. I shall leave every one in This Country astonish'd at my Patience & Forbearance of Injuries upon Injuries; & I do assure you that, if I could have return'd to London a Month after my arrival here, I should have done so, but I was commanded by my Spiritual friends to bear all, to be silent, & to go thro' all without murmuring, &, in fine, hope, till my three years should be almost accomplish'd; at which time I was set at liberty to remonstrate against former conduct & to demand Justice & Truth; which I have done in so effectual a manner that my antagonist is silenc'd completely, & I have compell'd what should have been of freedom—My Just Right as an Artist & as a Man; & if any attempt should be made to refuse me this, I am inflexible & will relinquish Any engagement of Designing at all, unless altogether left to my own Judgment, As you, My dear Friend, have always left me, for which I shall never cease to honour & respect you.

When we meet, I will perfectly describe to you my Conduct & the Conduct of others toward me, & you will see that I have labour'd hard indeed, & have been borne on angel's wings. Till we meet I beg of God our Saviour to be with you & me, & yours &

[1] *Ezekiel*, iii. 8–9. "Behold I have made thy face strong against their faces, and thy forehead strong against their foreheads. As an adamant harder than flint have I made thy forehead: fear them not, neither be dismayed at their looks, though they be a rebellious house."

mine. Pray give my & my wife's love to Mrs Butts & Family, &
believe me to remain,

Yours in truth & sincerity,

Will Blake

Felpham July 6. 1803

34. SCOFIELD'S INFORMATION AND COMPLAINT

15 AUGUST 1803

The Information and Complaint of John Scofield, a Private Soldier
in His Majesty's First Regiment of Dragoons, taken upon his Oath,
this 15th Day of August, 1803, before me One of His Majesty's
Justices of the Peace, in and for the County aforesaid.

Who saith that on the twelfth Day of this Instant, August, at the
Parish of Felpham, in the County aforesaid, one —— Blake, a
Miniature Painter, and now residing in the said Parish of Felpham,
did utter the following seditious expressions, viz, that we (meaning
the People of England) were like a Parcel of Children, that they
would play with themselves till they got scalded and burnt, that the
French knew our Strength very well, and if Bonaparte should come
he would be master of Europe in an Hour's Time, that England
might depend upon it, that when he set his Foot on English Ground
that every Englishman would have his choice, whether to have his
Throat cut, or to join the French, & that he was a strong Man, and
would certainly begin to cut Throats, and the strongest Man must
conquer—that he damned the King of England—his Country, &
his Subjects, that his Soldiers were all bound for Slaves, and all the
Poor People in general—that his Wife then came up, and said to
him, this is nothing to you at present, but that the King of England
would run himself so far into the Fire, that he might get himself out
again, & altho' she was but a Woman, she would fight as long as she
had a drop of Blood in her—to which the said —— Blake said, my
Dear, you would not fight against France—she replyed no, I would
for Bonaparte as long as I am able—that the said —— Blake, then
addressing himself to this Informant, said, tho' you are one of the
King's Subjects, I have told what I have said before greater People
than you, and that this Informant was sent by his Captain to Esquire
Hayley to hear what he had to say, & to go and tell them—that his
Wife then told her said Husband to turn this Informant out of the
Garden—that this Informant thereupon turned round to go peacably
out, when the said —— Blake pushed this Deponant out of the

71

Garden into the Road down which he followed this Informant, & twice took this Informant by the Collar without this Informant's making any Resistance, & at the same Time the said Blake damned the King, and said [his *del.*] the Soldiers were all Slaves——

John Scofield

35. TO THOMAS BUTTS

16 AUGUST 1803

Felpham, August 16. 1803

Dear Sir,

I send 7 Drawings, which I hope will please you; this, I believe, about balances our account. Our return to London draws on apace; our Expectation of meeting again with you is one of our greatest pleasures. Pray tell me how your Eyes do. I never sit down to work but I think of you & feel anxious for the sight of that friend whose Eyes have done me so much good. I omitted (very unaccountably) to copy out in my last Letter that passage in my rough sketch which related to your kindness in offering to Exhibit my 2 last Pictures in the Gallery in Berners Street; it was in these Words: "I sincerely thank you for your kind offer of Exhibiting my 2 Pictures; the trouble you take on my account I trust will be recompensed to you by him who seeth in secret; if you should find it convenient to do so, it will be gratefully remember'd by me among the other numerous kindnesses I have reciev'd from you."

I go on with the remaining Subjects which you gave me commission to Execute for you, but shall not be able to send any more before my return, tho' perhaps I may bring some with me finish'd. I am at Present in a Bustle to defend myself against a very unwarrantable warrant from a Justice of Peace in Chichester, which was taken out against me by a Private[1] in Capt\[n\] Leathes's troop of 1\[st\] or Royal Dragoons, for an assault & Seditious words. The wretched Man has terribly Perjur'd himself, as has his Comrade;[2] for, as to Sedition, not one Word relating to the King or Government was spoken by either him or me. His Enmity arises from my having turned him out of my Garden, into which he was invited as an assistant by a Gardener at work therein, without my knowledge that he was so invited. I desired him, as politely as was possible to go out of the Garden; he made me an impertinent answer. I insisted on his leaving the Garden; he refused. I still persisted in desiring his departure; he then threaten'd to knock out my Eyes, with many

---

[1] John Scofield, or Scholfield.
[2] Private Cock.

abominable imprecations & with some contempt for my Person; it affronted my foolish Pride. I therefore took him by the Elbows & pushed him before me till I had got him out; there I intended to have left him, but he, turning about, put himself into a Posture of Defiance, threatening & swearing at me. I, perhaps foolishly & perhaps not, stepped out at the Gate, &, putting aside his blows, took him again by the Elbows, &, keeping his back to me, pushed him forwards down the road about fifty yards—he all the while endeavouring to turn round & strike me, & raging & cursing, which drew out several neighbours; at length, when I had got him to where he was Quarter'd, which was very quickly done, we were met at the Gate by the Master of the house, The Fox Inn (who is the proprietor of my Cottage), & his wife & Daughter & the Man's Comrade & several other people. My Landlord compell'd the Soldiers to go in doors, after many abusive threats against me & my wife from the two Soldiers; but not one word of threat on account of Sedition was utter'd at that time. This method of Revenge was Plann'd between them after they had got together into the Stable. This is the whole outline. I have for witnesses: The Gardener, who is Hostler at the Fox & who Evidences that, to his knowledge, no word of the remotest tendency to Government or Sedition was utter'd: Our next door Neighbour, a Miller's wife, who saw me turn him before me down the road, & saw & heard all that happen'd at the Gate of the Inn, who Evidences that no Expression of threatening on account of Sedition was utter'd in the heart of their fury by either of the Dragoons; this was the woman's own remark, & does high honour to her good sense, as she observes that, whenever a quarrel happens, the offence is always repeated. The Landlord of the Inn & His Wife & daughter will Evidence the Same, & will evidently prove the Comrade perjur'd, who swore that he heard me, while at the Gate, utter Seditious words & D— the K—, without which perjury I could not have been committed; & I had no witness with me before the Justices who could combat his assertion, as the Gardener remain'd in my Garden all the while, & he was the only person I thought necessary to take with me. I have been before a Bench of Justices at Chichester this morning; but they, as the Lawyer who wrote down the Accusation told me in private, are compell'd by the Military to suffer a prosecution to be enter'd into: altho' they must know, & it is manifest, that the whole is a Fabricated Perjury. I have been forced to find Bail. Mr Hayley was kind enough to come forwards, & Mr Seagrave,[1] Printer at Chichester; Mr H. in 100£, & Mr S. in 50£; & myself am bound in 100£ for my appearance at the

---

[1] Joseph Seagrave, printer of Hayley's *Ballads, The Life of Cowper, The Triumphs of Temper*, and other books by Hayley.

73

Quarter Sessions, which is after Michaelmass. So I shall have the satisfaction to see my friends in Town before this Contemptible business comes on. I say Contemptible, for it must be manifest to every one that the whole accusation is a wilful Perjury. Thus, you see, my dear Friend, that I cannot leave this place without some adventure; it has struck a consternation thro' all the Villages round. Every Man is now afraid of speaking to, or looking at, a Soldier; for the peaceable Villagers have always been forward in expressing their kindness for us, & they express their sorrow at our departure as soon as they hear of it. Every one here is my Evidence for Peace & Good Neighbourhood; & yet, such is the present state of things, this foolish accusation must be tried in Public. Well, I am content, I murmur not & doubt not that I shall recieve Justice, & am only sorry for the trouble & expense. I have heard that my Accuser is a disgraced Sergeant; his name is John Scholfield; perhaps it will be in your power to learn somewhat about the Man. I am very ignorant of what I am requesting of you; I only suggest what I know you will be kind enough to Excuse if you can learn nothing about him, & what, I as well know, if it is possible, you will be kind enough to do in this matter.

Dear Sir, This perhaps was suffer'd to Clear up some doubts, & to give opportunity to those whom I doubted to clear themselves of all imputation. If a Man offends me ignorantly & not designedly, surely I ought to consider him with favour & affection. Perhaps the simplicity of myself is the origin of all offences committed against me. If I have found this, I shall have learned a most valuable thing, well worth three years' perseverance. I have found it. It is certain that a too passive manner, inconsistent with my active physiognomy, had done me much mischief. I must now express to you my conviction that all is come from the spiritual World for Good, & not for Evil.

Give me your advice in my perilous adventure; burn what I have peevishly written about any friend. I have been very much degraded & injuriously treated; but if it all arise from my own fault, I ought to blame myself.

O why was I born with a different face?
Why was I not born like the rest of my race?
When I look, each one starts! when I speak, I offend;
Then I'm silent & passive & lose every Friend.

Then my verse I dishonour, My pictures despise,
My person degrade & my temper chastise;
And the pen is my terror, the pencil my shame;
All my Talents I bury, and dead is my Fame.

I am either too low or too highly priz'd;
When Elate I am Envy'd, When Meek I'm despis'd.

This is but too just a Picture of my Present state. I pray God to keep you & all men from it, & to deliver me in his own good time. Pray write to me, & tell me how you & and your family enjoy health. My much terrified Wife joins me in love to you & Mrs Butts & all your family. I again take the liberty to beg of you to cause the Enclos'd Letter to be deliver'd to my Brother, & remain Sincerely & Affectionately Yours,

William Blake

36. TO THOMAS BUTTS*

20 AUGUST 1803

[An Account amounting to £14 14s. for eleven drawings, including The Three Maries,[1] delivered on July 8 and August 20, 1803.]

37. BLAKE'S MEMORANDUM AGAINST SCOFIELD

AUGUST 1803

Blake's Memorandum in Refutation of the Information and Complaint of John Scholfield, a private Soldier, &c.

The Soldier has been heard to say repeatedly, that he did not know how the Quarrel began, which he would not say if such seditious words were spoken.

Mrs. Haynes Evidences, that she saw me turn him down the Road, & all the while we were at the Stable Door, and that not one word of charge against me was uttered, either relating to Sedition or any thing else; all he did was swearing and threatening.

Mr. Hosier heard him say that he would be revenged, and would have me hanged if he could: He spoke this the Day after my turning him out of the Garden. Hosier says he is ready to give Evidence of this, if necessary.

The Soldier's Comrade swore before the Magistrates, while I was present, that he heard me utter seditious words, at the Stable Door, and in particular, said, that he heard me D—n the K—g. Now I

---

[1] Now in the Fitzwilliam Museum, Cambridge.

have all the Persons who were present at the Stable Door to witness that no Word relating to Seditious Subjects was uttered, either by one party or the other, and they are ready, on their Oaths, to say that I did not utter such Words.

Mrs. Haynes says very sensibly, that she never heard People quarrel, but they always charged each other with the Offence, and repeated it to those around, therefore as the Soldier charged not me with Seditious Words at that Time, neither did his Comrade, the whole Charge must have been fabricated in the Stable afterwards.

If we prove the Comrade perjured who swore that he heard me D—n the K—g, I believe the whole Charge falls to the Ground.

Mr. Cosens, owner of the Mill at Felpham, was passing by in the Road, and saw me and the Soldier and William standing near each other; he heard nothing, but says we certainly were not quarrelling.

The whole Distance that William could be at any Time of the Conversation between me and the Soldier (supposing such Conversation to have existed) is only 12 Yards, & W— says that he was backwards and forwards in the Garden. It was a still Day, there was no Wind stirring.

William says on his Oath, that the first Words that he heard me speak to the Soldier were ordering him out of the Garden; the truth is, I did not speak to the Soldier till then, & my ordering him out of the Garden was occasioned by his saying something that I thought insulting.

The Time that I & the Soldier were together in the Garden was not sufficient for me to have uttered the Things that he alledged.

The Soldier said to Mrs. Grinder, that it would be right to have my House searched, as I might have plans of the Country which I intended to send to the Enemy; he called me a Military Painter; I suppose [he *del*.] mistaking the Words Miniature Painter, which he might have heard me called. I think that this proves, his having come into the Garden with some bad Intention, or at least with a prejudiced Mind.

It is necessary to learn the Names of all that were present at the Stable Door, that we may not have any Witnesses brought against us, that were not there.

All the Persons present at the Stable Door were, Mrs. Grinder and her Daughter, all the Time; Mrs. Haynes & her Daughter all the Time; Mr. Grinder, part of the Time; Mr. Hayley's Gardener part of the Time.—Mrs. Haynes was present from my turning him out at my Gate, all the rest of the Time. What passed in the Garden, there is no Person but William & the Soldier, & myself can know.

There was not any body in Grinder's Tap-room, but an Old Man,

76

named Jones, who (Mrs. Grinder says) did not come out. He is the same Man who lately hurt his Hand, & wears it in a sling.

The Soldier after he and his Comrade came together into the Tap-room, threatened to knock William's Eyes out (this was his often repeated Threat to me and to my Wife) because W—refused to go with him to Chichester, and swear against me. William said that he would not take a false Oath, for that he heard me say nothing of the Kind (i.e. Sedition) Mr. Grinder then reproved the Soldier for threatening William, and Mr. Grinder said, that W— should not go, because of those Threats, especially as he was sure that no seditious Words were spoken.

William's timidity in giving his Evidence before the Magistrates, and his fear of uttering a Falsehood upon Oath, proves him to be an honest Man, & is to me an host of Strength. I am certain that if I had not turned the Soldier out of my Garden, I never should have been free from his Impertinence & Intrusion.

Mr. Hayley's Gardener came past at the Time of the Contention at the Stable Door, & going to the Comrade said to him, Is your Comrade drunk?—a Proof that he thought the Soldier abusive, & in an Intoxication of Mind.

If such a Perjury as this can take effect, any Villain in future may come & drag me and my Wife out of our House, & beat us in the Garden, or use us as he please, or is able, & afterwards go and swear our Lives away.

Is it not in the Power of any Thief who enters a Man's Dwelling, & robs him, or misuses his Wife or Children, to go & swear as this Man has sworn.

38. TO WILLIAM HAYLEY*

19 SEPTEMBER 1803

My admiration of Flaxman's genius is more and more—his industry is equal to his other great powers.

Speaks of his works in progress in his studio, and of various matters connected with art. [*Extracts from sale catalogue.*]

39. TO WILLIAM HAYLEY

7 OCTOBER 1803

London, October 7, 1803.

Dear Sir,

Your generous & tender solicitude about your devoted rebel

makes it absolutely necessary that he should trouble you with an account of his safe arrival, which will excuse his begging the favor of a few lines to inform him how you escaped the contagion of the Court of Justice—I fear that you have & must suffer more on my account than I shall ever be worth—Arrived safe in London, my wife in very poor health, still I resolve not to lose hope of seeing better days.

Art in London flourishes. Engravers in particular are wanted. Every Engraver turns away work that he cannot execute from his superabundant Employment. Yet no one brings work to me. I am content that it shall be so as long as God pleases. I know that many works of a lucrative nature are in want of hands; other Engravers are courted. I suppose that I must go a Courting, which I shall do awkwardly; in the mean time I lose no moment to complete Romney to satisfaction.[1]

How is it possible that a Man almost 50 Years of Age, who has not lost any of his life since he was five years old without incessant labour & study, how is it possible that such a one with ordinary common sense can be inferior to a boy of twenty, who scarcely has taken or deigns to take a pencil in hand, but who rides about the Parks or Saunters about the Playhouses, who Eats & drinks for business not for need, how is it possible that such a fop can be superior to the studious lover of Art can scarcely be imagin'd. Yet such is somewhat like my fate & such it is likely to remain. Yet I laugh & sing, for if on Earth neglected I am in heaven a Prince among Princes, & even on Earth beloved by the Good as a Good Man; this I should be perfectly contented with, but at certain periods a blaze of reputation arises round me in which I am consider'd as one distinguish'd by some mental perfection, but the flame soon dies again & I am left stupified and astonish'd. O that I could live as others do in a regular succession of Employment, this wish I fear is not to be accomplish'd to me—Forgive this Dirge-like lamentation over a dead horse, & now I have lamented over the dead horse let me laugh & be merry with my friends till Christmas, for as Man liveth not by bread alone, I shall live altho' I should want bread—nothing is necessary to me but to do my Duty & to rejoice in the exceeding joy that is always poured out on my Spirit, to pray that my friends & you above the rest may be made partakers of the joy that the world cannot concieve, that you may still be replenish'd with the same & be as you always have been, a glorious & triumphant Dweller in immortality. Please to pay for me my best

[1] Blake engraved a head of Romney for Hayley's *Life*, but it was not used. See further references below. No impression from the plate is now known.

78

thanks to Miss Poole: tell her that I wish her a continued Excess of Happiness—some say that Happiness is not Good for Mortals, & they ought to be answer'd that Sorrow is not fit for Immortals & is utterly useless to any one; a blight never does good to a tree, & if a blight kill not a tree but it still bear fruit, let none say that the fruit was in consequence of the blight. When this Soldier-like danger is over I will do double the work I do now, for it will hang heavy on my Devil who terribly resents it; but I soothe him to peace, & indeed he is a good natur'd Devil after all & certainly does not lead me into scrapes—he is not in the least to be blamed for the present scrape, as he was out of the way all the time on other employment seeking amusement in making Verses, to which he constantly leads me very much to my hurt & sometimes to the annoyance of my friends; as I percieve he is now doing the same work by my letter, I will finish it, wishing you health & joy in God our Saviour.

To Eternity yours,

Willm Blake

40. TO WILLIAM HAYLEY*

26 OCTOBER 1803

Dear Sir,

I hasten to write to you by the favour of Mr. Edwards. I have been with Mr. Saunders, who has now in his possession all Mr. Romney's pictures that remained after the sale at Hampstead; I saw "Milton and his Daughters", and "'Twas where the Seas were Roaring", and a beautiful "Female Head". He has promised to write a list of all that he has in his possession, and of all that he remembers of Mr. Romney's paintings, with notices where they now are, so far as his recollection will serve. The picture of "Christ in the Desert" he supposes to be one of those which he has rolled on large rollers. He will take them down and unroll them, but cannot do it easily, as they are so large as to occupy the whole length of his workshop, and are laid across beams at the top.

Mr. Flaxman is now out of town. When he returns I will lose no time in setting him to work on the same object.

I have got to work after Fuseli for a little Shakespeare.[1] Mr. Johnson, the bookseller, tells me that there is no want of work. So far you will be rejoiced with me, and your words, *"Do not fear you can want employment!"* were verified the morning after I received your

---

[1] *The Plays of William Shakespeare*, ed. Alexander Chalmers, 10 vols. London, 1805. Blake engraved two plates after Fuseli's designs for this edition—"Queen Katherine's Dream" (vol. VII, facing p. 235) and "Romeo and the Apothecary" (vol. X, facing p. 107).

kind letter; but I go on finishing Romney with spirit, and for the relief of variety shall engage in other little works as they arise.

I called on Mr. Evans,[1] who gives small hopes of our ballads; he says he has sold but fifteen numbers at the most, and that going on would be a certain loss of almost all the expenses. I then proposed to him to take a part with me in publishing them on a smaller scale, which he declined on account of its being out of his line of business to publish, and a line in which he is determined never to engage, attaching himself wholly to the sale of fine editions of authors and curious books in general. He advises that some publisher should be spoken to who would purchase the copyright: and, as far as I can judge of the nature of publication, no chance is left to one out of the trade. Thus the case stands at present.[2] God send better times! Everybody complains, yet all go on cheerfully and with spirit. The shops in London improve; everything is elegant, clean, and neat; the streets are widened where they were narrow; even Snow Hill is become almost level, and is a very handsome street, and the narrow part of the Strand near St. Clement's is widened and become very elegant.

My wife continues poorly, but fancies she is better in health here than by the seaside. We both sincerely pray for the health of Miss Poole, and for all our friends in Sussex, and remain, dear sir,

Your sincere and devoted servants,

W. and C. Blake

South Molton Street
26 October 1803

41. TO WILLIAM HAYLEY

13 DECEMBER 1803

Dear Sir,

I write in a violent hurry. Your Letter has never arrived to me. M[rs] Lambert has been with me, which is the first notice I had of the Letter or of the drawing. I have fetch'd the drawing from M[r] Rose & have shew'd it to M[r] Flaxman, who approves of it, wishing only that the Monument[3] itself may be more made out & the other

---

[1] R. H. Evans, bookseller, Pall Mall, London, is given on the title-page of the quarto *Ballads* as having the book on sale.

[2] A small 8⁰ edition of the *Ballads* with five plates was, in fact, published in 1805. See p. 114.

[3] Cowper's Monument in East Dereham Church, Norfolk. Blake engraved two plates of this for vol. III of Hayley's *Life of Cowper*, 1803–4: "A View of St. Edmund's Chapel in the Church of East Dereham, containing the Grave of William Cowper, Esq.", engraved from a drawing by Francis Stone, and "A Sketch of the

Little TOM the Sailor

And does then the Ocean possess
The promising, brave, little youth,
Who displays, on a scene of distress,
Such tenderness, Courage, and Truth?

Little Tom is a Cottagers Son;
His years not amounting to ten;
But the Dawn of his Manhood begun
With a Soul like the noblest of Men.

In an Hospital, distant from Home,
He lost his unfortunate Sire;
And his Mother was tempted to roam,
But to see that kind Father expire.

To depart from her Cottage was hard;
To desert the dear dying was worse,
Tho! She had, an Infant to guard,
And a sick little Infant to nurse.

The brave little Tom tried to cheer
The Grief that He shudderd to see,
"Go! Mother (He said) without Fear!
Go! and leave these poor Creatures to me!

Go, you my sick Father restore!
And I will take Care of these two,
I will not stir out of the Door,
For what without me could they do?

I will carefully dress them, and feed,
Go, you our dear Father to save,
I will not desert them indeed!"
And Tom kept the promise he gave.

But his Mother a Widow came back;
Want, and Sorrow her Portion must be;
And her Heart, on Necessitys Rack,
Has sent little Thomas to Sea.

O, Sea! Thou proud Servant of God!
The Children of Britain defend!
As a braver the Deck never trod,
Little Thomas will find Thee a Friend:

And when He is aloft in the Shrouds,
If a Storm threats aloud, to destroy,
His Fathers free Soul, in the Clouds,
Will watch over the venturous Boy;

I hear, when the Tempests uppall,
that Spirit paternal exclaim,
"O God! thou Protector of All!
Let me shelter this dear little Frame!

A Defender, with Honour, his Due!
In the Man, may his Country admire,
Since the Child was a Guardian so true
To the desolate Cot of his Sire"

Printed for & Sold by the Widow Spicer of Folkstone
for the Benefit of her Orphans
October 1800

VI. LITTLE TOM
THE SAILOR

broadside by
Hayley and Blake 1800

Monument in the back Ground kept in a lower tint. The little oval tablet on the side by Cowper's Monument he tells me is Mrs Unwin's[1]; of course that shall be distinguish'd.

I have a great many things to say & a great many heartfelt acknowledgements to express, particularly for your tens, which are hundreds to me, nay thousands. I am going on with success: business comes in & I shall be at ease if this infernal business of the soldier can be got over.

I have seen Mr Saunders & enquir'd of him whether he has any of Mr Romney's [Sketches *del*.] Historical Sketches: he says that he sent a great part of them to the North & explain'd the North by saying that [Mr Romney *del*.] Mr John Romney[2] has a dwelling in the north. Mr Flaxman supposes that if some of the most distinguish'd designs of Mr Romney, of which Mr Saunders has a good many, were Engrav'd, they would be an appropriate accompaniment to the Life of Romney; the expense would not be very great & the merit of the designs an object of consequence.

Mr Saunders will shortly write to you giving you every information in his power with notices of where Mr Romney's best pictures now are & other articles collected from every Fountain he can visit.

I send the five copies of Cowper's Plates, which you will recieve with this & have only time to say, because I shall be too late for the carriage,

God bless you & preserve you & reward your kindness to me

Will Blake

Tuesday night
13 Decr 1803

' *P.S.* My wife is better; we are very anxious about Miss Poole's health & shall be truly happy to hear that it is perfectly restored. Mr Romney's Portrait goes on with spirit. I do not send a proof because I cannot get one, the Printers [being *del*.] having been this afternoon unable or unwilling & my Press not yet being put up.

Farewell.

Monument Erected in the Church of East Dereham in Norfolk, in Memory of William Cowper, Esqre", from the original model by John Flaxman.

[1] Cowper's friend, with whom he lived at Olney.

[2] Romney's only surviving son (1758–1832). He afterwards quarrelled with Hayley and attacked him in his *Life of Romney*, 1830. He lived at Kendall.

42. SAMUEL ROSE: SPEECH IN DEFENCE OF BLAKE

11 JANUARY 1804

The Speech of Counsellor Rose In Defence of
Blake the Artist
at the Chichester Sessions Jan. 11 1804
taken in short Hand by the Revd.
Mr. Youatt

Gentlemen of the Jury,

I perfectly agree with my learned friend, with regard to the atrocity & malignity of the charge now laid before you. I am also much obliged to him, for having given me the credit, that no justification, or extenuation of such a charge would have been attempted by me, supposing the charge could have been proved to your satisfaction; & I must be permitted to say, that it is a credit which I deserve. If there be a man, who can be found guilty of such a transgression, he must apply to some other person to defend him, if a palliation of such an offence becomes part of the duty of his counsel. I certainly think that such an offence is incapable of extenuation. My task is to shew that my client is not guilty of the words imputed to him. It is not to shew that they are capable of any mitigated sense. We stand here not merely in form, but in sincerity & truth, to declare that we are *not guilty*. I am instructed to say, that Mr Blake is as loyal a subject as any man in this court:—that he feels as much indignation at the idea of exposing to contempt or injury the sacred person of his sovereign as any man:—that his indignation is equal to that, which I doubt not every one of you felt, when the charge was first stated to you.

Gentlemen, this is a very uncommon accusation—it is foreign to our natures & opposite to our habits.—Do you not hear every day from the mouths of thousands in the streets the exclamation of God save the King:—it is the language of every Englishman's lip—it is the effusion of every Englishman's heart. The charge therefore laid in the indictment is an offence of so extraordinary a nature, that evidence of the most clear, positive, & unobjectionable kind is necessary to induce you to believe it. Extraordinary vices, Gentlemen, are very rare, as well as extraordinary virtues; indeed the term extraordinary implies as much. There is no doubt that the crime which is laid to the charge of my client, is a crime of most extraordinary malignity. I choose the term malignity purposely— for if the offence be clearly proved I am willing to allow, that public malignity and indelible disgrace are fixed upon my client. If on the other hand when you have heard the witnesses which I shall call, you should be led to believe that it is a fabrication for the purpose of answering some scheme of revenge you will have little difficulty in deciding that it is still greater malignity on the part of the witness Scholfield.

Gentlemen, the greater the offence charged the greater the improbability of its being true. I will state to you the situation of Mr Blake & it will be for you to judge whether it is probable he should be guilty of the crime alledged.

He is an artist, who, tho' not a native here, has lived in your part of the country for 2 or 3 years. He is an engraver. He was brought into this country by Mr Hayley, a gentleman well known to you, & whose patriotism & loyalty have never been impeached. Blake was previously known to Mr Hayley. I think I need not state that Mr Hayley would never have brought Mr Blake into this part of the country, & given him encouragement, if he conceived it possible that he could have uttered these sentiments. Mr Hayley from his previous knowledge of him was certain that he was not the seditious character here represented.

Gentlemen, the story is very improbable, if we farther consider Mr Blake's situation. Mr Blake is engaged as an engraver. He has a wife [& family *del.*] to support: that wife & himself he has supported by his art—an art, which has a tendency, like all the other fine arts, to soften every asperity of feeling & of character, & to secure the bosom from the influence of those tumultuous & discordant passions, which destroy the happiness of mankind. If any men are likely to be exempt from angry passions it is such an one as Mr Blake. He had resided in this village for some time, when you have heard one day the witness Scholfield came into his garden for the purpose of delivering a message to the ostler, there he continues for some time without any apparent reason. But I will just make this observation in addition to what I have said of the great incredibility of so infamous a crime being committed by such an individual—the proof adduced ought to be uniform, consistent & clear, so much as to leave no doubt of the veracity of those persons who come forward—not only so—it should proceed from characters of unimpeachable credit —those who have acted in such a way, that you can be morally certain no temptation whatever will induce them to speak what is not true. The first witness is in a different situation from what he has been—he was once in a superior, but now appears in an inferior, rank. Now Gentlemen, merit always promotes a man—misconduct degrades him—misconduct not only degrades him in his situation, but in the consideration of all men, who know the circumstances. This Man was once a Serjeant—he is now a private. He says he was degraded an account of drunkeness. He is degraded, be it from what cause it may—& he certainly does not stand before you under the most favourable circumstances, nor is he entitled to that credit, which you would have given him, if by his good conduct he had continued in his former situation, or raised himself to a higher. He tells you a story, which to be sure requires a great deal of faith in order to believe it—because it is an unaccountable story. He was in Blake's garden talking to the Ostler—he came to tell him that he could not do the job he was to do, for he was order'd to march to Chichester—that he had but few words to say, & no time to spare, yet we find him lounging about leaning against the garden wall. That Mr Blake came out, & without any provocation, without one word being spoken on either side, began to utter these expressions (the words in the Indictment). These expressions divide themselves into 2 classes—some of them deserve the reprobation, which my learned friend has bestowed upon them—others are so absurd & unintelligible, that he with all his ingenuity has not attempted to explain them—as cut throat for cut throat. It does not appear what can be meant. If you are able to understand them, I honestly confess, that after no small pains bestowed on the point, I cannot. The witness at one time asserted, that these words were spoken to him, then he was doubting whether they were addressed to Mrs Blake— at last he asserts again that they were spoken to him. Gentlemen, you will take notice that the Ostler was all this time working in the Garden—this Garden I shall be able to prove to you did not contain above 10 yards square—no words consequently could have been uttered without every person in the Garden hearing them, especially when Scholfield acknowledged that they were talking rather high. The Ostler is allowed to have been in the Garden, he was in a situation to hear all that passed, & he will prove to you by & bye that he heard no such expressions uttered by Mr Blake.

Here, then, Gentlemen, is a charge attended with circumstances of the most extraordinary nature. A man comes out of his house for the purpose of addressing a malignant & unintelligible discourse to those who are most likely to injure him for it. A person exerting such an art, tending to render him indifferent to the factions & disputes of the world, uttering this discourse without any inducement whatsoever, & stated by the witness to have been uttered in the presence of one, who will presently tell you that no such words were uttered. All this as to the words which are represented to have been spoken to the soldier, & you will not forget that the man who has given you this testimony, is a man who so far from being thought worthy of reward, has been degraded.

The second witness states that there was a noise in the street, he was at work in the stable, & came out in consequence of the noise, he saw Mr Blake and Scholfield in the act of collaring each other, and Mrs Grinder separated them—that M^rs G—— was as near to Blake as Cock was, [because she was the person who separated them *del*.] he states that without any farther provocation or hearing any words from Scholfield or Blake, Blake uttered these words, damn the King, damn the country, you soldiers are all slaves. M^rs G—— I shall call to you & she will state that she was as near Mr Blake as Cock was, & heard no such words. I would observe, in order to shew that there is a small difference between the testimony of Cock & Scholfield, that when Scholfield was asked if any thing had been uttered beside the words which were spoken in the garden, he replied no. Scholfield confines himself to the words in the Garden— the other says they were uttered before the public house. If they were spoken in the Garden the Ostler must have heard them. If they were uttered before the public-house Mrs G. must have heard them too. I will call these witnesses & you shall hear their account—you will then agree with me that they totally overthrow the testimony of these Soldiers.

43. TO WILLIAM HAYLEY

14 JANUARY 1804

London Jany 14. 1804

Dear Sir,

I write immediately on my arrival. Not merely to inform you that I am safe arriv'd, but also to inform you that in a conversation with an old Soldier who came in the Coach with me I learned: that no one: not even the most expert horseman: ought ever to mount a Trooper's Horse; they are taught so many tricks such as stopping short, falling down on their knees, running sideways, & in various & innumerable ways endeavouring to throw the rider, that it is a miracle if a stranger escapes with Life,— All this I learn'd with some alarm & heard also what the soldier said confirm'd by another person in the coach. I therefore as it is my duty beg & intreat you never to mount that wicked horse again, nor again trust to one who has been so Educated. God our Saviour watch over you & preserve you.

I have seen Flaxman already as I took to him early this morning your present to his Scholar; he & his are all well & in high spirits & welcom'd Me with kind affection & generous exultation in my escape from the arrows of darkness. I intend to see Mrs Lambert & Mr Johnson bookseller this afternoon. My poor wife has been near the Gate of Death as was supposed by our kind & attentive fellow inhabitant, the young & very amiable Mʳˢ Enoch, who gave my wife all the attention that a daughter could pay to a mother, but my arrival has dispell'd the formidable malady & my dear & good woman again begins to resume her health & strength. Pray my dear Sir favour me with a line concerning your health & how you have escaped the double blow both from the wicked horse & from your innocent humble servant, whose heart & soul are more & more drawn out towards you & Felpham & its kind inhabitants. I feel anxious, & therefore pray to my God & father for the health of Miss Poole: hope that the pang of affection & gratitude is the Gift of God for good. I am thankful that I feel it; it draws the soul towards Eternal life & conjunction with Spirits of just men made perfect by love & gratitude—the two angels who stand at heaven's gate ever open, ever inviting guests to the marriage. O foolish Philosophy! Gratitude is Heaven itself; there could be no heaven without Gratitude. I feel it & I know it. I thank God & Man for it & above all You, My dear friend & benefactor in the Lord. Pray give my & my wife's duties to Miss Poole; accept them yourself & believe me to be,

Yours in sincerity,

Will ᵐ Blake

44. TO WILLIAM HAYLEY

27 JANUARY 1804

Dear Sir,

Your eager expectation of hearing from me compells me to write immediately, tho' I have not done half the business I wish'd owing to a violent cold which confin'd me to my bed 3 days & to my chamber a week. I am now so well (thank God) as to get out & have accordingly been to Mʳ Walker's[1] who is not in town being at Birmingham where he will remain 6 Weeks or 2 Months. I took my Portrait of Romney as you desired to shew him: his Son was likewise not at home: but I will again call on Mʳ Walker Junʳ & beg him to shew me the Pictures, & make every enquiry of him, If you think best:—Mʳ Sanders has one or two large Cartoons, The Subjects he does not know, they are folded up on the top of his workshop, the rest he pack'd up & sent into the North. I shew'd your Letter to Mʳ John Romney to Mʳ Flaxman who was perfectly satisfied with it. I seal'd & sent it immediately as directed by Mʳ Sanders to Kendall, Westmoreland. Mʳ Sanders expects Mʳ Romney in town soon. Note,

[1] Adam Walker (1731–1821), author and inventor, an old friend of Romney.

Your Letter to M[r] J. Romney I sent off the morning after I reciev'd it from you, being then in health. I have taken your noble present to M[r] Rose & left it with charge to the Servant of Great Care; the Writing looks very pretty. I was fortunate in doing it myself & hit it off excellently. I have not seen M[r] Rose,[1] tho' he is in town. M[r] Flaxman is not at all acquainted with S[r] Allan Chambre,[2] recommends me to enquire concerning him of M[r] Rose; my brother says he believes S[r] Allan is a Master in Chancery. Tho' I have call'd on M[r] Edwards twice for Lady Hamilton's[3] direction, was so unfortunate as to find him Out both times. I will repeat my call on him tomorrow morning.

My Dear Sir, I write now to satisfy you that all is in a good train. I am going on briskly with the Plates, find every thing promising. Work in Abundance; & if God blesses me with health doubt not yet to make a Figure in the Great Dance of Life that shall amuse the Spectators in the Sky. I thank you for my Demosthenes[4] which is now become a noble subject—My Wife gets better every Day: hope earnestly that you have entirely escaped the brush of my Evil Star, Which I believe is now for ever fallen into the Abyss—God bless & preserve You and our Good Lady Paulina with the Good things both of this life & of eternity & with you my much admired & respected Edward the Bard of Oxford[5] whose verses still sound upon my Ear like the distant approach of things mighty & magnificent; like the sound of harps which I hear before the Sun's rising, like the remembrance of Felpham's waves & of the Glorious & far beaming Turret, like the Villa of Lavant,[6] blessed & blessing. Amen. God bless you all O people of Sussex around your Hermit & Bard. So prays the Emulator of both his & your mild & happy tempers of Soul. Your devoted

Will Blake

S[th] Molton Street
Friday Jany 27, 1804

[1] Samuel Rose, Blake's counsel at his trial.

[2] Sir Alan Chambré (1739–1823), judge; Recorder of Lancaster; Baron of the Exchequer, 1799. His portrait was painted by Romney.

[3] Emma Hart, Lady Hamilton, Nelson's mistress and Romney's most frequent sitter.

[4] "The Death of Demosthenes", engraved by Blake after Thomas Hayley, for William Hayley's *Essay on Sculpture*, 1800, 4°.

[5] Edward Garrard Marsh, Fellow of Oriel College, Oxford, ordained in 1807, died 1862; author of hymns, published in 1837. See Gilchrist's *Life of Blake*, 1880, i., 203, and Morchard Bishop's *Blake's Hayley*, 1951, pp. 290–1.

[6] i.e. Miss Poole's villa.

45. TO WILLIAM HAYLEY

Dear Sir,

I call'd Yesterday on M[r] Braithwaite,[1] as you desired, & found him quite as chearful as you describe him, & by his appearance should not have supposed him to be near sixty, notwithstanding he was shaded by a green shade over his Eyes. He gives a very spirited assurance of M[r] John Romney's interesting himself in the great object of his Father's Fame, & thinks that he must be proud of such a work & in such hands. The Picture from Sterne,[2] which you desired him to procure for you, he has not yet found where it is. Supposes that it may be in the north, & that he may learn from M[r] Romney, who will be in town soon. M[r] B. desires I will present his Compliments to you, & write you that he has spoken with M[r] Read concerning the Life of Romney; he interests himself in it, & has promised to procure dates of premiums, Pictures, &[c], M[r] Read having a number of Articles relating to Romney, either written or printed, which he promises to copy out for your use, as also the Catalogue of Hampstead Sale. He shew'd me a very fine Portrait of M[rs] Siddons (by Romney) as the Tragic Muse, half-length, that is, the Head & hands, & in his best Style. He also desires me to express to you his wish that you would give the Public an Engraving of that Medallion by your Son's matchless hand,[3] which is placed over his chimney piece between two little pretty pictures, correct & enlarged copies from antique Gems, of which the center ornament is worthy; he says that it is by far, in his opinion, the most exact resemblance of Romney he ever saw. I have, furthermore, the pleasure of informing you that he knew immediately my Portrait of Romney, & assured me that he thought it a very great likeness.

I wish I could give you a Pleasant account of our beloved Counsellor;[4] he, Alas! was ill in bed when I call'd yesterday at about 12 O'clock, & the servant said that he remains very ill indeed.

M[r] Walker, I have been so unfortunate as not to find at home, but I will call again in a day or two. Neither M[r] Flaxman nor M[r] Edwards know Lady Hamilton's address; the house S[r] William

---

[1] Daniel Braithwaite, controller of the Foreign department of the Post Office, was Romney's earliest patron, in 1762; it was to him that Hayley dedicated his *Life of Romney*.

[2] Probably "The Introduction of Dr. Slop into the Parlour of Mr. Shandy", a scene from *Tristram Shandy*, painted c. 1757, which was engraved for the *Life of Romney* by W. Haines.

[3] The medallion of Romney by Thomas Hayley was engraved for the *Life* by Caroline Watson.

[4] Samuel Rose.

liv'd in in Piccadilly She left some time ago. Mr Edwards will procure her address for you, & I will send it immediately.

I have inclos'd for you the 22 Numbers of Fuseli's Shakespeare[1] that are out, & the book of Italian Letters from Mrs Flaxman, who with her admirable husband present their best Compliments to you; he is so busy that I believe I shall never see him again but when I call on him, for he has never yet, since my return to London, had the time or grace to call on me. Mrs Flaxman & her Sisters gave also their testimony to my Likeness of Romney. Mr Flaxman I have not yet had an opportunity of consulting about it, but soon will.

I inclose likewise the Academical Correspondence of Mr Hoare[2] the Painter, whose note to me I also inclose, for I did but express to him my desire of sending you a Copy of his work, & the day after I reciev'd it with the note Expressing his pleasure [of your *del.*] in your wish to see it. You would be much delighted with the Man, as I assure myself you will be with his work.

The plates of Cowper's Monument are both in great forwardness & you shall have Proofs in another week. I assure you that I will not spare pains, & am myself very much satisfied that I shall do my duty & produce two Elegant plates; there is, however, a great deal of work in them that must & will have time.

"Busy, Busy, Busy, I bustle along,
"Mounted upon warm Phoebus's rays,
"Thro' the heavenly throng."[3]

But I hasten'd to write to you about Mr Braithwaite; hope when I send my proofs to give as good an account of Mr Walker.

My wife joins me in Respects & Love to you, & desires with mine to present hers to Miss Poole.

I remain, Dear Sir, Your Sincere,

Will Blake

Sth Molton Street
23 Feby 1804

---

[1] *The Plays of Shakespeare*, ed. George Steevens and Alexander Chalmers, illustrated with engravings after designs by Fuseli, in 10 vols., 1804–5. Two of the plates, "Queen Katherine's Dream" (vol. VII) and "Romeo and the Apothecary" (vol. X) were engraved by Blake. See also pp. 91, 101.

[2] Prince Hoare (1755–1834), painter and author of several works, including *Academic Correspondence*, 1803, 4°, with frontispiece of a bust of Ceres engraved by Blake after Flaxman.

[3] From "The Rehearsal", Act V, by George Villiers second Duke of Buckingham. Identified by Morchard Bishop (*Times Literary Supplement*, 2 April, 1964).

46. TO WILLIAM HAYLEY

12 MARCH 1804

Dear Sir,

I begin with the latter end of your letter & grieve more for Miss Poole's ill-health than for my failure in sending proofs, tho' I am very sorry that I cannot send before Saturday's Coach. Engraving is Eternal work; the two plates[1] are almost finish'd. You will recieve proofs of them for Lady Hesketh, whose copy of Cowper's letters ought to be printed in letters of Gold & ornamented with Jewels of Heaven, Havilah, Eden & all the countries where Jewels abound. I curse & bless Engraving alternately, because it takes so much time & is so untractable, tho' capable of such beauty & perfection.

My wife desires me to Express her Love to you, Praying for Miss Poole's perfect recovery, & we both remain,

Your Affectionate,

March 12 1804   Will Blake

47. TO WILLIAM HAYLEY

16 MARCH 1804

Dear Sir,

According to your Desire I send proofs of the Monumental Plates tho' as you will percieve they have not the last touches especially the Plate of the Monument which I have drawn from Mr Flaxman's Model with all the fidelity I could & will finish with equal care, the writing being exactly copied from the tracing paper which was traced on the marble. The inscriptions to the Plates I must beg of you to send to me that I may Engrave them immediately.

The drawing of the Monument which Mr Johnson sent has the following Inscription—"Monument Erected to the Memory of William Cowper Esqre in St Edmunds Chapel East Dereham by the Lady Hesketh 1803"—But it strikes me that St Edmund's Chapel East Dereham may be understood to mean a Chapel in East Dereham *Town* & not to Express sufficiently that the Monument is in *East Dereham Church*. Owing to my determination of sending you Proofs I have not been able to consult Mr Flaxman about the Designs of Mr Romney which are at Saunders'. I call'd once of [on] Mr F. but he was not at home so could not spare more time, but will now immediately proceed in that business. The Pleasure I reciev'd from your kind Letter ought to make me assiduous & it does so. That Mr John Romney is so honest as to expose to you His whole absurd prejudice gives hopes that he may prove worthy of his father,

---

[1] The plates of Cowper's monument.

& that he should tell such inconsistent surmizes proves that they will soon be eradicated & forgotten. You who was his father's best friend will I hope become the most respected object of his love & admiration.

I call'd on Mʳ Hoare with your Elegant & Heart lifting Compliment; he was not at home. I left it with a short note, have not seen him since.

Mʳ Rose I am happy to hear is getting quite well. Hope to hear the same good account of our most admirable & always anxiously remember'd Miss Poole.

Mʳ Braithwaite call'd on me & brought two Prints which he desires may be sent to you (with his Compliments) (which you will find inclosed) one is a copy from that Miniature you kindly suffer'd me to make from the Picture of Romney which I am now Engraving & which was lent by Mʳ Long[1] for the purpose of being Engraved for the European Magⁿᵉ. The other is Mʳˢ Siddons from the Picture by Romney in Mʳ Braithwaite's possession, but as much unlike the original as possible.

My Wife joins me in best Affections to you

& I remain Sincerely Yours

16 March 1804   Will Blake

I enclose also N° 23 of the Shakespeare.

48. TO WILLIAM HAYLEY

21 MARCH 1804

Dear Sir,

I send two Proofs of Each of the Monumental Plates with the writing, which I hope will please. Should have sent the twelve of each if I had not wish'd to improve them still more, & because I had not enough paper in proper order for printing: beg pardon for the omission of Mʳ Baithwaite's two Prints, as also for omitting to mention Mʳ Hoare's grateful sensation on His reception of your very beautiful Verses. I now send you his note to Me, as I think it will give you a good idea of this good & excellent Man.

I have been to look at the Drawings & Picture, but Flaxman has not yet been able to go with me. Am sorry to inform you that one of the drawings which Mʳ Romney destined for you is Lost or at least

[1] William Long (1747–1818), F.R.S., F.S.A., assistant surgeon, St. Bartholomew's Hospital, and Master of the College of Surgeons in 1800. He was a friend of both Flaxman and Hayley, and possessed a copy of Blake's *Poetical Sketches* (see Keynes, *Blake Studies*, p. 35). He sat to Romney as his first subject for a portrait (see "William Long, F.R.S." by W. E. Thompson, *Annals of the Royal College of Surgeons*, xiii, 1951, p. 55).

cannot now be found: it is that of the Witch raising the Storm. Mr Romney says that in lieu of the lost drawing you shall have choice of either of the remaining ones of which Sanders says there are several, but I only saw one more because I would not give much trouble as Flaxman was not with me. The Drawing I saw is of a Female Figure with a Serpent in one hand & a torch in the other both held above her head & a figure kneeling at her feet; it is a very sublime drawing & would make an Excellent Print, but I will not advise any thing till Flaxman sees them. The drawing of Pliny in the Eruption of Vesuvius is very clever & indeed a Sublime, but very unfinish'd, Sketch—The Picture of the Man on horseback rescuing the drowning people is a beautiful Performance.[1] Mr Saunders says that he has orders from Mr Romney to deliver the Picture & two drawings to any person whom you shall authorize to recieve them. They are somewhat batter'd, but not so much as I expected, for I remember, & Saunders says, that they never were properly strained upon their straining frames.

We both rejoice that Miss Poole is better, but hope & pray for her intire recovery.

My wife joins me in sincere love to you: please to remember us both affectionately & gratefully to Miss Poole

& believe me to remain, Ever Yours,

Will Blake

Sth Molton Street
   March 21. 1804

49. TO WILLIAM HAYLEY

31 MARCH 1804

Dear Sir,

I did not recieve your Letter till Monday: of course could not have got them Printed to send by tuesday's Coach. But there is a real reason equally good why I have not yet sent. I hope you will believe me when I say that my solicitude to bring them to perfection has caused this delay, as also not being quite sure that you had Copies ready for them. I could not think of delivering the 12 Copies without giving the last touches, which are always the best. I have now, I hope, given them & we directly go to Printing. Consequently it will be by Tuesday's Coach that you will recieve 12 of Each. If you do not wish any more done before I deliver, then pray favor me with a line

---

[1] Romney's oil sketch, "The Shipwreck", engraved by Blake for Hayley's *Life of Romney*, 4°, 1809. Blake's sepia drawing done from the picture is now in the Print Room of the British Museum. The picture illustrates a story from the travels of Thunberg of a horseman, Wolfemad, who rescued shipwrecked people from the sea at the Cape of Good Hope.

that I may send the Plates to Johnson, who wants them to set the Printer to work upon.

I remain   In Engraver's hurry, which is
the worst & most unprofitable of hurries,
Your Sincere & Affectionate,

St Molton S^t   Will Blake
   March 31. 1804

50. TO WILLIAM HAYLEY*   2 APRIL 1804

2 April, 1804.

. . . Mr. Flaxman advises that the drawing of Mr. Romney's which shall be chosen instead of the Witch (if that cannot be recovered), be Hecate, the figure with the torch and snake, which he thinks one of the finest drawings. The twelve impressions of each of the plates which I now send ought to be unrolled immediately that you receive them and put under somewhat to press them flat. You should have had fifteen of each, but I had not paper enough in proper order for printing. There is now in hand a new edition of Flaxman's *Homer*,[1] with additional designs, two of which I am now engraving. I am uneasy at not hearing from Mr. Dally,[2] to whom I enclosed £15 in a letter a fortnight ago, by his desire. I write to him by this post to inquire about it. Money in these times is not to be trifled with. I have now cleared the way to Romney, in whose service I now enter again with great pleasure, and hope soon to show you my zeal with good effect. Am in hopes that Miss Poole is recovered, as you are silent on that most alarming and interesting topic in both your last letters. God be with you in all things. My wife joins me in this prayer.

I am, dear Sir,
Your sincerely affectionate,
Willm. Blake

[1] Flaxman's *Iliad of Homer*, 1805, with 40 plates, three of which were engraved by Blake.

[2] Mr. Dally has not been identified with certainty. It was formerly guessed that he might have been a solicitor in Chichester who had acted for Blake at his trial. No money was due for the services of Blake's counsel, Samuel Rose, who wrote to his father-in-law, Dr. Farr, on 5 May 1804: 'Mrs B. will probably have told you I was highly complimented by the Duke of Richmond for my Defense of Blake, and magnificently remunerated by Hayley' (see G. E. Bentley jr., *Notes & Queries*, March 1955). A more probable identification has been suggested by Mr John Adlard. He has pointed out to me that the name may refer to Richard Dally, author of *The Bognor, Arundel and Littlehampton Guide*, Chichester, 1828, and other works. T. W. Horsfield in his *History, Antiquities and Topography of the County of Sussex*, Lewes, 1835, p. 110, states that Dally knew Hayley intimately and often visited and corresponded with him. Yet, even with the help of the further reference on p. 100, it is not clear why Blake should have sent him £15.

Dear Sir,

You can have no Idea, unless you was in London as I am, how much your Name is lov'd & respected. I have the Extreme pleasure of transmitting to you one proof of this Respect which you will be pleased with & I hope will adopt & embrace. It comes thro' Mr Hoare from Mr Phillips[1] of St Pauls Church Yard; it is as yet an intire secret between M^r P, M^r H, & myself & will remain so till you have given Your Decision—Mr Phillips is a man of vast spirit & enterprize with a solidity of character which few have; he is the man who applied to Cowper for that sonnet in favor of a Prisoner at Leicester which I believe you thought fit not to Print. So you see he is spiritually adjoin'd with us. His connections throughout England & indeed Europe & America enable him to Circulate Publications to an immense Extent & he told Mr Hoare that on the present work which he proposes to commence with your assistance he can afford to expend 2,000 a year. Mr Phillips considers you as the Great Leading character in Literature & his terms to others will amount to only one Quarter of what he proposes to you. I send Inclos'd his Terms as Mr Hoare by my desire has given them to me in writing. Knowing your aversion to Reviews & Reviewing I consider the Present Proposal as peculiarly adapted to your Ideas; it may be call'd a Defence of Literature against those pests of the Press & a bulwark for Genius, which shall with your good assistance disperse those Rebellious Spirits of Envy & Malignity. In short: If you see it as I see it, you will embrace this Proposal on the Score of Parental Duty. Literature is your Child. She calls for your assistance! You: who never refuse to assist any, how remote soever, will certainly hear her Voice. Your answer to the Proposal you will if you think fit direct to Mr Hoare who is worthy of every Confidence you can place in him.

I am, dear Sir,
Your anxiously devoted

Sth Molton Street   Will Blake
April 7. 1804

    Mr Hoare's address is
      To Prince Hoare Esqre
        Buckingham Street
          Strand

[1] Sir Richard Phillips (1767–1840), bookseller and publisher, proprietor of *The Monthly Magazine*. The project described by Blake was never carried out. Phillips published the 1805 edition of Hayley's *Ballads*, with Blake's plates.

52. TO WILLIAM HAYLEY

27 APRIL 1804

Dear Sir,

I have at length seen Mr Hoare after having repeatedly call'd on him every day & not finding him. I now understand that he reciev'd your reply to P.'s Proposal at Brighton where he has a residence from whence he sent it to London to Mr Phillips; he has not seen P. since his return & therefore cannot tell me how he understood your Answer. Mr H. appears to me to consider it as a rejection of the Proposal altogether. I took the liberty to tell him that I could not consider it so, but that as I understood you, You had accepted the Spirit of P's intention which was to leave the whole conduct of the affair to you & that you had accordingly nominated one of your Friends & agreed to nominate others, but if P. meant that you should yourself take on you the drudgery of the ordinary business of a Review his Proposal was by no means a generous one. Mr H. has promised to see Mr Phillips immediately & to know what his intentions are, but he says Perhaps Mr P. may not yet have seen your letter to him, & that his multiplicity of business may very well account for the delay.

I have seen our Excellent Flaxman lately; he is well in health but has had such a burn on his hand as you had once which has hinder'd his working for a fortnight, it is now better; he desires to be most Affectionately remember'd to you, had begun a letter to you a week ago, perhaps by this time you have reciev'd it, but he is also a laborious votary of Endless Work. Engraving is of so Slow Process I must beg of you to give me the earliest possible notice of what Engraving is to be done for The Life of Romney. Endless Work is the true title of Engraving as I find by the things I have in hand day & night.

We feel much easier to hear that you have parted with your Horse, hope soon to hear that you have got a living one of brass, a pegasus of Corinthian metal & that Miss Poole is again in such health as when she first mounted me on my beloved Bruno.

I forgot to mention that Mr Hoare desires his most respectful Compliments to you. Speaks of taking a ride across the country to Felpham as he always keeps a Horse at Brighton.

my wife joins me in love to you

I remain Yours Sincerely

Willm Blake

Sth Molton Street
27 (26 *del.*) April 1804

53. TO WILLIAM HAYLEY*

Dear Sir,

I thank you sincerely for Falconer,[1] an admirable poet, and the admirable prints to it by Fittler. Whether you intended it or not, they have given me some excellent hints in engraving; his manner of working is what I shall endeavour to adopt in many points. I have seen the elder Mr. Walker. He knew and admired without any preface my print of Romney, and when his daughter came in he gave the print into her hand without a word, and she immediately said, "Ah! Romney! younger than I knew him, *but very like indeed.*" Mr. Walker showed me Romney's first attempt at oil painting; it is a copy from a Dutch picture—Dutch Boor Smoking; on the back is written, "This was the first attempt at oil painting by G. Romney." He shew'd me also the last performance of Romney. It is of Mr. Walker and family,[2] the draperies put in by somebody else. It is a very excellent picture, but unfinished. The figures as large as life, half length, Mr. W., three sons, and, I believe, two daughters, with maps, instruments, &c. Mr. Walker also shew'd me a portrait of himself (W.), whole length, on a canvas about two feet by one and a half; it is the first portrait Romney ever painted. But above all, a picture of *Lear and Cordelia*, when he awakes and knows her,—an incomparable production, which Mr. W. bought for five shillings at a broker's shop; it is about five feet by four, and exquisite for expression; indeed, it is most pathetic; the heads of Lear and Cordelia can never be surpassed, and Kent and the other attendant are admirable; the picture is very highly finished. Other things I saw of Romney's first works: two copies, perhaps from Borgognone, of battles; and Mr. Walker promises to collect all he can of information for you. I much admired his mild and gentle benevolent manners; it seems as if all Romney's intimate friends were truly amiable and feeling like himself.

I have also seen Alderman Boydel,[3] who has promised to get the number and prices of all Romney's prints as you desired. He has sent a Catalogue of all his Collection, and a Scheme of his Lottery; desires his compliments to you; says he laments your absence from

---

[1] *The Shipwreck*, by William Falconer, 1804, with seven engravings by J. Fittler, A.R.A., after N. Pocock. Russell (*Letters*, 1906, p. 152) sees evidence of Fittler's influence in Blake's engraving of "The Shipwreck" in Hayley's *Life of Romney* (see p. 132).

[2] A large canvas, now in the National Portrait Gallery, of Walker seated at a table with his wife and daughter, his three sons standing behind them.

[3] John Boydell, engraver and printseller, for whose *Graphic Illustration of the Works of Shakespeare* Blake had engraved a plate after Opie, dated 1803, for *Romeo and Juliet*, Act IV, Scene V.

VII. THOMAS BUTTS
MRS. BUTTS
THOMAS BUTTS JR.
miniatures by Blake c. 1804

London, as your advice would be acceptable at all times, but especially at the present. He is very thin and decay'd, and but the shadow of what he was; so he is now a Shadow's Shadow; but how can we expect a very stout man at eighty-five, which age he tells me he has now reached? You would have been pleas'd to see his eyes light up at the mention of your name.

Mr. Flaxman agrees with me that somewhat more than outline is necessary to the execution of Romney's designs, because his merit is eminent in the art of massing his lights and shades. I should propose to etch them in a rapid but firm manner, somewhat, perhaps, as I did the *Head of Euler*;[1] the price I receive for engraving Flaxman's outlines of *Homer* is five guineas each. I send the Domenichino, which is very neatly done. His merit was but little in light and shade; outline was his element, and yet these outlines give but a faint idea of the finished prints from his works, several of the best of which I have. I send also the French monuments, and inclose with them a catalogue of Bell's Gallery, and another of the Exhibition, which I have *not* yet seen. I mentioned the pictures from Sterne to Mr. Walker; he says that there were several; one, a garden scene, with Uncle Toby and Obadiah planting in the garden; but that of Lefevre's Death he speaks of as incomparable, but cannot tell where it now is, as they were scattered abroad, being disposed of by means of a raffle. He supposes it is in Westmoreland; promises to make every inquiry about it. Accept, also, of my thanks for Cowper's third volume, which I got, as you directed, of Mr. Johnson. I have seen Mr. Rose; he looks, tho' not so well as I have seen him, yet tolerably, considering the terrible storm he has been thro'! He says that the last session was a severe labour; indeed it must be so to a man just out of so dreadful a fever. I also thank you for your very beautiful little poem on the King's recovery; it is one of the prettiest things I ever read, and I hope the King will live to fulfil the prophecy and die in peace; but at present, poor man, I understand he is poorly indeed, and times threaten worse than ever. I must now express my sorrow and my hopes for our good Miss Poole, and so take my leave for the present, with the joint love of my good woman, who is still stiff-knee'd but well in other respects.

I am, dear Sir,

Yours most sincerely,

William Blake

4th May 1804

---

[1] Frontispiece to Euler's *Elements of Algebra*, J. Johnson, London, 1797.

97

54. TO WILLIAM HAYLEY*

28 MAY 1804

Dear Sir,

I thank you heartily for your kind offer of reading, &c. I have read the book thro' attentively and was much entertain'd and instructed, but have not yet come to the *Life of Washington*.[1] I suppose an American would tell me that Washington did all that was done before he was born, as the French now adore Buonaparte and the English our poor George; so the Americans will consider Washington as their god. This is only Grecian, or rather Trojan, worship, and perhaps will be revised [?] in an age or two. In the meantime I have the happiness of seeing the Divine countenance in such men as Cowper and Milton more distinctly than in any prince or hero. Mr. Phillips has sent a small poem; he would not tell the author's name, but desired me to inclose it for you with Washington's *Life*.

Mr. Carr[2] called on me, and I, as you desired, gave him a history of the reviewing business as far as I am acquainted with it. He desires me to express to you that he would heartily devote himself to the business in all its laborious parts, if you would take on you the direction; and he thinks it might be done with very little trouble to you. He is now going to Russia; hopes that the negotiations for this business is not wholly at an end, but that on his return he may still perform his best, as your assistant in it. I have delivered the letter to Mr. Edwards, who will give it immediately to Lady Hamilton. Mr. Walker I have again seen; he promises to collect numerous particulars concerning Romney and send them to you; wonders he has not had a line from you; desires me to assure you of his wish to give every information in his power. Says that I shall have *Lear and Cordelia* to copy if you desire it should be done; supposes that Romney was about eighteen when he painted it; it is therefore doubly interesting. Mr. Walker is truly an amiable man; spoke of Mr. Green[3] as the oldest friend of Romney, who knew most concerning him of any one; lamented the little difference that subsisted between you, speaking of you both with great affection. Mr. Flaxman has also promised to write all he knows or can collect concerning Romney, and send to you. Mr. Sanders has promised to write to Mr. J. Romney immediately, desiring him to give us liberty to copy any of his

[1] *Life of George Washington* by John Marshall, Philadelphia, 1804–7.

[2] John (later Sir John) Carr (1772–1832,) barrister of the Middle Temple and traveller, who published accounts of his tours in France, Holland, Ireland and Scotland. His journey in 1804 was described in *A Northern Summer, or Travel round the Baltic*, 1805 (see D. V. Erdman's "Blake's 'Nest of Villains' ", *Keats-Shelley Journal*, II, 1953, p. 61).

[3] Thomas Greene, of Slyne, Lancaster (1737–1810), solicitor, of whom Romney painted several portraits.

father's designs that Mr. Flaxman may select for that purpose; doubts not at all of Mr. Romney's readiness to send any of the cartoons to London you desire; if this can be done it will be all that could be wished. I spoke to Mr. Flaxman about choosing out proper subjects for our purpose; he has promised to do so. I hope soon to send you Flaxman's advice upon this article. When I repeated to Mr. Phillips your intention of taking the books you want from his shop, he made a reply to the following purpose: "I shall be very proud to have Mr. Hayley's name in my books, but please to express to him my hope that he will consider me as the sincere friend of Mr. Johnson, who is (I have every reason to say) both the most generous and honest man I ever knew, and with whose interest I should be so averse to interfere, that I should wish him to have the refusal first of anything before it should be offered to me, as I know the value of Mr. Hayley's connexion too well to interfere between my best friend and him." This Phillips spoke with real affection, and I know you will love him for it, and will also respect Johnson the more for such testimony; but to balance all this I must, in duty to my friend Seagrave,[1] tell you that Mr. Rose repeated to me his great opinion of Mr. Johnson's integrity, while we were talking concerning Seagrave's printing; it is but justice, therefore, to tell you that I perceive a determination in the London booksellers to injure Seagrave in your opinion, if possible. Johnson may be very honest and very generous, too, where his own interest is concerned; but I must say that he leaves no stone unturn'd to serve that interest, and often (I think) unfairly; he always has taken care, when I have seen him, to rail against Seagrave, and I perceive that he does the same by Mr. Rose. Mr. Phillips took care to repeat Johnson's railing to me, and to say that the country printers could not do anything of consequence. Luckily he found fault with the paper which Cowper's *Life* is printed on, not knowing that it was furnish'd by Johnson. I let him run on so far as to say that it was scandalous and unfit for such a work; here I cut him short by asking if he knew who furnish'd the paper. He answered: "I hope Mr. J. did not." I assured him that he did, and here he left off, desiring me to tell you that the *Life of Washington* was not put to press till the 3rd of this month (May), and on the 13th he had deliver'd a dozen copies at Stationer's Hall, and by the 16th five hundred were out. This is swift work if literally true, but I am not apt to believe literally what booksellers say; and on comparing *Cowper* with *Washington*, must assert that, *except paper* (which is Johnson's fault), *Cowper* is far the best, both as to type and printing. Pray look at *Washington* as far as page 177, you will find that the type is smaller than from 177 to 308, the whole middle of the

[1] Joseph Seagrave, printer of Chichester (see p. 73).

book being printed with a larger and better type than the two extremities; also it is carefully hot-pressed. I say thus much, being urged thereto by Mr. Rose's observing some defects in Seagrave's work, which I conceive were urged upon him by Johnson; and as to the time the booksellers would take to execute any work, I need only refer to the little job which Mr. Johnson was to get done for our friend Dally.[1] He promised it in a fortnight, and it is now three months and is not yet completed. I could not avoid saying thus much in justice to our good Seagrave, whose replies to Mr. Johnson's aggravating letters have been represented to Mr. Rose in an unfair light, as I have no doubt; because Mr. Johnson has, at times, written such letters to me as would have called for the sceptre of Agamemnon rather than the tongue of Ulysses, and I will venture to give it as my settled opinion that if you suffer yourself to be persuaded to print in London you will be cheated every way; but, however, as some little excuse, I must say that in London every calumny and falsehood utter'd against another of the same trade is thought fair play. Engravers, Painters, Statuaries, Printers, Poets, we are not in a field of battle, but in a City of Assassinations. This makes your lot truly enviable, and the country is not only more beautiful on account of its expanded meadows, but also on account of its benevolent minds. My wife joins with me in the hearty wish that you may long enjoy your beautiful retirement.

I am, with best respects to Miss Poole, for whose health we constantly send wishes to our spiritual friends,

Yours sincerely,
William Blake

28 May 1804

P.S.—Mr. Walker says that Mr. Cumberland is right in his reckoning of Romney's age. Mr. W. says Romney was two years older than himself, consequently was born 1734.

Mr. Flaxman told me that Mr. Romney was three years in Italy; that he returned twenty-eight years since. Mr. Humphry,[2] the Painter, was in Italy the same time with Mr. Romney. Mr. Romney lodged at Mr. Richter's, Great Newport Street,[3] before he went; took the house in Cavendish Square immediately on his return; but as Flaxman has promised to put pen to paper, you may expect a full account of all he can collect. Mr. Sanders does not know the time when Mr. R. took or left Cavendish Square house.

---

[1] Probably Richard Dally, friend of Hayley (see p. 93).
[2] Ozias Humphry, miniaturist.
[3] Henry James Richter, painter.

55. TO WILLIAM HAYLEY

Dear Sir,

I have got the three Sublime Designs of Romney now in my Lodgings, & find them all too Grand as well as too undefined for meer outlines; & indeed it is not only my opinion but that of Mr Flaxman & Mr Parker,[1] both of whom I have consulted, that to give a true Idea of Romney's Genius, nothing less than some Finish'd Engravings will do, as Outline intirely omits his chief beauties; but there are some which may be executed in a slighter manner than others, & Mr Parker, whose Eminence as an Engraver makes his opinion deserve notice, has advised that 4 should be done in the highly finished manner, & 4 in a less Finish'd—& on my desiring him to tell me for what he would undertake to Engrave One in Each manner, the size to be about 7 Inches by 5¼, which is the size of a Quarto printed Page, he answer'd: "30 Guineas the finish'd, & half the sum for the less finish'd; but as you tell me that they will be wanted in November, I am of opinion that if Eight different Engravers are Employ'd, the Eight Plates will not be done by that time; as for myself" (Note Parker now speaks), "I have to-day turned away a Plate of 400 Guineas because I am too full of work to undertake it, & I know that all the Good Engravers are so Engaged that they will be hardly prevail'd upon to undertake more than One of the Plates on so short a notice." This is Mr Parker's account of the matter, & perhaps may discourage you from the Pursuit of so Expensive an undertaking; it is certain that the Pictures deserve to be Engraved by the hands of Angels, & must not by any means be done in a careless or too hasty manner. The Price Mr Parker has affix'd to each is Exactly what I myself had before concluded upon. Judging as he did that if the Fuseli Shakespeare is worth 25 Guineas, these will be at least worth 30, & that the inferior ones cannot be done at any rate under 15.

Mr Flaxman advises that the best Engravers should be engaged in the work, as its magnitude demands all the Talents that can be procured.

Mr Flaxman named the following Eight as proper subjects for Prints:

1. The Vision of Atossa from Eschylus.
2. Apparition of Darius.
3. Black Ey'd Susan, a figure on the Sea shore embracing a Corse.

---

[1] James Parker, apprenticed at the same time as Blake to Basire. He and Blake were in partnership as printsellers and engravers, from 1784 to 1787.

4. The Shipwreck, with the Man on Horseback &c., which I have.[1]
5. Hecate: a very fine thing indeed, which I have.
6. Pliny: very fine, but very unfinish'd, Which I have.
7. Lear & Cordelia, belonging to Mr Walker.
8. One other which I omitted to write down & have forgot, but think that it was a Figure with Children, which he call'd a Charity.

I write immediately on recieving the Above Information, because no time should be lost in this truly interesting business.

Richardson is not yet Published. My Head of Romney is in very great forwardness. Parker commends it highly. Flaxman has not yet seen it, but shall soon, & then you shall have a Proof of it for your remarks also. I hope by this time Flaxman has written to you, & that you will soon recieve such documents as will enable you to decide on what is to be done in our desirable & arduous task of doing Justice to our admired Sublime Romney. I have not yet been able to meet Mr Braithwaite at home, but intend very soon to call again, & (as you wish) to write all I can collect from him—be so good as to give me your Earliest decision on what would be safe & not too venturesome in the number of projected Engravings, that I may put it into a train to be properly Executed.

We both rejoice in the generous Paulina's return, with recover'd strength, to her delightful Villa; please to present our sincerest Affections to her. My Wife continues to get better, & joins me in my warmest love & acknowledgments to you, as do my Brother & Sister.

I am, dear Sir, Yours Sincerely,

William Blake

Sth Molton Street
  22 June 1804

56. TO WILLIAM HAYLEY

16 JULY 1804

Dear Sir,

We are both happy to hear that Miss Poole is better, sincerely Pray that she may soon be perfectly restored. I call'd on Mr Rose in Chancery Lane on Friday, hear that he is in Sussex & is well, suppose that he does not tell the worst to his family, hope that so

[1] Engraved by Blake for Hayley's *Life of Romney*, Chichester: Printed by W. Mason for T. Payne, 1809; Blake's drawing is reproduced here facing p. 92.

valuable a life will be preserv'd in health & strength—I send Richardson[1] accompanied by a Proof of Romney in Still an unfinish'd state; but it will have the great advantage to [of] Time to its completion. I also send a Sketch of the Heroic Horseman as you wish'd me to do, the size the Print is to be.

M[r] Phillips desired I would present his most respectful Compliments to you & inform you that he with M[r] Hoare intended to have visited you together—that terrible wet Tuesday, but could not for the Deluges of Rain. M[r] P. was at Brighton with M[r] Hoare, fears that so good an opportunity of seeing you may not occur soon again —M[r] P. refuses to recieve payment for Books & says that he will not recieve it in Money but in some how else more agreeable still, of course he means to pursue his court to Your [*altered from* his] Coy Muse. I wish him success.

I omitted to get Richardson[2] till last Friday having call'd thrice unsuccessfully & before publication, have only had time to skim it but cannot restrain myself from speaking of M[rs] Klopstock's letters Vol. 3, which to my feelings are the purest image of Conjugal affection honesty & Innocence I ever saw on paper. Richardson has won my heart. I will again read Clarissa &[c].,[3] they must be admirable. I was too hasty in my perusal of them to percieve all their beauty. I admire Miss Watson's[4] head of Richardson, it is truly delicate,

"The patient touches of unweari'd Art".[5]

I am now Earnestly employ'd on the Heroic Horseman endeavouring to do justice to so admirable a Picture.

My Wife joins me in love to you.

I remain Dear Sir
Your sincere &
Obliged Serv[t]

Will Blake

Sth Molton S[t]
16 July 1804

---

[1] Probably the head of Richardson engraved for the *Life of Romney*.

[2] *The Correspondence of Samuel Richardson Selected by Anne Laetitia Barbauld*, for R. Phillips, London, 6 vols, 1804. See vol. III, pp. 139–158 for the letters to and from Mrs. Klopstock.

[3] Samuel Richardson's three novels, *Pamela, Clarissa Harlowe* and *Sir Charles Grandison*.

[4] Caroline Watson (1761–1814), stipple engraver.

[5] From Pope's *Temple of Fame*, line 199: "with patient touches of unweary'd art."

57. TO WILLIAM HAYLEY*

It is certainly necessary that the best artists that can be engaged should be employed on the work of Romney's Life. . . . Money flies from me. Profit never ventures upon my Threshold, tho' every other man's doorstone is worn down into the very Earth by the footsteps of the fiends of commerce. [*Extracts from sale catalogue.*]

58. TO WILLIAM HAYLEY*

9 AUGUST 1804

[Unpublished.]

Signed: W. & C. Blake

59. TO WILLIAM HAYLEY

28 SEPTEMBER 1804

Dear Sir,

I hope you will Excuse my delay in sending the Books which I have had some time, but kept them back till I could send a Proof of the Shipwreck which I hope will please. It yet wants all its last & finishing touches, but I hope you will be enabled by it to judge of the Pathos of the Picture.

I send Washington's 2^d Vol:[1]—5 Numbers of Fuseli's Shakespeare, & two Vols. with a Letter from Mr Spilsbury,[2] with whom I accidentally met in the Strand: he says that he relinquish'd Painting as a Profession, for which I think he is to be applauded: but I concieve that he may be a much better Painter if he practises secretly & for amusement, than he could ever be if employ'd in the drudgery of fashionable daubing for a poor pittance of money in return for the sacrifice of Art & Genius: he says he never will leave to Practise the Art, because he loves it, & This Alone will pay its labour by Success, if not of money, yet of True Art, which is All.

I had the pleasure of a call from Mrs Chetwynd & her Brother, a Giant in body, mild & polite in soul, as I have, in general, found great bodies to be; they were much pleased with Romney's Designs. Mrs C. sent to me the two articles for you, & for the safety of which

---

[1] *The Life of Washington* by John Marshall, R. Phillips, London, 1804–1807, 5 vols., each volume was printed from the MS as received by the publisher.

[2] Probably Jonathan Spilsbury (brother of John Spilsbury, the engraver), who exhibited portraits at the Royal Academy from 1776 to 1807.

by the Coach I had some fears, till Mr Meyer[1] obligingly undertook
to convey them safe: he is now, I suppose, enjoying the delights of
the Turret of Lovely Felpham; please to give my affectionate compliments to him.

I cannot help suggesting an Idea which has struck me very
forcibly, that the Tobit & Tobias[2] in your bedchamber would make
a very beautiful Engraving, done in the same manner as the Head
of Cowper,[3] after Lawrence. The Heads to be finish'd, & the figures
left exactly in imitation of the first strokes of the Painter. The Expression of those truly Pathetic heads would thus be transmitted to
the Public, a singular Monument of Romney's Genius in that
Highest branch of Art.

I must now tell my wants, & beg the favour of some more of the
needful: the favor of ten Pounds more will carry me thro' this Plate
& the Head of Romney, for which I am already paid. You shall soon
see a Proof of Him in a very advanc'd state. I have not yet proved it,
but shall soon, when I will send you one. I rejoice to hear from M^r
Meyer of Miss Poole's continued recovery. My wife desires with me
her respects to you, & her, & to all whom we love, that is, to all
Sussex.

  I remain,
    Your Sincere & Obliged Hble Servant,
             Will Blake

Sth Molton St
 28 Septr 1804

60. TO WILLIAM HAYLEY*

            23 OCTOBER 1804

Dear Sir,

I received your kind letter with the note to Mr. Payne, and have
had the cash from him. I should have returned my thanks immediately on receipt of it, but hoped to be able to send, before now,
proofs of the two plates, the *Head* of R[omney] and the *Shipwreck*,
which you shall soon see in a much more perfect state. I write immediately because you wish I should do so, to satisfy you that I have
received your kind favour.

I take the extreme pleasure of expressing my joy at our good Lady
of Lavant's[4] continued recovery: but with a mixture of sincere

---

[1] William Meyer, son of the miniaturist, who was Romney's friend.

[2] According to *Romney*, by Humphry Ward and W. Roberts (vol. II, p. 202),
this picture was painted at Eartham, Hayley and his son serving as models.

[3] Engraved by Blake for Hayley's *Life of Cowper*, 1803.

[4] Miss Harriet Poole.

sorrow on account of the beloved Councillor.[1] My wife returns her heartfelt thanks for your kind inquiry concerning her health. She is surprisingly recovered. Electricity is the wonderful cause; the swelling of her legs and knees is entirely reduced. She is very near as free from rheumatism as she was five years ago, and we have the greatest confidence in her perfect recovery.

The pleasure of seeing another poem from your hands has truly set me longing (my wife says I ought to have said us) with desire and curiosity; but, however, "Christmas is a-coming."

Our good and kind friend Hawkins[2] is not yet in town—hope soon to have the pleasure of seeing him, with the courage of conscious industry, worthy of his former kindness to me. For now! O Glory! and O Delight! I have entirely reduced that spectrous Fiend[3] to his station, whose annoyance has been the ruin of my labours for the last passed twenty years of my life. He is the enemy of conjugal love and is the Jupiter of the Greeks, an iron-hearted tyrant, the ruiner of ancient Greece. I speak with perfect confidence and certainty of the fact which has passed upon me. Nebuchadnezzar had seven times passed over him; I have had twenty; thank God I was not altogether a beast as he was; but I was a slave bound in a mill among beasts and devils; these beasts and these devils are now, together with myself, become children of light and liberty, and my feet and my wife's feet are free from fetters. O lovely Felpham, parent of Immortal Friendship, to thee I am eternally indebted for my three years' rest from perturbation and the strength I now enjoy.

[1] Samuel Rose.

[2] John Hawkins (1758–1841), youngest son of Thomas Hawkins of Trewin and St. Erith, Cornwall, M.P. for Grampound and F.R.S. John Flaxman, in a letter written to William Hayley about 1784, wrote: "Mr. Hawkins, a Cornish gentleman, has shown his taste and liberality in ordering Blake to make several drawings for him; and is so convinced of his uncommon talents that he is now endeavouring to raise a subscription to send him to finish studies in Rome: if this can be at all, it will be determined on before the 10th of May next, at which time Mr. Hawkins is going out of England. His generosity is such that he would bear the whole charge of Blake's travels; but he is only a younger brother, and can therefore, only bear a large proportion of the expense." Flaxman was at the same time reporting that Romney considered Blake's "historical drawings ranked with those of Michael Angelo" (see Blake's *Letters*, ed. Russell, 1906, p. 52). The plan for Blake to travel to Rome was never realised. Hawkins, although only a younger brother, bought Bignor Park, in 1808, and became Sheriff of Sussex.

[3] Blake uses the term "Spectre" in more than one sense, though in general it represents "the critical reason, antagonistic to vision, an exercise of the spirit of man in analysing, and so dissipating, experience, not in unifying or relating them into a spiritual harmony". In the present context the "rationalizing spectre" of industry has been subdued by Blake's accession of inspiration, so as to compel it to serve in spiritual works (see Sloss & Wallis, ii, 228–30). The rest of the letter develops this theme.

Suddenly, on the day after visiting the Truchsessian Gallery[1] of Pictures, I was again enlightened with the light I enjoyed in my youth, and which has for exactly twenty years been closed from me as by a door and by window-shutters. Consequently I can, with confidence, promise you ocular demonstration of my altered state on the plates I am now engraving after Romney, whose spiritual aid has not a little conduced to my restoration to the light of Art. O the distress I have undergone, and my poor wife with me: incessantly labouring and incessantly spoiling what I had done well. Every one of my friends was astonished at my faults, and could not assign a reason; they knew my industry and abstinence from every pleasure for the sake of study, and yet—and yet—and yet there wanted the proofs of industry in my works. I thank God with entire confidence that it shall be so no longer—he is become my servant who domineered over me, he is even as a brother who was my enemy. Dear Sir, excuse my enthusiasm or rather madness, for I am really drunk with intellectual vision whenever I take a pencil or graver into my hand, even as I used to be in my youth, and as I have not been for twenty dark, but very profitable years. I thank God that I courageously pursued my course through darkness. In a short time I shall make my assertion good that I am become suddenly as I was at first, by producing the *Head of Romney* and the *Shipwreck* quite another thing from what you or I ever expected them to be. In short, I am now satisfied and proud of my work, which I have not been for the above long period.

If our excellent and manly friend Meyer is yet with you, please to make my wife's and my own most respectful and affectionate compliments to him, also to our kind friend at Lavant.

I remain, with my wife's joint affection,

Your sincere and obliged servant,

Will Blake

23 October 1804

61. TO WILLIAM HAYLEY

4 DECEMBER 1804

Dear Sir,

I have omitted so long to thank you for your kind & admirable

[1] The Truchsessian Gallery was a collection of pictures brought to England by Joseph, Count Truchsess, and exhibited in London in August 1803, with a view to selling the pictures to a company for the benefit of the public. Many great masters were supposed to be represented in the collection, but Lawrence, when he went to see them, thought very poorly of them (see *The Farington Diary*, II, 137). When the pictures were sold in 1806 in 676 lots, they made very small sums.

Present in hopes to send Proofs of my plates, but can no longer wait for them but must express my own & my wife's high gratification in the perusal of your elegant & pathetic Poem.[1] To say that Venusia is as beautiful as Serena is only expressing private opinion which will vary in each individual, but to say that she is Your Daughter & is like You, to say "'tis a Girl, promising Boys hereafter", & to say God bless her, for she is a peerless Jewel for a Prince to wear & that we are both highly delighted is what I could not longer omit to say. —Proofs of my Plates will wait on you in a few days; in the mean while I conclude this hasty scrawl with sincere thanks for your kind proposal in your Last letter. I have not yet been able to meet Phillips—Wilkes[2] was not out when I call'd nor any more of Washington. But I have mention'd your Proposal to our Noble Flaxman whose high & generous Spirit relinquishing the whole to me was in some measure to be Expected, but that he has reasons for not being able to furnish any designs You will readily believe, he says his Engagements are so multiform that he should not be able to do them Justice, but that he will overlook & advise & do all that he can to make my designs (should they ever be attempted) what he can, & I know his *What he Can* will be full as much as he pretends, so that I should not fear to produce somewhat in this way that must be satisfactory, the only danger will be that I shall put my Name to his Designs, but if it should fall out so he has Enough & to Spare; the World will know his at once & I shall glory in the Discovery, for Friendship with such a one is better than Fame!—I was about to have written to you to express my wish that two so unequal labourers might not be yoked to the same Plow & to desire you if you could to get Flaxman to do the whole, because I thought it would be (to say the best of myself) like putting John Milton with John Bunyan; but being at Flaxman's taking his advice about our Engravings he mention'd his having reciev'd a Letter from you on the same Day I reciev'd mine & said somewhat, I cannot tell what, that made me think you had open'd your Proposal to him—I thought at any rate it would not be premature to tell him what you had said about the Designs for Edward the first, & he advised it to be done as above related.

I will soon speak with Phillips about it if you will favor me with a line of direction how to proceed—Hope in a few days to send Proofs of Plates which I must say are far beyond Any thing I have ever done. For O happiness never enough to be grateful for! I have lost my Confusion of Thought while at work & am as much myself when I take the Pencil or Graver into my hand as I used to be in my

---

[1] *The Triumph of Music*, Joseph Seagrave, Chichester, 1804.
[2] *Correspondence and Papers of John Wilkes*, ed. J. Almon, London, 1805,

Youth. I have indeed fought thro' a Hell of terrors & horrors (which none could know but myself) in a Divided Existence; now no longer Divided, nor at war with myself I shall travel on in the strength of the Lord God as Poor Pilgrim says.

My wife joins me in Love to you & to our dear Friend and Friends at Lavant & in all Sussex.

I remain Dear Sir Your Sincere and obliged

Will Blake

Sth Molton St

4 Decr. 1804

62. TO WILLIAM HAYLEY*

18 DECEMBER 1804

Dear Sir,

I send, with some confidence, proofs of my two plates, having had the assistance and approbation of our good friend Flaxman. He approves much (I cannot help telling you so much) of the *Shipwreck*. Mrs. Flaxman also, who is a good connoisseur in engraving, has given her warm approbation, and to the plate of the *Portrait*, though not yet in so high finished a state. I am sure (mark my confidence), with Flaxman's advice, which he gives with all the warmth of friendship both to you and me, it must be soon a highly finished and properly finished print; but yet I must solicit for a supply of money, and hope you will be convinced that the labour I have used on the two plates has left me without any resource but that of applying to you. I am again in want of ten pounds; hope that the size and neatness of my plate of the *Shipwreck* will plead for me the excuse for troubling you before it can be properly called finished, though Flaxman has already pronounced it so. I beg your remarks also on both my performances, as in their present state they will be capable of very much improvement from a few lucky or well advised touches. I cannot omit observing that the price Mr. Johnson gives for the plates of Fuseli's *Shakespeare* (the concluding numbers of which I now send) is twenty-five guineas each. On comparing them with mine of the *Shipwreck*, you will perceive that I have done my duty, and put forth my whole strength.

Your beautiful and elegant daughter *Venusea*[1] grows in our estimation on a second and third perusal. I have not yet received the *History of Chicester*.[2] I mention this not because I would hasten

---

[1] *Venusia*, a character in Hayley's *Triumph of Music*, published by Joseph Seagrave, Chichester, 1804.

[2] Alexander Hay, *The History of Chichester*, Chichester, J. Seagrave, 1804. Blake's copy, if he received it, has not been identified.

its arrival before it is convenient, but fancy it may have miscarried. My wife joins me in wishing you a merry Christmas. Remembering our happy Christmas at lovely Felpham, our spirits seem still to hover round our sweet cottage and round the beautiful Turret. I have said *seem*, but am persuaded that distance is nothing but a phantasy. We are often sitting by our cottage fire, and often we think we hear your voice calling at the gate. Surely these things are real and eternal in our eternal mind and can never pass away. My wife continues well, thanks to Mr. Birch's Electrical Magic, which she has discontinued these three months.

I remain your sincere and obliged,
William Blake

63. TO WILLIAM HAYLEY

28 DECEMBER 1804

Dear Sir,

The Death of so Excellent a Man as my Generous Advocate[1] is a Public Loss, which those who knew him can best Estimate, & to those who have an affection for him like Yours, is a Loss that only can be repair'd in Eternity, where it will indeed with such abundant felicity, in the meeting Him a Glorified Saint who was a Suffering Mortal, that our Sorrow is swallow'd up in Hope. Such Consolations are alone to be found in Religion, the Sun & the Moon of our Journey; & such sweet Verses as yours in your last beautiful Poem must now afford you their full reward.

Farewell, Sweet Rose! thou hast got before me into the Celestial City. I also have but a few more Mountains to pass; for I hear the bells ring & the trumpets sound to welcome thy arrival among Cowper's Glorified Band of Spirits of Just Men made Perfect.

Now, My Dear Sir, I will thank you for the transmission of ten Pounds to the Dreamer over his own Fortunes: for I certainly am that Dreamer; but tho' I dream over my own Fortunes, I ought not to Dream over those of other Men, & accordingly have given a look over my account Book, in which I have regularly written down Every Sum I have reciev'd from you; & tho' I never can balance the account of obligations with you, I ought to do my best at all times & in all circumstances. I find that you was right in supposing that I had been paid for all I have done; but when I wrote last requesting ten pounds, I thought it was Due on the Shipwreck (which it was), but I did not advert to the Twelve Guineas which you Lent Me when I made up 30 Pounds to pay our Worthy Seagrave in part of his

[1] Samuel Rose.

Account. I am therefore that 12 Guineas in your Debt: Which If I had consider'd, I should have used more consideration, & more ceremony also, in so serious an affair as the calling on you for more Money; but, however, your kind answer to my Request makes me Doubly Thank you.

The two Cartoons[1] which I have of Hecate & Pliny are very un-equal in point of finishing: the Pliny in [is] a Sketch, tho' admirably contrived for an Effect equal to Rembrandt. But the Hecate is a finish'd Production, which will call for all the Engraver's nicest attention; indeed it is more finish'd than the Shipwreck; it is every body['s] favourite who have seen it, & they regularly prefer it to the Shipwreck as a work of Genius. As to the [Plates del.] Price of the Plates, Flaxman declares to me that he will not pretend to set a price upon Engraving. I think it can only be done by Some Engraver. I consulted Mr Parker on the Subject before I decided on the Ship-wreck, & it was his opinion, & he says it still is so, that a Print of that size cannot be done under 30 Guineas, if finish'd, &, if a Sketch, 15 Guineas; as, therefore, Hecate must be a Finish'd Plate, I consider 30 Guineas as its Price, & the Pliny 15 Guineas.

Our Dear Friend Hawkins is out of Town, & will not return till April. I have sent to him, by a parcel from Col. Sibthorpe's,[2] your Desirable Poetical Present for Mrs Hawkins. His address is this—To John Hawkins, Esqr., Dallington, near Northampton. Mr Edwards is out of Town likewise.

I am very far from shewing the Portrait of Romney as a finish'd Proof; be assured that with our Good Flaxman's good help, & with your remarks on it in addition, I hope to make it a Supernaculum. The Shipwreck, also, will be infinitely better the next proof. I feel very much gratified at your approval of my Queen Catherine: beg to observe that the Print of Romeo & the Apothecary[3] annex'd to your copy is a shamefully worn-out impression, but it was the only one I could get at Johnson's. I left a good impression of it when I left Felpham last in one of Heath's Shakespeare: you will see that it is not like the same Plate with the worn out Impression. My Wife joins me in love & in rejoicing in Miss Poole's continued health. I am, dear Sir,

Yours sincerely,
Will Blake

Sth Molton Street
28 Decr 1804

[1] By Romney.
[2] Colonel Humphry Waldo Sibthorp, father-in-law of John Hawkins.
[3] These two plates were engraved by Blake after Fuseli for *The Plays of Shakes-peare*, ed. Alexander Chalmers, 1805 (see p. 79).

P.S. I made a very high finish'd Drawing of Romney as a Companion to my drawing of the head of Cowper (you remember), with which Flaxman is very much satisfied, & says that when my Print is like that I need wish it no better, & I am determin'd to make it so at least.

W. B.

64. TO WILLIAM HAYLEY

19 JANUARY 1805

Saturday

Dear Sir,

I at length send the Books which I have in vain call'd for at the Publishers[1] 3 several times; but his removal from St Pauls to a noble House in Bridge Street Blackfriars perhaps hinder'd his sending & perhaps his wish that I might again call. I have however seen him this morning, & he has in the most open & explicit manner offer'd his service to you Expressing his desire that I will repeat to you his regret that your last beautiful Poem was not Publish'd in the Extensive way (I speak his own words) that a Poem of Confessedly the first Poet of England ought to be given to the Public (speaking so I must own he won my heart). He said I knew that Dodsley was Mr Hayley's Publisher, but hope that as Mr D. is dead & if Mr H. has no Engagement with any London Bookseller I may myself be appoint'd by him in so honourable a concern as the Publication of his Labours. He then Proceeded to find fault with the Printing of our friend the Chichester Printer. Here I consider'd it my duty to interfere. I express'd my own respect for our Good Seagrave & said I knew your chief intentions in Employing him were 1st to Encourage a Worthy Man & 2^d For the Honour of Chichester. Mr P. immediately replied, if Mr Hayley should think fit to employ me as his Publisher I should have no objection but a pleasure in employing his Printer & have no doubt I could be of service to him in many ways, but I feel for the Honour of London Booksellers & consider them as losing a great deal of Honour in Losing the first Publication of any work of Mr Hayley's & the Public likewise are deprived of the advantage of so extensive a diffusal as would be promoted by the methods which they use to Publish & disperse Copies into all parts to a very great amount. He then said: If Mr Hayley is willing to dispose of this his New Poem I will Purchase it & at his own Price or any other of his Works—For I do assure you I feel it a duty to my Profession that I should do my Endeavour to give Mr Hayley's works

[1] Richard Phillips.

VIII. THE SHIPWRECK

sepia drawing by Blake after Romney 1804

the first rate Elegance in Printing & Paper as they hold the First in internal value. I then said, Is it agreeable to you that I repeat what you have said to me, To Mr Hayley, or will you yourself, for I dare say he will be much pleas'd to hear from you, but said I, I will if you wish (as I shall write soon) give him (as near as I can remember) what you have said, & hope that he will see the matter in the light you do.—He desired I would, expressing (for which I thank him) confidence in my discretion—Such was our conversation as near as I can recollect, I thought it best to keep silent as to anything like a hint of a proposal relating to Edwd 1st or the Ballads having come from you; accordingly I did not say that I knew of any Poem, but left all to you intirely. I do think from the Liberality of this Enter-prizing Man that all Parties, I mean our Friend Seagrave together with the Author & Publisher (& also the Public), may be mutually & extensively benefitted. His connexions are Universal; his present House is on the most noble scale & will be in some measure a Worthy Town Vehicle for your Beautiful Muse. But Mr Phillips said, Mr Hayley shall have whatever I publish sent to him if he pleases & he may return them when he has read them. Such is his determination to do every thing to engage himself to you if possible. He desired I would present you from him with the little volume of poems inclos'd; they are by a Lady of Fortune. I suppose he sends it as a specimen of Printing. P's chief objection to the manner in which the Triumphs of Music[1] are printed—were the strong Metal Rules at the Ends of the Canto's, but he confess'd to me that the first Page of the Poem was beautifully executed & could not be better done.

Pray might I not shew Phillips the four Numbers of Ballads? or will you write to him? or will you think it best to commission me to answer him? whatever you command I will zealously perform, & depend upon it I will neither Do nor say but as you Direct.

I feel extremely happy that you think My Prints will do me Credit & at the very idea of another journey to Sweet Felpham. O that I could but bring Felpham to me or go to her in this World as easy as I can in that of Affection & Remembrance. I feel it is necessary to be very circumspect how we advance with Romney; his best Works only ought to be engraved for your Work.

Pray accept My & My Wife's sincerest affection & believe me to remain Yours sincerely

Will Blake

S^th Molton Street
19 Jany 1805

[1] *The Triumph of Music* by William Hayley, Chichester, 1804.

113

65. TO WILLIAM HAYLEY*

Dear Sir,

I hope this letter will outstrip Mr. Phillips', as I sit down to write immediately on returning from his house. He says he is agreeable to every proposal you have made, and will himself immediately reply to you. I should have supposed him mad if he had not: for such clear and generous proposals as yours to him he will not easily meet from anyone else. He will, of course, inform you what his sentiments are of the proposal concerning the three dramas. I found it unnecessary to mention anything relating to the purposed application of the profits, as he, on reading your letter, expressed his wish that you should yourself set a price, and that he would, in his letter to you, explain his reasons for wishing it. The idea of publishing one volume a year he considers as impolitic, and that a handsome general edition of your works would be more productive. He likewise objects to any periodical mode of publishing any of your works, as he thinks it somewhat derogatory, as well as unprofitable. I must now express my thanks for your generous manner of proposing the *Ballads* to him on my account, and inform you of his advice concerning them; and he thinks that they should be published *all together* in a volume the size of the small edition of the *Triumphs of Temper*, with six or seven plates.[1] That one thousand copies should be the first edition, and, if we choose, we might add to the number of plates in a second edition. And he will go equal shares with me in the expense and the profits, and that Seagrave is to be the printer. That we must consider all that has been printed as lost, and begin anew, unless we can apply some of the plates to the new edition. I consider myself as only put in trust with this work, and that the copyright is for ever yours. I therefore beg that you will not suffer it to be injured by my ignorance, or that it should in any way be separated from the grand bulk of your literary property. Truly proud I am to be in possession of this beautiful little estate; for that it will be highly productive I have no doubt, in the way now proposed; and I shall consider myself a robber to retain more than you at any time please to grant. In short, I am tenant at will, and may write over my door, as the poor barber did, 'Money for live here.'

I entreat your immediate advice what I am to do, for I would not for the world injure this beautiful work, and cannot answer P.'s proposal till I have your directions and commands concerning it;

---

[1] *Ballads*, by William Hayley, Esq., founded on Anecdotes relating to Animals, with [five] Prints designed and engraved by William Blake. Chichester: printed by J. Seagrave, for Richard Phillips, Bridge Street, Blackfriars, London, 1805, 8°.

for he wishes to set about it immediately, and has desired that I will give him my proposal concerning it in writing.

I remain, dear Sir,

Your obliged and affectionate

Will Blake

22 January 1805

66. TO THOMAS BUTTS 22 JANUARY 1805

22: Janry 1805

Received of Mr Butts twelve Pounds twelve Shillings on further account

William Blake

£12–12

67. TO WILLIAM HAYLEY 25 APRIL 1805

Friday

Dear Sir,

This Morning I have been with Mr Phillips & have entirely settled with him the plan of Engraving for the new Edition of the Ballads. The Prints 5 in Number I have Engaged to finish by 28 May: they are to be as highly finish'd as I can do them, the Size the same as the Serena plates,[1] the Price 20 Guineas Each, half to be paid by P—The Subjects I cannot do better than those already chosen, as they are the most eminent among Animals Viz. The Lion, The Eagle, The Horse, The Dog. Of the Dog Species the Two Ballads are so pre-eminent & my Designs for them please me so well that I have chosen that design in our Last Number of the Dog & Crocodile, & that of the Dog defending his dead Master from the Vultures; of these five I am making little high finish'd Pictures the size the Engravings are to be, & am hard at it to accomplish in time what I intend. M^r P— says he will send Mr Seagrave the Paper directly.

The Journeyman Printers throughout London are at War with their Masters & are likely to get the better. Each Party meet to consult against the other; nothing can be greater than the Violence on both sides. Printing is suspended in London Except at private

---

[1] i.e. the six plates engraved by Blake for Hayley's *Triumphs of Temper*, twelfth edition, Chichester, 1803, from designs by Maria Flaxman. Serena was the heroine of Hayley's poem.

Presses. I hope this will become a source of Advantage to our Friend Seagrave.

The Idea of Seeing an Engraving of Cowper by the hand of Caroline Watson[1] is, I assure you, a pleasing one to me; it will be highly gratifying to see another Copy by another hand & not only gratifying, but Improving, which is better.

The Town is Mad. Young Roscius[2] like all Prodigies is the talk of Every Body. I have not seen him & perhaps never may. I have no curiosity to see him, as I well know what is within the compass of a boy of 14, & as to Real Acting it is Like Historical Painting, No Boy's Work.

Fuseli is made Master of the Royal Academy. Banks[3] the Sculptor is Gone to his Eternal Home. I have heard that Flaxman means to give a Lecture on Sculpture at the Royal Academy on the Occasion of Banks's Death; he died at the Age of 75 of a Paralytic Stroke. Now I concieve Flaxman stands without a competitor in Sculpture.

I must not omit to tell you that on leaving Mr Phillips I ask'd i he had any Message to you as I meant to write immediately; he said Give my best Respects & tell Mr Hayley that I wish very much to be at work for him. But perhaps I ought to tell you what he said to me previous to this in the course of our Conversation; his words were, I feel, somewhat Embarras'd at the Idea of setting a value on any work of Mr Hayley's & fear that he will wish me to do so. I asked him how a Value was set on any Literary work; he answer'd The Probable sale of the work would be the measure of Estimating the Profits & that would lead to a Valuation of the Copy right. This may be of no Consequence, but I could not omit telling it you.

My Wife Continues in health & desires to join me in every Grateful Wish to you & to our Dear Respected Miss Poole.

I remain

Yours with Sincerity
William Blake

P.S. Your Desire that I should write a little Advertisement[4] at the Beginning of the Ballads has set my Brains to work & at length produc'd the following. Simplicity, as you desired has been my first object. I send it for your Correction or Condemnation, begging you to supply its deficiency or to New Create it according to your wish.

[1] Caroline Watson (1761–1814) engraved for the octavo edition of Hayley's *Life of Cowper* the crayon portrait of the poet engraved by Blake for the quarto edition of 1803, vol II.

[2] Master Betty, i.e. William Henry West Betty (1791–1874), actor from 1803 to 1864.

[3] Thomas Banks, R.A., had died on 2 February, 1805.

[4] This was not printed in the book.

The Public ought to be inform'd that [The following *del*.] These
Ballads were the Effusions of Friendship to Countenance what their
Author is kindly pleased to call Talents for Designing and to relieve
my more laborious [employment *del*.] engagement of Engraving
those Portraits which accompany The Life of Cowper. Out of a
number of Designs I have selected Five [and] hope that the Public
will approve of my rather giving few highly labour'd Plates than a
greater number & less finish'd. If I have succeeded in these more may
be added at Pleasure.

Will Blake

68. ACCOUNT WITH THOMAS BUTTS

12 MAY 1805–3 MARCH 1806

Mr Butts D^r,		C^r
May 12 1805	Jany 12	
Due on Account . . 0.4.0	By Cash 12.12.0	
12 Drawings[1] Viz		
1 Famine 2 War 3 Moses striking		
the Rock 4 Ezekiel's Wheels 5 Christ		
girding himself with strength 6 Four		
& twenty Elders 7 Christ Baptizing		
8 Samson breaking bonds 9 Samson		
subdu'd 10 Noah & Rainbow 11		
Wise & foolish Virgins 12 Hell be-		
neath is moved for thee &^{c} from		
Isaiah 12.12.0		
5 July	5 July	
4 Prints[2] Viz	By d^o _____ 5.7.0	
1 Good & Evil Angel 2 House of		
Death 3 God Judging Adam 4		
Lamech 4.4.0		
21 Augst		
4 N^{os} of Hayley's		
Ballads 0.10.0		
7 Sept^r	7 Sept^r	
4 Prints[3] Viz	By d^o 4.4.0	

[1] Of these water-colour drawings nos. 1, 3, 5, 6, 7, 9, 11, were afterwards in the
Graham Robertson collection. No. 6 is now in the Tate Gallery; the remainder
have been dispersed.

[2] These four colour prints were afterwards in the collection of Graham Robertson, who gave them, with others, to the Tate Gallery in 1939.

[3] Of these four prints nos. 1–3 were acquired by Graham Robertson and given
to the Tate Gallery in 1939. The print of no. 4 now in the Tate Gallery, "Christ
appearing to the Apostles", was a different impression acquired later from another
source and bequeathed by Graham Robertson to the Gallery. No. 3 is the print

68. ACCOUNT WITH THOMAS BUTTS (*contd.*)

1 Nebuchadnezzar 2 Newton 3 God
Creating Adam 4 Christ appear-
ing 4.4.0
Decr 12
   Touch^g up Christ
   Baptizing   1.1.0

Should be 22.15	£21.15.0	Should be £22.3	£21.3.0

Dr Mr Butts		C^r	
Bro^t over	£22.15.–	Bro^t over	£22.3.–
Drawings &c sent from Felpham	}14.14.–	Balance due from me previous to my going to Felpham	14.10.8
Urizen,^{1} Heaven^2 &c & Songs of Experience for balance	–.10.6	By Coals to 5: Octr 1805	}12.19.–
3 Hayley's Ballads per Brother	7.6		
3 Ditto — Mr Birch	7.6		
4 Ditto	10.–	Balance paid	
History of Mast^r Malkin^3	10.6	to Mr Blake	16.7.4
Decr 25 1805			
On Account of teaching your Son at 25 Guineas per Annum to commence on this Day	}26.5.0		
	£66.0.–		£66.0.0

[*Receipt*]
Reciev'd of Mr Butts, March 3. 1806 the Sum of Sixteen Pounds
Seven & Four pence Balance to this day as per Annexed Account
                                      William Blake
£16. 17. 4

69. TO WILLIAM HAYLEY*   17 MAY 1805

"Reading in the Bible of the Eyes of the Almighty, I could not help
putting up a petition for yours." Speaks of his rough sketch of an

---

formerly known as "Elijah in the Fiery Chariot", now correctly named as "God
judging Adam".
   ^{1} This copy of *The First Book of Urizen* has not been identified.
   ^{2} *The Marriage of Heaven and Hell*, copy C in the *Census*, afterwards in the Crewe
collection and now in America.
   ^{3} *A Father's Memoirs of his Child*. By T. H. Malkin. London 1806. The frontispiece
was engraved by Cromek after a design by Blake.

advertisement (the direction of which has been improved). . . . "if any of my writings should hereafter appear before the Public, they will fall far short of this first specimen." [*Extracts from sale catalogue.*]

70. TO WILLIAM HAYLEY*

4 JUNE 1805

Dear Sir,

I have fortunately, I ought to say providentially, discovered that I have engraved one of the plates for that ballad of *The Horse* which is omitted in the new edition; time enough to save the extreme loss and disappointment which I should have suffered had the work been completed without that ballad's insertion.[1] I write to entreat that you would contrive so as that my plate may come into the work, as its omission would be to me a loss that I could not now sustain, as it would cut off ten guineas from my next demand on Phillips, which sum I am in absolute want of; as well as that I should lose all the labour I have been at on that plate, which I consider as one of my best; I know it has cost me immense labour. The way in which I discovered this mistake is odd enough. Mr. Phillips objects altogether to the insertion of my Advertisement, calling it an appeal to charity, and says it will hurt the sale of the work, and he sent to me the last sheet by the penny (that is, the twopenny) post, desiring that I would forward it to Mr. Seagrave. But I have inclosed it to you, as you ought and must see it. I am no judge in these matters, and leave all to your decision,[2] as I know that you will do what is right on all hands. Pray accept my and my wife's sincerest love and gratitude.

Will Blake

71. TO THOMAS BUTTS

5 JULY 1805

July 5 1805

Received of M^r. Butts five Pounds seven Shillings on further account

William Blake

£5 „ 7 „ –

[1] "The Horse" was included as the last ballad in the volume, together with the plate—Blake had also made a tempera painting of the same subject fomerly at Upholland College, Wigan, now in the Paul Mellon collection.

[2] The Advertisement was not included.

72. TO THOMAS BUTTS

7: Septr 1805

Received of M^r. Butts four Pounds four Shillings on further account

WILLIAM BLAKE

£4 „ 4

73. TO WILLIAM HAYLEY

27 NOVEMBER 1805

Dear Sir,

Mr Cromek the Engraver came to me desiring to have some of my Designs; he nam'd his Price & wish'd me to Produce him Illustrations of The Grave, A Poem by Robert Blair; in consequence of this I produced about twenty Designs which pleas'd so well that he, with the same liberality with which he set me about the Drawings, has now set me to Engrave them. He means to Publish them by Subscription with the Poem as you will see in the Prospectus which he sends you in the same Pacquet with the Letter. You will, I know, feel as you always do on such occasions, not only warm wishes to promote the Spirited Exertions of my Friend Cromek. You will be pleased to see that the Royal Academy have Sanctioned the Style of work. I now have reason more than ever to lament your Distance from London, as that alone has prevented our Consulting you in our Progress, which is but of about two Months Date. I cannot give you any Account of our Ballads, for I have heard nothing of Phillips this Age. I hear them approved by the best, that is, the most serious people, & if any others are displeas'd it is also an argument of their being Successful as well as Right, of which I have no Doubt; for what is Good must Succeed first or last, but what is bad owes success to something beside or without itself, if it has any.

My Wife joins me in anxious wishes for your Health & Happiness, desiring to be particularly remember'd by You & our Good Lady Paulina over a dish of Coffee. I long to hear of your Good Health & that of our dear friend of Lavant & of all our friends (to whom we are grateful & desire to be remember'd) In Sussex.

I am, Dear Sir,

Yours ever Affectionately,

Will. Blake

27 Nov^r.
1805

Dear Sir,

I cannot omit to Return you my sincere & Grateful Acknowledgments for the kind Reception you have given my New Projected
Work. It bids fair to set me above the difficulties I have hitherto
encounter'd. But my Fate has been so uncommon that I expect
Nothing. I was alive & in health & with the same Talents I now
have all the time of Boydell's, Macklin's, Bowyer's, & other Great
Works. I was known by them & was look'd upon by them as Incapable of Employment in those Works; it may turn out so again,
notwithstanding appearances. I am prepared for it, but at the same
time sincerely Grateful to Those whose Kindness & Good opinion
has supported me thro' all hitherto. You, Dear Sir, are one who has
my Particular Gratitude, having conducted me thro' Three that
would have been the Darkest Years that ever Mortal Suffer'd, which
were render'd thro' your means a Mild & Pleasant Slumber. I speak
of Spiritual Things, Not of Natural; Of Things known only to Myself & to Spirits Good & Evil, but Not Known to Men on Earth.
It is the passage thro' these Three Years that has brought me into
my Present State, & *I know* that if I had not been with You I must
have Perish'd. Those Dangers are now Passed & I can see them
beneath my feet. It will not be long before I shall be able to present
the full history of my Spiritual Sufferings to the Dwellers upon
Earth & of the Spiritual Victories obtain'd for me by my Friends.
Excuse this Effusion of the Spirit from One who cares little for this
World, which passes away, whose Happiness is Secure in Jesus our
Lord, & who looks for Suffering till the time of complete deliverance.
In the mean While I am kept Happy, as I used to be, because I
throw Myself & all that I have on our Saviour's Divine Providence.
O What Wonders are the Children of Men! Would to God that they
would Consider it. That they would Consider their Spiritual Life,
Regardless of that faint Shadow Call'd Natural Life, & that they
would Promote Each other's Spiritual Labours, Each according to
its Rank, & that they would know that Recieving a Prophet As a
Prophet is a Duty which If omitted is more Severely Avenged than
Every Sin & Wickedness beside. It is the Greatest of Crimes to
Depress True Art & Science. I know that those who are dead from
the Earth, & who mock'd & Despised the Meekness of True Art
(and such, I find, have been the situations of our Beautiful, Affectionate Ballads),[1] I know that such Mockers are Most Severely
Punish'd in Eternity. I know it, for I see it & dare not help. The

---

[1] The volume of *Ballads* had been ridiculed by some of the reviewers, including
Robert Southey in *The Annual Register*.

Mocker of Art is the Mocker of Jesus. Let us go on, Dear Sir, following his Cross: let us take it up daily, Persisting in Spiritual Labours & the Use of that Talent which it is Death to Bury, & of that Spirit to which we are called.

Pray Present My Sincerest Thanks to our Good Paulina, whose kindness to Me shall recieve recompense in the Presence of Jesus. Present also my Thanks to the Generous Seagrave, In whose debt I have been too long, but percieve that I shall be able to settle with him soon what is between us. I have deliver'd to Mr Sanders the 3 Works of Romney, as Mrs Lambert told me you wished to have them: a very few touches will finish the Shipwreck. Those few I have added upon a Proof before I parted with the Picture. It is a Print that I feel proud of, on a New inspection. Wishing you & All Friends in Sussex a Merry & a Happy Christmas,

I remain, Ever Your Affectionate,

Will Blake & his Wife Catherine Blake

Sth Molton Street
Decemb^r. 11. 1805

75. TO RICHARD PHILLIPS[1]*

JUNE 1806

Sir,

My indignation was exceedingly moved at reading a criticism in *Bell's Weekly Messenger* (25th May) on the picture of Count Ugolino, by Mr. Fuseli, in the Royal Academy Exhibition; and your Magazine being as extensive in its circulation as that Paper, and as it also must from its nature be more permanent, I take the advantageous opportunity to counteract the widely diffused malice which has for many years, under the pretence of admiration of the arts, been assiduously sown and planted among the English public against true art, such as it existed in the days of Michael Angelo and Raphael. Under pretence of fair criticism and candour, the most wretched taste ever produced has been upheld for many, very many years; but now, I say, now its end is come. Such an artist as Fuseli is invulnerable, he needs not my defence; but I should be ashamed not to set my hand and shoulder, and whole strength, against those wretches who, under pretence of criticism, use the dagger and the poison.

My criticism on this picture is as follows: Mr. Fuseli's Count Ugolino is the father of sons of feeling and dignity, who would not sit looking in their parent's face in the moment of his agony, but would rather retire and die in secret, while they suffer him to in-

[1] Sir Richard Phillips, publisher, and proprietor of *The Monthly Magazine*. Blake's letter appeared in the number for 1 July 1806.

dulge his passionate and innocent grief, his innocent and venerable madness and insanity and fury, and whatever paltry, cold-hearted critics cannot, because they dare not, look upon. Fuseli's Count Ugolino is a man of wonder and admiration, of resentment against man and devil, and of humiliation before God; prayer and parental affection fill the figure from head to foot. The child in his arms, whether boy or girl signifies not (but the critic must be a fool who has not read Dante, and who does not know a boy from a girl), I say, the child is as beautifully drawn as it is coloured—in both, inimitable! and the effect of the whole is truly sublime, on account of that very colouring which our critic calls black and heavy. The German flute colour, which was used by the Flemings (they call it burnt bone), has possessed the eye of certain connoisseurs, that they cannot see appropriate colouring, and are blind to the gloom of a real terror.

The taste of English amateurs has been too much formed upon pictures imported from Flanders and Holland; consequently our countrymen are easily browbeat on the subject of painting; and hence it is so common to hear a man say: 'I am no judge of pictures.' But O Englishmen! know that every man ought to be a judge of pictures, and every man is so who has not been connoisseured[1] out of his senses.

A gentleman who visited me the other day, said, "I am very much surprised at the dislike that some connoisseurs shew on viewing the pictures of Mr. Fuseli; but the truth is, he is a hundred years beyond the present generation." Though I am startled at such an assertion, I hope the contemporary taste will shorten the hundred years into as many hours; for I am sure that any person consulting his own eyes must prefer what is so supereminent; and I am as sure that any person consulting his own reputation, or the reputation of his country, will refrain from disgracing either by such ill-judged criticisms in future.

Yours,
Wm. Blake

76. TO THOMAS BUTTS   30 JUNE 1806

30: June 1806
Received of Mr. Butts twenty one pounds ten Shillings on account for sundry Drawings

Will m Blake

£21 ,, 10 ,, 0

[1] cp. Blake's punning fragment in the MS Note Book: "The cunning-sures & the aim-at-yours . . ."

77. TO THOMAS BUTTS

9 SEPTEMBER 1806

9 Septr. 1806
Receiv'd of M^r. Butts six Pounds six Shillings for Drawings Songs
of Innocence &c

William Blake

£6 ,, 6 ,,

78. TO THOMAS BUTTS

15 OCTOBER 1806

15: Octr. 1806
Received of Mr Butts five Pounds 5/- on further account

Willm Blake

£5 ,, 5 ,,

79. TO THOMAS BUTTS

29 JANUARY 1807

29: Janry 1807
Received of Mr Butts Twenty one Pounds on further account

William Blake

£21 —

80. TO THOMAS BUTTS

3 MARCH 1807

Receivd March 3. 1807 of M^r. Butts the Sum of Twenty Eight
Pounds Six Shillings on Account

Willm Blake

28–6–0
[*Added in pencil*]

Tom[1]—	26.	5		28.	6.	
Drawings in			}28–6	25.	4.	6.
full to this	2.	1.				
day—				3.	1.	6.

[1] Blake was teaching Thomas Butts jr. to engrave.

124

81. R. H. CROMEK TO BLAKE*

MAY 1807

Sir,

I received, not without great surprise, your letter demanding four guineas for the *sketched* vignette dedicated to the Queen.[1] I have returned the drawing with this note, and I will briefly state my reasons for so doing. In the first place I do not think it merits the price you affix to it, *under any circumstances*. In the next place, I never had the remotest suspicions that you would for a moment entertain the idea of writing *me* to supply money to create an honour in which I cannot possibly participate. The Queen allowed *you*, not *me*, to dedicate the work to *her*! The honour would have been yours exclusively; but that you might not be deprived of any advantage likely to contribute to your reputation, I was willing to pay Mr. Schiavonetti *ten* guineas for etching a plate from the drawing in question.

Another reason for returning the sketch is, that I *can do without it*, having already engaged to give a greater number of etchings than the price of the book will warrant; and I neither have, nor ever had, any encouragement from *you* to place you before the public in a more favourable point of view than that which I have already chosen. You charge me with *imposing upon you*. Upon my honour I have no recollection of anything of the kind. If the world and I were to settle accounts tomorrow, I do assure you the balance would be considerably in my favour. In this respect I am more sinned against than sinning; but if I cannot recollect any instances wherein I have imposed upon *you*, several present themselves in which I have imposed upon myself. Take two or three that press upon me.

When I first called on you, I found you without reputation; I *imposed* on myself the labour, and a herculean one it has been, to create and establish a reputation for you. I say the labour was herculean, because I had not only to contend with, but I had to battle with a man who had pre-determined not to be served. What public reputation you have, the reputation of eccentricity excepted, I have acquired for you; and I can honestly and conscientiously assert, that if you had laboured through life for yourself as zealously and as earnestly as I have done for you, your reputation as an artist would not only have been enviable, but it would have put it out of the power of an individual as obscure as myself either to add to or take from it. I *also imposed on myself*, when I believed what you so often have told me, that your works were equal, nay superior, to a Raphael or to a Michael Angelo! Unfortunately, for me as a publisher, the

---

[1] This water-colour drawing is now in the Print Room at the British Museum. It was not used in Cromek's edition of Blair's *Grave*.

public awoke me from this state of stupor, this mental delusion. That public is willing to give you credit for what real talent is to be found in your productions, *and for no more.*

I *have imposed on myself* yet more grossly in believing you to be one altogether abstracted from this world, holding converse with the world of spirits! simple, unoffending, a combination of the *serpent* and the *dove.* I really blush when I reflect how I have been cheated in this respect. The most effectual way of benefiting a designer whose aim is general patronage, is to bring his designs before the public, through the medium of engraving. Your drawings have had the *good* fortune to be engraved by one of the first artists in Europe,[1] and the specimens already shown have already produced you orders that I verily believe you otherwise would not have received. Herein I have been gratified; for I was determined to bring you food as well as reputation, though, from your late conduct, I have some reason to embrace your wild opinion, that to manage genius, and to cause it to produce good things, it is absolutely necessary to starve it; indeed, this opinion is considerably heightened by the recollection that your best work, the illustrations of *The Grave*, was produced when you and Mrs. Blake were reduced so low as to be obliged to live on half a guinea a week!

Before I conclude this letter, it will be necessary to remark, when I gave you the order for the drawings from the poem of *The Grave*, I paid you for them more than I could afford; more in proportion than you were in the habit of receiving, and what you were perfectly satisfied with; though, I must do you the justice to confess, much less than I think is their real value. Perhaps you have friends and admirers who can appreciate their merit and worth as much as I do. I am decidedly of opinion that the twelve for *The Grave* should sell at least for sixty guineas. If you can meet with any gentleman who will give you this sum for them, I will deliver them into his hands on the publication of the poem. I will deduct the twenty guineas I have paid you from that sum, and the remainder forty ditto shall be at your disposal.

I will not detain you more than one minute. Why did you so *furiously rage* at the success of the little picture of "The Pilgrimage"?[2] Three thousand people have now *seen it and have approved of it.* Believe me, yours is *"the voice of one crying in the wilderness!"*

You say the subject is *low* and *contemptibly treated.* For his excellent mode of treating the subject, the poet has been admired for the last 400 years; the poor painter has not yet the advantage of antiquity

---

[1] Schiavonetti, engraver of Blake's designs for Blair's *Grave.*

[2] This refers to Stothard's painting of "The Canterbury Pilgrims", which had been exhibited with great success to the public.

on his side, therefore, with some people, an apology may be necessary for him. The conclusion of one of Squire Simkin's letters to his mother in the *Bath Guide*[1] will afford one. He speaks greatly to the purpose:

> "Very well know,
> Both my subject and verse is exceedingly low;
> But if any *great critic* finds fault with my letter,
> *He has nothing to do but to send you a better.*"

With much respect for your talents, I remain, Sir, your real friend and well-wisher,

R. H. Cromek

64 Newman Street
  May, 1807

82. TO THOMAS BUTTS

2 JUNE 1807

2: June 1807

Received of M^r. Butts twelve Pounds 1/6 on further account

William Blake

£12 ,, 1 ,, 6

83. TO THOMAS BUTTS

13 JULY 1807

13: July 1807

Received of M^r. Butts fifteen Pounds 15/– on further account

William Blake

£15 ,, 15 ,, –

84. TO THOMAS BUTTS

6 OCTOBER 1807

6: Octr. 1807

Received of M^r. Butts Ten Guineas on further account

William Blake

£10 ,, 10 ,, –

[1] Christopher Anstey's *New Bath Guide*, Bath, 1807, pp. 27–8.

85. TO RICHARD PHILLIPS

Oct 14

Sir,

A circumstance has occurred which has again raised my Indignation.

I read in the Oracle & True Briton of Octr 13, 1807, that a Mr Blair, a Surgeon, has, *with the Cold fury of Robespierre*, caused the Police to sieze upon the Person & Goods or Property of an Astrologer & to commit him to Prison. The Man who can Read the Stars often is opressed by their Influence, no less than the Newtonian who reads Not & cannot Read is opressed by his own Reasonings & Experiments. We are all subject to Error: Who shall say, Except the Natural Religionists, that we are not all subject to Crime?

My desire is that you would Enquire into this Affair & that you would publish this in your Monthly Magazine. I do not pay the postage of this Letter, because you, as Sheriff, are bound to attend to it.[1]

William Blake

17 S^th Molton S^t

86. TO THOMAS BUTTS

14: Janry 1808
Received of M^r· Butts twenty six pounds 5/– on further account
for W^m· Blake
Cathrine
Blake

£26 ,, 5 ,,

87, 88. TO OZIAS HUMPHRY [first draft and duplicate]

To Ozias Humphry Esqre·

The Design of The Last Judgment, which I have completed by your recommendation [*under a fortunate star*] for the Countess [*(del.)*

---

[1] The letter is marked: W. B. Rec^d· Oct^r· 27th 1807. With Mr P.'s Comps. It was not published in *The Monthly Magazine*.

IX. TO THE QUEEN
drawing for Blake's Dedication, 1807,
of the illustrations to Blair's *Grave* 1808

Earl (in another hand)] of Egremont,[1] it is necessary to give some account of: & its various parts ought to be described, for the accomodation of those who give it the honor of attention.

Christ seated on the Throne of Judgment: The Heavens in Clouds rolling before him & around him, like a scroll ready to be consumed in the fires of the Angels; who descend before his feet with their four trumpets sounding to the four Winds.

Beneath; the Earth is convuls'd with the labours of the Resurrection. In the caverns of the Earth is the Dragon with seven heads & ten horns, Chained by two Angels & above his Cavern[s] on the Earth's surface, is the Harlot also siezed & bound [*chain'd*] by two Angels with Chains while her Palaces are falling into [*in*] ruins & her Councellors & Warriors are descending into the Abyss in wailing & despair.

Hell opens beneath the Harlot's seat on the left hand into which the Wicked are descending [*while others rise from their Graves on the brink of the Pit*].

The right hand of the Design is appropriated to the Resurrection of The Just; the left hand of the Design is appropriated to the Resurrection & Fall of the Wicked.

Immediately before the Throne of Christ is Adam & Eve, kneeling in humiliation, as representatives of the whole Human Race; Abraham & Moses kneel on each side beneath them; from the Cloud on which Eve kneels & beneath Moses & from the Tables of Stone which utter lightnings, is seen Satan wound round by the Serpent & falling headlong; the Pharisees appear on the left hand pleading their own righteousness before the Throne of Christ: The Book of Death is open'd on Clouds by two Angels; many groupes of Figures are falling from before the Throne & from the Sea of Fire which flows before the steps of the Throne, on which are seen the Seven Lamps of the Almighty burning before the Throne: many Figures Chain'd & bound together fall thro' the air, & some are scourged by Spirits with flames of fire into the Abyss of Hell which opens to recieve them beneath, on the left hand of the Harlot's seat, where others are howling & descending into the flames & in the act of dragging each other into Hell & of contending in fighting with each other on the [*very*] brink of Perdition.

Before the Throne of Christ on the right hand the Just in humiliation & exultation, rise thro' the air, with their Children & Families: some of whom are bowing before the Book of Life which is open'd by two Angels on Clouds: many Groupes arise with Exultation [*in*

---

[1] This water-colour painting is still at Petworth House, Sussex, with one draft of the manifesto. The chief variations in the Petworth draft are printed here in italic within square brackets.

joy]: among them is a Figure crowned with Stars & the moon beneath her feet with six infants around her She represents the Christian Church: The Green Hills appear beneath: with the Graves of the Blessed, which are seen bursting with their births of immortality; Parents & Children embrace & arise together & in exulting attitudes tell each other, that The New Jerusalem is ready to descend upon Earth; they arise upon the air rejoicing: others newly awaken'd from the Grave stand upon the Earth embracing & shouting to the Lamb who cometh in the Clouds with Power & great Glory.

The whole upper part of the Design is a view of Heaven opened: around the Throne of Christ, Four Living Creatures filled with Eyes, attended by Seven Angels with the Seven Vials of the Wrath of God, & above these [*there are*] Seven Angels with the Seven Trumpets compose [*composing*] the Cloud, which by its rolling away displays the opening Seats of the Blessed, on the right & the left of which are seen the Four & Twenty Elders seated on Thrones to Judge the Dead.

Behind the Seat & Throne of Christ appears [*appear*] the Tabernacle with its Veil opened: [*&*] the Candlestick on the right: the Table with Shew Bread, on the left: & in the midst, the Cross in place of the Ark, with the two Cherubim bowing over it.

On the right hand of the Throne of Christ is Baptism. On his left is the Lord's Supper: the two introducers into Eternal Life. Women with Infants approach the Figure of an aged Apostle which represents Baptism; & on the left hand the Lord's Supper is administer'd by Angels, from the hands of another aged Apostle; these Kneel on each side of the Throne which is surrounded by a glory, in the glory many Infants appear, representing Eternal Creation flowing from The Divine Humanity in Jesus: who opens the Scroll of Judgment upon his knees before the Living & the Dead.

Such is the Design which you, my Dear Sir, have been the cause of my producing & which: but for you might have slept till the Last Judgment.

William Blake

18 January 1808

89. TO OZIAS HUMPHRY [*second draft*]

FEBRUARY 1808

To Ozias Humphry Esqre
The Design of The Last Judgment, which I have completed by your recommendation for The Countess of Egremont, it is necessary

to give some account of: & its various parts ought to be described for the accomodation of those who give it the honor of attention.

Christ, seated on the Throne of Judgment; before his feet & around him, the heavens in clouds are rolling like a scroll ready to be consumed in the fires of the Angels who descend with the Four Trumpets sounding to the Four Winds.

Beneath: Earth is convulsed with the labours of the Resurrection —in the Caverns of the Earth is the Dragon with Seven heads & ten Horns chained by two Angels, & above his Cavern on the Earth's Surface is the Harlot, siezed & bound by two Angels with chains, while her Palaces are falling into ruins & her councellors & warriors are descending into the Abyss in wailing & despair. Hell opens beneath the Harlot's seat on the left hand; into which the Wicked are descending.

The right hand of the Design, is appropriated to the Resurrection of the Just: the left hand of the Design, is appropriated to the Resurrection & Fall of the Wicked.

Immediately before the Throne of Christ, is Adam & Eve, kneeling in humiliation as representatives of the whole Human Race, Abraham & Moses kneel on each side beneath them: from the cloud on which Eve kneels, is seen Satan, wound round by the Serpent & falling headlong: the Pharisees appear on the left hand, pleading their own righteousness before the Throne of Christ & before the Book of Death which is open'd on clouds by two Angels, & many groupes of Figures are falling from before the Throne, & from before the Sea of Fire which flows before the steps of the Throne; on which is seen the seven Lamps of the Almighty burning before the Throne: many Figures chained & bound together & in various attitudes of Despair & Horror: fall thro' the air: & some are scourged by Spirits with flames of fire into the Abyss of Hell, which opens beneath, on the left hand of the Harlot's Seat: where others are howling & dragging each other into Hell & in contending in fighting with each other on the brink of Perdition.

Before the Throne of Christ on the Right hand the Just in humiliation & in exultation rise thro' the Air with their Children & Families: some of whom are bowing before the Book of Life which is open'd on clouds by two Angels: many groupes arise in exultation, among them is a Figure crown'd with Stars & the Moon beneath her feet with six infants around her. She represents the Christian Church; Green hills appear beneath with the Graves of the Blessed, which are seen bursting with their births of immortality: Parents & Children, Wives & Husbands embrace & arise together & in exulting attitudes of great joy tell each other that the New Jerusalem is ready to descend upon Earth: they arise upon the Air rejoicing:

others newly awaken'd from the Grave, stand upon the Earth embracing & shouting to the Lamb who cometh in the Clouds in power & great Glory.

The Whole upper part of the Design is a View of Heaven opened around the Throne of Christ: in the Cloud which rolls away, are the Four Living Creatures filled with Eyes, attended by Seven Angels with the Seven Vials of the Wrath of God; & above these Seven Angels with the Seven Trumpets, these compose the Cloud which by its rolling away displays the opening seats of the Blessed, on the right & left of which are seen the Four & twenty Elders, seated on Thrones to Judge the Dead.

Behind the Seat & Throne of Christ appears the Tabernacle with its Veil opened, the Candlestick on the right: the Table with the Shew bread on the left: in midst is the Cross in place of the Ark, the Cherubim bowing over it.

On the Right hand of the Throne of Christ is Baptism, on the left is the Lord's Supper, the two introducers into Eternal Life: Women with Infants approach the Figure of an Aged Apostle which represents Baptism, & on the left hand the Lord's Supper is administer'd by Angels from the hands of another Apostle: these kneel on each side of the Throne which is surrounded by a Glory: many Infants appear in the Glory, representing the Eternal Creation flowing from the Divine Humanity in Jesus, who opens the Scroll of Judgment upon his knees before the Living & the Dead.

Such is the design which you, my dear Sir, have been the cause of my producing & which but for you might have slept till the Last Judgment

William Blake

Feby 1808

90. TO THOMAS BUTTS 29 FEBRUARY 1808

29: Febry 1808

Received of Mr Butts Ten Pounds on further account

William Blake

£10 „ –

91. TO THOMAS BUTTS 29 JULY 1808

29: July 1808

Received of Mr. Butts Ten Pounds on further account

William Blake

£10

92. TO THOMAS BUTTS

3: Novem^r 1808

Received of Mr. Butts five Guineas on further account

Willm Blake

£5 ,, 5 ,, –

93. TO THOMAS BUTTS   7 DECEMBER 1808

7: Decr. 1808

Received of Mr. Butts five Guineas on further account

William Blake

£5 ,, 5 ,, –

94. GEORGE CUMBERLAND TO BLAKE
18 DECEMBER 1808

Dear Blake,

A gentleman of my acquaintance, to whom I was shewing your incomparable etchings last night, was so charmed with them, that he requested me to get him a compleat set of all you have published in the way of Books colour'd as mine are;[1] and at the same time he wishes to know what will be the price of as many as you can spare him, if all are not to be had, being willing to wait your own time in order to have them as those of mine are.

With respect to the Money, I will take care that it shall be reced and sent to you through my Son as fast as they are procured.

I find by a Letter from my son that the picture you sent, he asked you for, which is what I do not approve, as I certainly had no such thing in contemplation when I sent you those very slight sketches from Raffael—I am glad, however, that you found them acceptable, and shall certainly send you a few more as soon as I can light on them among my papers. The Holy family[2] is, like all your designs, full of Genius and originality. I shall give it a handsome frame and shew it to all who come to my house.

[1] Cumberland is known to have possessed at least five of the Illuminated Books; see the *Census*, New York, 1953.

[2] Perhaps a water-colour drawing of "The Holy Family with John the Baptist and a lamb", which was afterwards in the possession of Alexander A. Weston. Its present whereabouts are not known.

When you answer this, pray tell me if you have been able to do anything with the Bookseller—something of that kind would be no bad thing, and might turn out a great one if a competition could be raised by that means among the genuine qymeliars[1] of talents of every sort. You talked also of publishing your new method of engraving—send it to me and I will do my best to prepare it for the Press—perhaps when done you might, with a few specimens of Plates, make a little work for subscribers for it—as Du-Crow did of his Aqua-tinta—selling about 6 Pages for [half *del.*] a guinea to non subscribers—but if you do not chuse that method, we might insert it in Nicholson's Journal or the Monthly Magazine, with reference to you for explanations—

with best regards to you & yours, I am always,

your sincere friend,

G. Cumberland

Culworth 18 Dec. 1808

95. TO GEORGE CUMBERLAND

19 DECEMBER 1808

Dear Cumberland,

I am very much obliged by your kind ardour in my cause, & should immediately Engage in revising my former pursuits of printing [alone *del.*] if I had not now so long been turned out of the old channel into a new one, that it is impossible for me to return to it without destroying my present course. New Vanities, or rather new pleasures, occupy my thoughts. New profits seem to arise before me so tempting that I have already involved myself in engagements that preclude all possibility of promising any thing. I have, however, the satisfaction to inform you that I have Myself begun to print an account of my various Inventions in Art, for which I have procured a Publisher,[2] & am determin'd to pursue the plan of publishing what I may get printed without disarranging my time, which in future must alone be devoted to Designing & Painting; when I have got my Work printed I will send it you first of any body; in the mean time, believe me to be

Your Sincere friend,

Will Blake

19 Dec[r] 1808

[1] A doubtful word, perhaps intended for "cymeliarchs" from κειμηλιάρχος, a treasurer, or storekeeper, as suggested by the late W. E. Moss.

[2] Nothing further is known of this projected work, unless perhaps the reference is to *A Descriptive Catalogue*, printed in 1809.

134

96. TO OZIAS HUMPHRY

1809

Dear Sir,

You will see in this little work[1] the cause of difference between you & me; you demand of me to Mix two things that Reynolds has confess'd cannot be mixed. You will percieve that I not only detest False Art, but have the Courage to say so Publickly & to dare all the Power on Earth to oppose—Florentine & Venetian Art cannot exist together. Till the Venetian & Flemish are destroy'd, the Florentine & Roman cannot Exist; this will be shortly accomplish'd; till then I remain Your Grateful, altho' seemingly otherwise, I say Your Grateful & Sincere

William Blake

I inclose a ticket of admission if you should honour my Exhibition with a Visit.

97. TO THOMAS BUTTS

7 APRIL 1809

7: April 1809

Received of M^r· Butts Twenty one Pounds on further account

William Blake

£21

98. TO THOMAS BUTTS

29 JUNE 1809

Received of Mr Butts ten Guineas on further account

William Blake

£10 ,, 10 ,,

99. TO THOMAS BUTTS   10 JULY 1809

10: July 1809

Received of M^r· Butts ten Guineas on further account

William Blake

£10 ,, 10 ,, –

[1] *A Descriptive Catalogue,* 1809.

100. TO THOMAS BUTTS

10: August 1809

Received of Mr. Butts ten Guineas on further account

Willm Blake

£10 ,, 10 ,, –

101. TO THOMAS BUTTS   4 OCTOBER 1809

4: Octo^{r.} 1809

Received of Mr. Butts ten Guineas on further account

Willm Blake

£10 ,, 10 ,, –

102. TO THOMAS BUTTS

25 NOVEMBER 1809

25: Novr. 1809

Received of Mr. Butts twenty Pounds on further account

William Blake

£20

103. TO THOMAS BUTTS

16 JANUARY 1810

16 Janry 1810

Received of Mr. T. Butts twenty one Pounds on further account

William Blake

£21

104. TO THOMAS BUTTS

3 MARCH 1810

3: March 1810

Received of Mr. Butts ten Guineas on further account

William Blake

£10 ,, 10 ,, –

105. TO THOMAS BUTTS

14 APRIL 1810

14: April 1810

Received of Mr. Butts twenty one Pounds on further account

William Blake

£21

106. TO THOMAS BUTTS

30 JUNE 1810

30: June 1810

Received of Mr. Butts five Guineas on further account

Willm Blake

£5 „ 5 „ –

107. TO THOMAS BUTTS

14 JULY 1810

14: July 1810

Received of Mr. Butts fifteen Guineas on further account

William Blake

£15 „ 15 „ –

108. TO THOMAS BUTTS

20 SEPTEMBER 1810

20: Septr. 1810

Received of Mr. Butts ten Pounds ten Shillings on further account

William Blake

£10 „ 10 „ –

109. TO THOMAS BUTTS

18 DECEMBER 1810

18: Decr. 1810

Received of Mr. Butts ten Pounds ten Shillings on further account

William Blake

£10 „ 10 „ –

110. JOSIAH WEDGWOOD TO BLAKE

Etruria, 29 July 1815

Sir,—I return the drawing you have been so good to send me, which I entirely approve in all respects. I ought to have mentioned when the Terrine was sent you that the hole for the ladle in the cover should not be represented & which you will be so good to omit in the engraving.

I presume you would make a drawing of each article that is to be engraved, & if it will be agreeable to you to complete the drawings before the engraving is begun, I think it may enable me to make the best arrangement of the articles on the copper plates, but if this is not quite as agreeable to you as going on with the drawing & engraving together, I will only beg you to make two or three drawings, & I will in that case in the mean time consider of the arrangement. I have directed a Terrine to be sent you, presuming you will prefer having only one vessell at a time. If you would have more, be so good as to let Mr. Mowbray at my house know, who has a list of more articles.

I am, Sir,
Your mo. obt. svt.,
Josiah Wedgwood[1]

M\u1d63 Blake, 17 South Molton St.

111. TO JOSIAH WEDGWOOD

Sir,

I send Two more drawings with the First that I did, altered, having taken out that part which expressed the hole for the ladle.

It will be more convenient to me to make all the drawings first, before I begin Engraving them, as it will enable me also to regulate a System of working that will be uniform from beginning to end. Any Remarks that you may be pleased to make will be thankfully reciev'd by, Sir

Your humble Servant
17 South Molton Street   William Blake
8 Septemb\u1d63 1815

---

[1] Josiah Wedgwood the younger, second son of the founder of the pottery works at Etruria, Staffordshire. Blake had been recommended to the Wedgwoods by Flaxman in order to make drawings and engravings of their pottery for a pictorial catalogue, intended only for their own use. Blake engraved 185 figures on 18 plates during the years 1815–1816, and 13 more plates were engraved by others. For further details of the transactions see *Blake Studies*, 1949, pp. 67–75.

112. TO DAWSON TURNER

Sir,

I send you a List of the different Works you have done me the honour to enquire after—unprofitable enough to me, tho' Expensive to the Buyer. Those I Printed for Mr Humphry[1] are a selection from the different Books of such as could be Printed without the Writing,[2] tho' to the Loss of some of the best things. For they when Printed perfect accompany Poetical Personifications & Acts, without which Poems they never could have been Executed.

				£	s.	d.
America	.	.	.	18 Prints folio	. 5	5	0
Europe	.	.	.	17 do. folio.	. 5	5	0
Visions &^c	.	.	.	8 do. folio.	. 3	3	0
Thel	.	.	.	6 do. Quarto	. 2	2	0
Songs of Innocence	.	.	28 do. Octavo	. 3	3	0
Songs of Experience	.	.	26 do. Octavo	. 3	3	0
Urizen	.	.	.	28 Prints Quarto	. 5	5	0
Milton	.	.	.	50 do. Quarto	. 10	10	0

12 Large Prints,[3] Size of Each about 2 feet by 1 & ½, Historical & Poetical, Printed in Colours . . Each 5 5 0

These last 12 Prints are unaccompanied by any writing.

The few I have Printed & Sold are sufficient to have gained me great reputation as an Artist, which was the chief thing Intended. But I have never been able to produce a Sufficient number for a general Sale by means of a regular Publisher. It is therefore necessary to me that any Person wishing to have any or all of them should send me their Order to Print them on the above terms, & I will take care that they shall be done at least as well as any I have yet Produced.

[1] Ozias Humphry, the miniaturist.

[2] This probably refers to the two series of colour-printed designs known as the *Large* and *Small Book of Designs*, now in the Print Room at the British Museum. These consist for the most part of designs printed from the plates of the illuminated books, but omitting the text, and are thus incomplete, as Blake points out. The two books in the British Museum have now been broken up, so that the plates may be examined separately. Another series of the prints appears also to have been broken up, perhaps by Blake himself, and the contents scattered.

[3] These are the large colour-printed monotypes of which there is a set, lacking only two, in the Tate Gallery. The twelve subjects were "God creating Adam", "Lamech and his two Wives", "The Good and Evil Angels", "God judging Adam", "Ruth parting from Naomi", "Satan exulting over Eve", "Nebuchadnezzar", "Pity, like a naked newborn babe". "Christ appearing to the Apostles", "Newton" "The Lazar House", and "Hecate".

I am, Sir, with many thanks for your very Polite approbation of my works,

Your most obedient Servant,

William Blake

9 June 1818
17 South Molton Street

113. TO THOMAS BUTTS [?]

c. 1818

The Order in which the Songs of Innocence & of Experience ought to be paged & placed.[1]

Page
1. General Title
2. Frontispiece of Piper
3. Title page to Songs of Innocence
4. Introduction—Piping down the Valleys & ^c
5. Ecchoing Green
6. Ditto
7. The Lamb
8. The Shepherd
9. Infant Joy
10. Little Black Boy
11. Ditto
12. Laughing Song
13. Spring
14. Ditto
15. Cradle Song
16. Ditto
17. Nurse's Song
18. Holy Thursday
19. The Blossom
20. The Chimney Sweeper
21. The Divine Image
22. Night
23. Ditto
24. A Dream

[1] It is not certainly known for whom Blake drew up this Index to the *Songs*. The order was, however, adopted only in one copy (V in the *Census*), which belonged to Thomas Butts and is printed on paper with a watermark dated 1818.

114. TO JOHN LINNELL

12 AUGUST 1818

Reciev'd.   12 Augst 1818 of Mr Linnell

Two Pounds   W. Blake

114a. TO JOHN LINNELL   11 SEPTEMBER 1818

Reciev'd 11 Septemb^r 1818 of Mr Linnell the Sum of Five Pounds
on account of Mr Upton's Plate

William Blake

£5.   o.   o

115. TO JOHN LINNELL   19 SEPTEMBER 1818

19 Septemb^r 1818 Mr Linnell D^r To Willm· Blake
For Laying in the Engraving of Mr Upton's
portrait[1] _____   15.   15.   0
     Reciev'd on this account   7.   0.   0

                                         8.   15.   0

116. TO JOHN LINNELL   9 NOVEMBER 1818

Recievd 9 Novr 1818 of Mr Linnell
The Sum of Five Pounds on Account

William Blake

5.   o.   o.

117. TO JOHN LINNELL   31 DECEMBER 1818

Recieved 31 Decemb^r 1818 of Mr Linnell the Sum of Three Pounds
Fifteen Shillings
the Balance of Account of Mr Upton's Plate.

William Blake

3.   15.   0

118. TO JOHN LINNELL   27 AUGUST 1819
    August 27, 1819
Reciev'd One Pound Nineteen & Sixpence of M^r. Linnell for Songs
of Innocence & Experience.[2]
One Copy   William Blake
1.   19.   6.

---

[1] That is, etching the first outline of an engraving from Linnell's portrait of a
Baptist minister named Upton.

[2] Linnell gave this copy of Blake's *Songs* to his son William in 1863. It is now in
the Fitzwilliam Museum, Cambridge, having been bequeathed by William
Linnell's daughter, Mrs. T. H. Riches.

119. TO JOHN LINNELL [?]

11 OCTOBER 1819

Dear Sir,

I will have the Pleasure of meeting you on Thursday at 12 O'Clock; it is quite as Convenient to me as any other day. It appears to me that neither Time nor Place can make any real difference as to perfect Independence of Judgment, & If it is more Convenient to Mr Heaphy[1] for us to meet at his House let us accomodate him in what is Indifferent but not at all in what is of weight & moment to our Decision: hoping that I may meet you again in perfect Health & Happiness

I remain Dear Sir
Yours Truly
William Blake

Oct. 11 1819
Monday Evening

120. TO JOHN LINNELL

30 DECEMBER 1819

Reciev'd 30 Decemb^r 1819 of Mr Linnell the sum of Fourteen Shillings for Jerusalem Chap 2.[2]

Willm Blake

0. 14. 0.

121. TO JOHN LINNELL

30 APRIL 1821

Recievd April 30: 1821 of Mr Linnell the Sum of Two Guineas for Heaven & Hell[3]

Willm Blake

£2. 2. 0.

[1] Thomas Heaphy (1775–1835), engraver and water-colour artist.

[2] Probably part of the Linnell copy of *Jerusalem*, printed in black, formerly in the collection of the late Frank Rinder; now the property of his daughter, Mrs. Esther Harvey.

[3] This copy of *The Marriage of Heaven and Hell*, first printed in 1790, is perhaps the most beautiful in existence, the text, as well as the designs, being illuminated in brilliant colours. It was sold with the Linnell collection at Christie's, 18 March 1918 (lot 195, Riches, £756), and is now in the T. H. Riches collection in the Fitzwilliam Museum, Cambridge.

143

122. TO JOHN LINNELL

1 MARCH 1822

Reciev'd 1 March 1822 of Mr Linnell Three Pounds on $Acco^t$·

William Blake

£3. 0. 0.

122a. JOHN LINNELL'S CASH ACCOUNT BOOK
MARCH 1822–DECEMBER 1836

(This book contains the following entries among Linnell's general and household accounts. Some of these are duplicated among the other receipts and accounts following.)

1822 March 3	to Mr Blake	2	–	–
5	to Mr Blake	2	–	–
May 2	to Mr Pontifex for two copper Plates		13	6
8	to Mr Blake on acc^t	5	–	–
	(signed) W Blake			
do do		2	–	–
June 19	to Mr Blake on acc^t	1	–	–
1823 March 14	to Mr Blake on acc^t of Engraving of Job	5	–	–
May 3	to Mr Blake on acc^t of Job	3	–	–
5	do do	10	–	–
July 10	to Mr Blake on acc^t of Job	3	–	–
Aug 17	to Mr Blake on acc^t	1	–	–
Sept 3	to Mr Blake on acc^t	2	–	–
Oct 20	to Mr Blake on acc^t of Job	1	–	–
Nov 6	to Mr Blake on acc^t	1	–	–
13	to Mr Blake on acc^t	1	–	–
16	to Mr Blake on acc^t	6	–	–
Dec 15	to Mr Blake on acc^t	5	–	–
1824 Jan 10	to Mr Blake on acc^t of Job	7	–	–
Feb 2	to Mr Blake on acc^t	5	–	–
11	to Mr Blake on acc^t of Job	10	–	–
March 29	to Mr Blake on acc^t of Job	5	–	–
May 7	to Mr Blake on acc^t of Job	10	–	–
12	to Mr Blake on acc^t of Job	5	–	–
July 6	to Mr Blake on acc^t of Job	5	5	–
Sept 11	to Mr Blake for Mr Stephen	1	1	–
Nov 10	to Mr Blake on acc^t of the plate of the Portrait of Mr Lowry	5	–	–
1825 Jan 28	to Mr Blake on acc^t	10	–	–
March 12	to Mr Blake on account of Job	5	–	–
April 8	to Mr Blake on acc^t of Job	3	10	–

		£	s	d
May 3	to Mr Blake on acct of Job	5	–	–
5	of coals to be sent to Mr Blake	2	13	6
June 6	to Mr Blake on acct of Job	2	–	–
Aug 21	to Mr Blake on acct of Job	3	–	–
Sept 5	to Mr Blake on acct of Job	10	–	–
Oct 1	to Mr Blake on acct of Job	1	–	–
6	to Mr Blake on acct of drawings of Paradise Regained	5	–	–
30	to Mr Blake on acct of Job	5	–	–
	do do by Mr Flaxman's payment	3	3	–
Nov 19	to Mr Blake on acct of Paradise regd	5	–	–
Dec 21	to Mr Blake on acct of Dante	3	–	–
1826 March 9	to Mr Lahee for printing & paper of 150 sets of Book of Job on India paper[1]	50	–	–
9	to Mr Blake on acct of Dante	2	–	–
25	to Mr Blake (on acct)	5	–	–
April 15	to Mr Blake the money for the Songs of Innocence	5	5	–
29	to Mr Leighton balance of acct for Binding books for Job	4	2	6
	of Mr Butts for his copy of Job	3	3	–
	of Mr Riviere bal for do	1	12	6
	of Mr Parker for do	2	12	6
	of Mr Leigh (Strand) for do		12	6
	of Mr Chantry for copy of Job	5	5	–
	of Mr Westmacott for do	5	5	–
	of Mr F Tatham for his copy of Job	2	12	6
	of Mr Geo Young for do	3	3	–
	of Dr H Ley for do	3	3	–
May	of Mr Bury for copy of Job	5	5	–
20	to Mr Lahee (his Bill) final	40	–	–
30	to Mr Blake on acct	2	12	6
	Do	1	12	6
	Do	2	–	–
June 29	of Mr Behnes for Book of Job	2	12	6
July	to Mr Blake on acct	5	–	–
12	to Mrs Blake	3	–	–
29	to Mr Blake for Songs of Inc. Mrs Aders	5	5	–
Aug 17	to Mr Blake for Aders Cant Pilgrims	2	2	–
29	to Mr Blake on acct	5	–	–
Oct 31	of Ed Denny Esq for a copy of Job 5 5 – proofs & Blair's Grave 2 12 6	7	17	6
Nov 23	for Blair's Grave & to Blake on acct	2	–	–
Dec 16	to Blake on acct	3	–	–
1827 Jan 9	to Mr Blake on acct	5	–	–
18	to Mr Blake on acct	5	–	–
Feb 21	to Mr Blake	2	–	–

[1] Lahee's receipt for £49 19 11 is among the Linnell papers.

145

Year	Date		£	s	d
	April	to Lahee acc^t to this date	27	15	–
		to Mr Blake on acc^t	10	–	–
	June 1	to Mr Blake on acc^t	1	–	–
	25	of Messrs Budd & Calkin Booksellers for the copy of Job sent to the King	10	10	
		to Mr Blake	10	–	–
		do		10	–
		to Lahee for proofs &c		8	10
	Aug 3	to Mr Blake on acc^t	2	–	–
	11	to Mrs Blake money from Mr Ottley	5	5	–
		to Do money from Mr Stephen	2	2	–
	Sept 4	to Lahee for proofs		6	2
	29	of Mr Flower for print Cant. Pilgrims India	2	–	–
		to Mrs Blake The same	2	–	–
		of Mr Flower for balance p^d to M^{rs} B		12	–
	Nov 21	of Mr Daniel for Book of Job p^{fs}	5	–	–
1828	Jan 7	of Mr Cumberland for a Copy of Job	2	12	6
	26	to Mrs Blake for to pay to Mr Palmer for Mr Blake's funeral	10	18	–
		of Mr Younger for a Copy of Job	5	5	–
	July 6	to Mrs Blake (by M^r F Tatham)	10	–	–
	Sept 8	of Mr Johns by the Hands of Mr Calvert for a copy of Job	3	–	–
	16	to Mrs Blake by F Tatham	7	–	–
1829	Jan 26	to Mrs Blake on acc^t for a Drawing of Heads by M^r B & two by Fuseli	1	–	–
	May 15	to Mrs Blake by F Tatham for Homer's Iliad & Odyssey Tran. by Chapman	1	11	6
1830	July 30	of Mr Richd Jebb[1] for a set of Blake's Job &c small	3	3	–
1831	Aug 25	to Mrs Blake for Catalogue		2	6
		Do for Poems		2	6
1832	April 30	of Mr Brett for a copy of Job	2	12	6
1835	March 30	of Saml Boddington Esq for a plain copy of Blake's Canterbury Pilgrims	4	13	–
1836	Jan 22	of J Palmer for Job — 1 5 – & Blake woodcuts — 5 –	1	10	–

123. TO JOHN LINNELL

25 MARCH 1823

Memorandum of Agreement between William Blake and John Linnell.

March 25th 1823.

W. Blake agrees to Engrave the set of Plates from his own designs of Job's Captivity in number twenty, for John Linnell—and John

[1] Irish judge, brother of Bishop John Jebb.

146

Linnell agrees to pay William Blake five Pounds per Plate or one hundred Pounds for the set part before and the remainder when the Plates are finished as M^r· Blake may require it, besides which J. Linnell agrees to give W. Blake one hundred pounds more out of the Profits of the work as the receipts will admit of it.

Signed   J. Linnell   Willm Blake

N.B. J. L. to find copper Plates.

1823 March 25th

Cash on acc^t of Plates in the foregoing agreement

£5–0–0 W. B.

124. ACCOUNTS BETWEEN BLAKE & JOHN LINNELL

MARCH 1823–NOVEMBER 1825

[Most of the entries are initialled by Blake]

[Page 2r.]			1823			£.	s.
March 20	To Mr Blake 1st payment on account of Job: see memorandum of agreement &c.				WB	5.	o.
May	2	Cash	D°		WB	3.	o.
		D°	D°		WB	10.	o.
July	11	D°	D°		WB	3.	o.
Aug^t	2	D°	D°		WB	2.	o.
	17	D°	D°		WB	1.	o.
Sep	3	D°	D°		WB	2.	o.
	14	D°	D°		WB	1.	o.
	25	D°	D°		WB	2.	o.
Oc^t	12	D°	D°		WB	1.	o.
	20	D°	D°		WB	1.	o.
Nov^r	6	D°	D°		WB	1.	o.
						£32.	o.

[Page 2v.]		1823		£.	s.	
Nov^r		Cash Paid to Mr Blake on account of Job Bro^t over		32.	o.	
	13	Cash	WB	1.	o.	
	15	D° Balmanno's Sub.	WB	1.	o.	
	18	D°	WB	6.	o.	
Dec^r	15	D°	WB	5.	o.	
1824		Mr Leigh's Sub.	WB	2.	o.	
Jan	10	Cash	WB	5.	o.	o
		Coals	WB	3.	5.	9

				£	s.	
Feb	2^{d}	Cash	WB	5.	0.	0
	21	D^{o}	WB	10.	0.	
March	29	D^{o}	WB	5		
May	4	D^{o} Mr Muss's sub	WB	1		
	6	D^{o}	WB	10		
June	11	D^{o}	WB	5.		
		1 Chaldron of Coals	WB	1.	17.	
July	6	Cash by Dr Thornton's order	WB	5.	5.	
				98.	7.	9

[Page 1r.]

Augt 18th 1824			£
	Cash on account of The Portrait of Mr Lowry[1]	WB	5.
November 10th	D^{o} D^{o}	WB	5.
Decr 25	D^{o} D^{o}	WB	5.
Jan 28 1825	D^{o} D^{o}	WB	5.
	for Sketches of Subjects from Dante, carried to page 5		5.
Oc^{t} 10th	on acc^{t} of Drawings of Paradise regained[2]	WB	5.
Novr 19th	D^{o} D^{o}		5.

[Page 3r.]

Jany 1825		Brot over		98.	7.	9
	28th	Cash on acc^{t} of Job	WB	5.		
March	12	D^{o} D^{o}	WB	5.		
April	8	D^{o} D^{o}	WB	3.	10.	
May	3^{d}	D^{o} D^{o}	WB	5.		
June	6	D^{o} D^{o}	WB	2.		
		By Coals sent in May	WB	2.	13.	6
Aug^{t}	21	Cash	WB	3.		
Sep	3	D^{o}	WB	1.		
	4	D^{o}	WB	10.		
Oct	1st	D^{o}	WB	1.		
	30	D^{o}		5.		
		D^{o} by Mr Flaxman's Sub		3.	3.	
		D^{o} Mr Calvert's D^{o}		1.		
		by Sir Thos Lawrence D^{o} for one Copy. The extra 5 gs. which Sir T. L. gave is not reckoned against Mr Blake. Sir T. L. perhaps intended it for the copy presented to him for the library of the Royal Academy.		5.	5.	
				150.	19.	3

[1] Wilson Lowry, F.R.S. (1762–1824), engraver and inventor.

[2] The twelve water-colour drawings for *Paradise Regained* remained in the Linnell collection until it was sold at Christie's, 15 March 1918. They were then acquired by T. H. Riches and are now in the Fitzwilliam Museum, Cambridge.

125. SUBSCRIBERS TO THE BOOK OF JOB & EXPENSES

Subscribers & Purchasers of The Book of Illustrations of
The History of Job Designed & Engraved
By William Blake
Begun 1823 & Published March 1826
by The Author & J. Linnell

1823		Plain		
Oct 2	Ed. Hodges Baily Esq. R.A.			
	Sub. for one Copy plain	2.	12.	6
	— Balmanno Esq. D°	2.	12.	6
	Leigh, Booksellers from			
	Mr Willowby	2.	12.	6
	J. Flaxman Esq. R.A.			
	one copy plain	3.	3.	
Oct 2	Mr Riviere D°	2.	12.	6
	Mr Harrison, Tower St.	2.	12.	6
	Mr Butts, Fitzroy Sqr.			
	1 Copy of Proofs for	3.	3.	
	because he lent the Drawings to Copy			
	H. Robinson Esqr. of the Temple			
	3 copies	9.	9.	
	Mr Prosser, Charing X			
	one copy plain	3.	3.	
	C. H. Tatham Esqr.			
	one copy plain	2.	12.	6
	Dr H Ley 1 copy plain			
	Half Moon St, Piccadilly	2.	12.	6
	Mr Behnes, Dean St., Soho			
	1 copy plain	2.	12.	6
	Mr Waters D°	2.	12.	6
	Parker, Bookseller, Oxford			
	1 copy plain	2.	12.	6
	Mr Calvert, Brixton			
	1 copy plain	2.	12.	6
	Clunould, Booksellers, Spring Gardens			
	1 copy plain	2.	12.	6
1826		Proofs		
	Sir Henry Torrens			
	proofs	5.	5.	
	Revd Edw. Bury D°	5.	5.	
	Anthony Stewart Esq	4.	14.	6
	Chas Aders Esq. D°	5.	5.	
	T. G. Wainwright Esq. D°	5.	5.	
	James Vine Esq.	5.	5.	

Sir Tho⁵ Lawrence
    one copy of Proofs for himself   5.   5.
    one copy given to the Royal Academy—but Sir
    T. L. sent 10 gs. to Mr Blake—5 gs. of which
    was given to Mr B. although S. T. L. might have
    intended it for the Copy presented to him for the
    Royal Academy
The King 1 copy of Proofs Sent by the order of Sir
    Wᵐ Knighton & Dr Gooch, & for which 10 gs. was
    ordered to be paid, & was pd. by Messrs Budd &
    Calkin Pall Mall—
    given to Mr Blake   10. 10.
Josiah Taylor Esq. 1 copy of Proofs went to the House
    of Correction by F. Tatham—Taylor being Sᵈ H.
    of C. for swindling   5.   5.
Mr Young of Devonshire by Mr Johns, 1 copy   5.
                                                              Plain
    Mr Johns of Devonshire, 1 copy   3.
    Mr Flower of Islington, 1 copy   3.   3.
    Mr Geo Young, surgeon, brother of Young, the actor
        1 copy   3.   3.
    Mr Revᵈ Jebb   3.   3.
    Mr Bird   2. 12.   6
Augᵗ 1832   H. W. Lizars, Edinburgh, for a friend   2. 12.   6
                                                             Proofs

    H. Meredith Esq., Harley Place
        1 copy of Proofs   5.   5.
    Revᵈ L. Daniel of Norwich
        1 copy sent to Oxford   5.
    Westmacott, R.A.
        1 c. Proof   5.   5.
    Chantry, R.A.
        1 c. Proof   5.   5.
    Mr S. Woodburn
        one copy Proof   5.   5.
    Sir Geo. Pocock Bt.
        1 c. proof   5.   5.
    W. S. Davidson Esq.
        1 c. proof   5.   5.
1833   The Earl of Egremont   6.   6.

[There are a few other undated entries of copies supplied to booksellers and
    to Colnaghi & Co.]

Account of Expenses of the Book of Job by Mr Blake.
1823   £   s.   d.
        6 copper plates for Job   1.
        6   Dᵒ   Dᵒ   1.   2.

150

	6	D°	D°	1. 3.	7
1825	2	D°	D°	6.	
	proofs			1.	
	D° at Dixons & paper			1.	
	D° at Lahee & —			10.	
Sep	Proofs	& —		2.	
Oct	D°	& —		2.	
Nov	Binding 3 sets			7.	6
				9. 19.	1

March 1826	Paid to Mr Lahee for 150 sets of Proofs on Indian paper	56. 5.	
	to Freeman the workman	1.	
	to Mr White for Boarding	2. 4.	6
	1 ream of paper for D°	1. 6.	
	To Mr Leighton for Binding & paper &c	13. 17.	
May	To Lahee for 65 sets of Job on french paper	16. 3.	
1826	To D° for 50 sets on Drawing paper	10. 10.	
	To D° for D°	10. 10.	
		111. 15.	6

126. TO JOHN LINNELL

[1825]

Dear Sir,

A return of the old shivering fit[1] came on this Morning as soon as I awaked & I am now in Bed, Better & as I think almost well. If I can possibly, I will be at Mr Lahee's[2] tomorrow Morning; these attacks are too serious at the time to permit me to be out of Bed, but they go off by rest, which seems to be All that I want. I send the Pilgrims[3] under your Care with the Two First Plates of Job.

I am, Yours Sincerely,

Willm Blake

12 O'clock
Wednesday

127. TO JOHN LINNELL

[7 JUNE 1825]

Dear Sir,

I return you thanks for The Two Pounds you now send me. As to

[1] Probably due to gallstones and inflammation of the gall-bladder from which he afterwards died.

[2] Lahee was a copper-plate printer, who was employed by Linnell to print the engravings for *Illustrations of the Book of Job* (see above).

[3] Probably an impression of the engraving of Chaucer's Canterbury Pilgrims.

Sʳ T. Lawrence,[1] I have not heard from him as yet, & hope that he has a good opinion of my willingness to appear grateful, tho' not able, on account of this abominable Ague, or whatever it is. I am in Bed & at Work; my health I cannot speak of, for if it was not for the Cold weather I think I should soon get about again. Great Men die equally with the little. I am sorry for Lᵈ· Lᵈ·; he is a man of very singular abilities, as also for the D. of C.;[2] but perhaps, & I verily believe it, Every death is an improvement of the State of the Departed. I can draw as well a-Bed as Up, & perhaps better; but I cannot Engrave. I am going on with Dante,[3] & please myself.

I am, dʳ Sir, yours sincerely,

William Blake

Tuesday Night

128. TO MRS. LINNELL

11 OCTOBER 1825

Dear Madam,

I have had the Pleasure to see Mʳ Linnell set off safe in a very comfortable Coach, & I may say I accompanied him part of the way on his Journey in the Coach, for we both got in together & with another Passenger enter'd into Conversation, when at length we found that we were all three proceeding on our Journey; but as I had not paid & did not wish to pay for or take so long a Ride, we, with some difficulty, made the Coachman understand that one of his Passengers was unwilling to Go, when he obligingly permitted me to get out, to my great joy; hence I am now enabled to tell you that I hope to see you on Sunday morning as usual, which I could not have done if they had taken me to Gloucester.

I am, dʳ· Madam, yours Sincerely,

William Blake

Tuesday
11 October 1825

[1] Sir Thomas Lawrence was an admirer of Blake's work, and about this time bought a copy of *Songs of Innocence and of Experience*, and water-colour drawings of "Queen Catherine's Dream" and "The Wise and Foolish Virgins". The second of these was stated by a friend of Lawrence to have been his favourite drawing which he commonly kept on a table in his studio (see Mona Wilson, *Life of Blake*, 1948, p. 278).

[2] The D. of C. is identified by the late H. M. Margoliouth as The Dean of Canterbury, Gerrard Andrewes, who died on 2 June 1825. Lᵈ· Lᵈ· is probably Lord Lilford, who died 4 July 1825.

[3] That is, the water-colour drawings for Dante's *Divina Commedia* on which he was still engaged at the time of his death.

129. TO JOHN LINNELL

Dear Sir,

I have, I believe, done nearly all that we agreed on & ᶜ. If you should put on your considering Cap, just as you did last time we met, I have no doubt that the Plates would be all the better for it. I cannot get Well & am now in Bed, but seem as if I should be better to-morrow; rest does me good. Pray take care of your health this wet weather, & tho' I write, do not venture out on such days as to-day has been. I hope a few more days will bring us to a conclusion.

I am, dear Sir,
Yours Sincerely,
William Blake

Thursday Evening
10 Novʳ 1825
  Fountain Court
    Strand

130. TO JOHN LINNELL

Dear Sir,

I am forced to write, because I cannot come to you, & this on two accounts. First, I omitted to desire you would come & take a Mutton chop with us the day you go to Cheltenham, & I will go with you to the Coach; also, I will go to Hampstead to see Mrs. Linnell on Sunday, but will return before dinner (I mean if you set off before that), & Second, I wish to have a Copy of Job to shew to Mʳ Chantry.[1]

For I am again laid up by a cold in my stomach; the Hampstead Air, as it always did, so I fear it always will do this, Except it be the Morning air; & That, in my Cousin's[2] time, I found I could bear with safety & perhaps benefit. I believe my Constitution to be a good one, but it has many peculiarities that no one but myself can know. When I was young, Hampstead, Highgate, Hornsea, Muswell Hill, & even Islington & all places North of London, always laid me up the day after, & sometimes two or three days, with precisely the same Complaint & the same torment of the Stomach, Easily removed, but excruciating while it lasts & enfeebling for some time

---

[1] Francis Legatt Chantrey, R.A. (1781–1842), sculptor; knighted in 1835; founder of the Chantrey Bequest.

[2] There is no clue as to the identity of Blake's cousin.

after. Sr Francis Bacon[1] would say, it is want of discipline in Mountainous Places. Sr Francis Bacon is a Liar. No discipline will turn one Man into another, even in the least particle, & such discipline I call Presumption & Folly. I have tried it too much not to know this, & am very sorry for all such who may be led to such ostentatious Exertion against their Eternal Existence itself, because it is Mental Rebellion against the Holy Spirit, & fit only for a Soldier of Satan to perform.

Though I hope in a morning or two to call on you in Cirencester Place, I feared you might be gone, or I might be too ill to let you know how I am, & what I wish.

I am, dear Sir,
Yours Sincerely,

Feby 1. 1826 William Blake

131. TO MRS. LINNELL   [? FEBRUARY] 1826

London Sunday Morning

Dear Madam,

Mr. Linnell will have arrived at his Journey's end[2] before the time I now write; he set off Last night before Eight o'clock from the Angel Inn near St. Clements Church, Strand, on one of the Strongest & Handsomest Built Stages I ever Saw. I should have written Last Night, but as it would not come before now, I do as Mr. Linnell desired I would do by the First Stage. My Wife desires her kindest remembrances to you & I am

Yours sincerely
Willm Blake

Excuse the writing. I have delayed too long.

132. TO JOHN LINNELL   31 MARCH 1826

Friday Evening, March 31, 1826.

Dear Sir,

I have been very ill since I saw you, but am again well enough

---

[1] Bacon, the scientist, materialist, and courtier, had long been the object of Blake's hatred. He annotated an edition of Bacon's *Essays*, dated 1798, and wrote on the title-page "Good Advice for Satan's Kingdom" (*Complete Writings*, 1966, p. 396).

[2] It seems probable that this refers to the same journey as is the subject of the first part of the letter of 1 February. Blake there stated his intention of seeing Mrs. Linnell on the following Sunday, but probably he was not well enough to go, and so wrote this note instead.

to go on with my work, but not well enough to venture out; the Chill of the weather soon drives me back into that shivering fit which must be avoided till the Cold is gone.

Mr Robinson[1] certainly did Subscribe for Prints only & not for Proofs,[2] for I remember that he offer'd to pay me Three Guineas for each of the Copies.

However, if the weather should be warm I will endeavour to come to you before Tuesday, but much fear that my present tottering state will hold me some time yet.

I am, dear Sir, yours sincerely
Willm· Blake

133. TO JOHN LINNELL

19 MAY 1826

Dear Sir,

I have had another desperate Shivering Fit; it came on yesterday afternoon after as good a morning as I ever experienced. It began by a gnawing Pain in the Stomach, & soon spread a deathly feel all over the limbs, which brings on the shivering fit, when I am forced to go to bed, where I contrive to get into a little perspiration, which takes it quite away. It was night when it left me, so I did not get up, but just as I was going to rise this morning, the shivering fit attacked me again & the pain, with its accompanying deathly feel. I got again into a perspiration, & was well, but so much weaken'd that I am still in bed. This entirely prevents me from the pleasure of seeing you on Sunday at Hampstead, as I fear the attack again when I am away from home.

I am, d^r· Sir,
Yours sincerely,
William Blake

Friday Evening
May 19 1826

134. TO JOHN LINNELL

2 JULY 1826

My dearest Friend,

This sudden cold weather has cut up all my hopes by the roots. Everyone who knows of our intended flight into your delightful Country concur in saying: "Do not Venture till summer appears again". I also feel Myself weaker than I was aware, being not able,

[1] Henry Crabb Robinson.
[2] The engravings of *Illustrations of the Book of Job*.

as yet, to sit up longer than six hours at a time; & also feel the Cold too much to dare venture beyond my present precincts. My heartiest Thanks for your care in my accomodation, & the trouble you will yet have with me. But I get better & stronger every day, tho' weaker in muscle & bone than I supposed. As to pleasantness of Prospect, it is All pleasant Prospect at North End. Mrs Hurd's[1] I should like as well as any—But think of the Expense & how it may be spared, & never mind appearances.

I intend to bring with me, besides our necessary change of apparel, Only My Book of Drawings from Dante & one Plate shut up in the Book. All will go very well in the Coach, which, at present, would be a rumble I fear I could not go thro'. So that I conclude another Week must pass before I dare Venture upon what I ardently desire— the seeing you with your happy Family once again, & that for a longer Period than I had ever hoped in my healthfull hours.

I am, dear Sir,
Yours most gratefully,
William Blake

135. TO JOHN LINNELL   5 JULY 1826

5 July 1826.

Dear Sir,

I thank you for the Receit of Five Pounds this Morning, & Congratulate you on the receit of another fine Boy; am glad to hear of Mrs Linnell's health & safety.

I am getting better every hour; my Plan is diet only; & if the Machine is capable of it, shall make an old man yet. I go on just as if perfectly well, which indeed I am, except in those paroxysms, which I now believe will never more return. Pray let your own health & convenience put all solicitude concerning me at rest. You have a Family, I have none; there is no comparison between our necessary avocations.

Believe me to be, d^{r.} Sir,
Yours sincerely,
William Blake

136. TO JOHN LINNELL

14 JULY 1826

Dear Sir,

I am so much better that I have hopes of fulfilling my expectation & desire of Visiting Hampstead. I am nevertheless very consider-

[1] Linnell's lodgings, before he went to Collins' Farm, North End, Hampstead.

ably weaken'd by the Last severe attacks. Pray remember me with Kind Love to Mrs Linnell & her lovely Family.

Yours Sincerely,

July 14. 1826   William Blake

To Mr John Linnell—July 14: 1826

I hereby declare That Mr John Linnell has Purchased of Me The Plates & Copy-right of Job, & the same is his sole Property.

Witness   William Blake

Edwd Jno Chance[1]

136a. TO JOHN LINNELL   14 JULY 1826

London July 14: 1826.

Recievd of Mr John Linnell, the Sum of One Hundred & fifty Pounds for the Copy-right & Plates (Twenty-two in number) of the Book of Job. Publish'd March 1825 by Me. William Blake Author of the Work.

N° 3 Fountain Court Strand.

Witness: *Edwd Jno Chance*

137. TO JOHN LINNELL

16 JULY 1826

Dear Sir,

I have been, ever since taking Dr Young's Addition to Mr Fincham's Practise with me (the Addition is dandelion), In a species of delirium & in Pain too much for Thought. It is now passed, as I hope. But the moment I got ease of Body, began Pain of Mind, & that not a small one. It is about The Name of the Child,[2] which Certainly ought to be Thomas, after Mrs Linnell's Father. It will be brutal, not to say worse, for it is worse In my opinion & on my Part. Pray Reconsider it, if it is not too late. It very much troubles Me, as a Crime in which I shall be [a *del.*] The Principal. Pray Excuse this hearty Expostulation, & believe me to be, Yours sincerely,

William Blake

Sunday Afternoon
July 16. 1826

P.S. Fincham is a Pupil of Abernethy's;[3] this is what gives me great pleasure. I did not know it before yesterday, from Mr Fincham.

[1] A son-in-law of Linnell working as a print dealer at 28 London St., Fitzroy Square.

[2] It was finally named James, the next son being called William.

[3] John Abernethy (1764–1831), surgeon to St. Bartholomew's Hospital.

138. TO JOHN LINNELL

29 JULY 1826

Dear Sir,

Just as I had become Well, that is, subdued the disease tho' not its Effects, Weakness & ᶜ, Comes Another to hinder my Progress, call'd The Piles, which, when to the degree I have had them, are a most sore plague & on a Weak Body truly afflictive. These Piles have now also as I hope run their Period, & I begin to again feel returning Strength; on these accounts I cannot yet tell when I can start for Hampstead like a young Lark without feathers. Two or Three days may be sufficient or not; all now will depend on my bones & sinews. Muscle I have none, but a few days may do, & have done, miracles in the Case of a Convalescent who prepares himself ardently for his return to Life & its Business among his Friends.

With whom he makes his first Effort.

Dear Sir, Yours Ever,
William Blake

29 July 1826

*

139. TO MRS. CHARLES ADERS   29 JULY 1826

Recieved 29 July 1826 of M ʳˢ Aders[1] by the hands of M ʳ Linnell the Sum of Two Pounds Five Shillings for the Songs of Innocence.[2]

William Blake

£2. 5. 0.

140. TO JOHN LINNELL

1 AUGUST 1826

Dear Sir,

If this Notice should be too short for your Convenience, please to let me know. But finding myself Well enough to come, I propose to set out from here as soon after ten as we can on Thursday Morning.

---

[1] Mrs. Aders, the daughter of Raphael Smith, the mezzotint engraver, had married a wealthy merchant of German extraction. They lived in Euston Square and there entertained many artists and literary men. It was at their house that Blake first met Henry Crabb Robinson in 1825.

[2] This copy of the *Songs of Innocence and of Experience* was afterwards bought back by John Linnell, who gave it to his son James in 1863. It was sold with the Linnell collection at Christie's, 18 March 1918 (lot 215, Carfax, £735) and is now in the T. H. Riches collection in the Fitzwilliam Museum, Cambridge.

Our Carriage will be a Cabriolet, for tho' getting better & stronger, I am still incapable of riding in the Stage, & shall be, I fear, for some time, being only bones & sinews, All strings & bobbins like a Weaver's Loom. Walking to & from the State would be, to me, impossible; tho' I seem well, being entirely free from both pain & from that Sickness to which there is no name. Thank God, I feel no more of it, & have great hopes that the disease is Gone.

I am, dear Sir, Yours Sincerely,

William Blake

Augst 1 1826

140a. TO MRS. CHARLES ADERS

29 DECEMBER 1826

Mr Blake's respectful Compliments to Mrs Ade[r]s: is sorry to say that his Illness is so far from gone that the least thing brings on the symptoms of the original complaint: he does not dare to leave his room by any means: he had another desperate attack of the Aguish trembling last night & is certain that at present any venture to go out must be of bad, perhaps of fatal, consequence. Is very sorry indeed that he is deprived of the happiness of visiting again & also of seeing again those Pictures of the old Masters, but must submit to the necessity & be Patient till warm weather Comes.

3 Fountain Court, Strand

29 Decr 1826

141. TO JOHN LINNELL

27 JANUARY 1827

Dear Sir,

I ought to have acknowledg'd the Receit of Five Pounds from you on 16 Jany 1827; that part of your Letter in which you desired I would send an acknowledg'd it [sic] I did not see till the next morning, owing to its being writ on the outside double of your letter; nevertheless I ought to have sent it, but must beg you to Excuse such Follies, which tho' I am enough asham'd of & hope to mend, can only do so at present by owning the Fault.

I am, dear Sir, yours Sincerely,

William Blake

Saturday Night

Jany 27 1827

142. TO JOHN LINNELL

[February, 1827.]

Dear Sir,

I thank you for the Five Pounds recieved to day: am getting better every Morning, but slowly, as I am still feeble & tottering, tho' all the Symptoms of my complaint seem almost gone as the fine weather is very beneficial & comfortable to me. I go on, as I think, improving my Engravings of Dante[1] more & more, & shall soon get Proofs of these Four which I have, & beg the favour of you to send me the two Plates of Dante which you have, that I may finish them sufficiently to make some Shew of Colour & Strength.

I have Thought & Thought of the Removal & cannot get my Mind out of a state of terrible fear at such a step; the more I think, the more I feel terror at what I wish'd at first & thought it a thing of benefit & Good hope; you will attribute it to its right Cause—Intellectual Peculiarity, that must be Myself alone shut up in Myself, or Reduced to Nothing. I could tell you of Visions & dreams upon the Subject. I have asked & intreated Divine help, but fear continues upon me, & I must relinquish the step that I had wish'd to take, & still wish, but in vain.

Your Success in your Profession is above all things to me most gratifying; may it go on to the Perfection you wish & more. So wishes also

Yours Sincerely,
William Blake

143. TO JOHN LINNELL

[? FEBRUARY] 1827

Dear Sir,

I call'd this Morning for a Walk & brought my Plates with me to prevent the trouble of your Coming thro' Curiosity to see what I was about. I have got on very forward with 4 Plates, & am getting better or I could not have Come at all.

Yours,
Willm Blake

---

[1] Blake had engraved seven of the plates for Dante before he died, and sets of the prints were sold by Linnell in their unfinished state. These were still obtainable from the Linnell trustees up to the time of the sale of the Linnell collection in March 1918. The copper-plates are now in the Lessing Rosenwald collection, National Gallery, Washington, D.C.

XI. THE LAST JUDGMENT

water colour drawing 1808

144. TO JOHN LINNELL

Dear Sir,

This is to thank you for Two Pounds, now by me reciev'd on account. I have reciev'd a Letter from Mr Cumberland, in which he days he will take one Copy of Job for himself, but cannot, as yet, find a Customer for one, but hopes to do somewhat by perseverance in his Endeavours; he tells me that it is too much Finish'd, or over Labour'd, for his Bristol Friends, as they think. I saw Mr Tatham,[1] Senr., yesterday; he sat with me above an hour, & look'd over the Dante; he express'd himself very much pleas'd with the designs as well as the Engravings. I am getting on with the Engravings & hope soon to get Proofs of what I am doing.

I am, dear Sir, Yours Sincerely,

William Blake

15 March 1827

145. TO MARIA DENMAN[2]

14 MARCH 1827

Mr Blake's respectful Compliments to Miss Denman—has found 15 Proofs of The Hesiod:[3] as they are duplicates to others which he has, they are intirely at Miss Denman's Service if she will accept of them: what Proofs he has remaining are all Printed on both sides of the Paper & so are unfit for to make up a set, especially as many of the backs of the paper have on them impressions from other Plates for Booksellers, which he was employ'd about at the same time.

Wednesday Morning
18 [14] March 1827[4]
3 Fountain Court, Strand

146. TO JOHN LINNELL

1827

Dear Sir,

I am still far from recover'd, & dare not get out in the cold air. Yet I lose nothing by it. Dante goes on the better, which is all I care about.

---

[1] C. H. Tatham, architect, father of Blake's friend, Frederick Tatham. Blake had known the elder Tatham at least since 1799, when he gave him a copy of *America*, and his name appears in the list of subscribers to Tatham's *Etchings of Ancient Ornamental Architecture*, London, 1799, f^o.

[2] Sister-in-law of John Flaxman.

[3] Blake had engraved 38 plates for Flaxman's *Compositions from the Works Days and Theogony of Hesiod*, London, 1817.   [4] 18 March 1827 was a Sunday.

Mr Butts is to have a Proof Copy for Three Guineas; this is his own decision, quite in Character. He call'd on me this Week.

Yours sincerely,

William Blake

147. TO GEORGE CUMBERLAND

12 APRIL 1827

Dear Cumberland,

I have been very near the Gates of Death & have returned very weak & an Old Man feeble & tottering, but not in Spirit & Life, not in The Real Man The Imagination which Liveth for Ever. In that I am stronger & stronger as this Foolish Body decays. I thank you for the Pains you have taken with Poor Job. I know too well that a great majority of Englishmen are fond of The Indefinite which they Measure by Newton's[1] Doctrine of the Fluxions of an Atom, A Thing that does not Exist. These are Politicians & think that Republican Art is Inimical to their Atom. For a Line or Lineament is not formed by Chance: a Line is a Line in its Minutest Subdivisions: Strait or Crooked It is Itself & Not Intermeasurable with or by any Thing Else. Such is Job, but since the French Revolution Englishmen are all Intermeasurable One by Another, Certainly a happy state of Agreement to which I for One do not Agree. God keep me from the Divinity of Yes & No too, The Yea Nay Creeping Jesus,[2] from supposing Up & Down to be the same Thing as all Experimentalists must suppose.

You are desirous I know to dispose of some of my Works & to make them Pleasin[g]. I am obliged to you & to all who do so. But having none remaining of all that I had Printed I cannot Print more Except at a great loss, for at the time I printed those things I had a whole House to range in: now I am shut up in a Corner therefore am forced to ask a Price for them that I scarce expect to get from a Stranger. I am now Printing a Set of the Songs of Innocence & Experience for a Friend at Ten Guineas which I cannot do under Six Months consistent with my other Work, so that I have little hope of doing any more of such things. The Last Work I produced is a Poem Entitled Jerusalem the Emanation of the Giant

---

[1] Newton was for Blake the type of materialism and abstract philosophy, and therefore antipathetic to imagination and Art. See p. 51, note.

[2] cp. "The Everlasting Gospel", c:

> If he had been Antichrist, Creeping Jesus,
> He'd have done anything to please us:

(see Complete Writings, 1966, p. 750).

Albion, but find that to Print it will Cost my Time the amount of Twenty Guineas. One I have Finish'd. It contains 100 Plates but it is not likely that I shall get a Customer for it.[1]

As you wish me to send you a list with the Prices of these things they are as follows

	£	s	d
America	6.	6.	0
Europe	6.	6.	0
Visions & c	5.	5.	0
Thel	3.	3.	0
Songs of Inn. & Exp.	10.	10.	0
Urizen	6.	6.	0

The Little Card[2] I will do as soon as Possible but when you Consider that I have been reduced to a Skeleton from which I am slowly recovering you will I hope have Patience with me.

Flaxman[3] is Gone & we must All soon follow, every one to his Own Eternal House, Leaving the Delusive Goddess Nature & her Laws to get into Freedom from all Law of the Members into The Mind, in which every one is King & Priest in his own House. God send it so on Earth as it is in Heaven.

I am, Dear Sir, Yours Affectionately

12 April 1827   William Blake
N 3 Fountain Court Strand

148. TO JOHN LINNELL

25 APRIL 1827

Dear Sir,

I am going on better Every day, as I think, both in hea[l]th & in work. I thank you for The Ten Pounds which I recieved from you this day, which shall be put to the best use; as also for the prospect of M͏ʳ Ottley's[4] advantageous acquaintance. I go on without daring

---

[1] This is the unique coloured copy of *Jerusalem* now in the Paul Mellon collection. A complete facsimile in colour was issued by the Trustees of the William Blake Trust in 1952.

[2] A small engraved copper-plate, with a design surrounding the name of "Mr. Cumberland". A note in Cumberland's hand on the blank sheet of this letter is as follows: "My little Message card was the last thing to be executed, and he dated it thus: *W. Blake inv. & sc. Æ 70 1827*; the widow charged me £3. 3 for it. and £3. 3s. for the Job",

[3] Flaxman had died on 7 December 1826.

[4] William Young Ottley (1771–1836), author of a *History of Engraving*, Keeper of the Prints in the British Museum, 1833–1836. See also p. 146 above.

to count on Futurity, which I cannot do without doubt & Fear that ruins Activity, & are the greatest hurt to an Artist such as I am. As to Ugolino,[1] & ᶜ, I never supposed that I should sell them; my Wife alone is answerable for their having Existed in any finish'd State. I am too much attach'd to Dante to think much of anything else. I have Proved the Six Plates, & reduced the Fighting devils ready for the Copper.[2] I count myself sufficiently Paid if I live as I now do, & only fear that I may be Unlucky to my friends, & especially that I may not be so to you.

I am, sincerely yours,
William Blake

25 April 1827

149. TO JOHN LINNELL

3 JULY 1827

Dear Sir,

I thank you for the Ten Pounds you are so kind as to send me at this time. My journey to Hampstead on Sunday brought on a relapse which is lasted till now. I find I am not so well as I thought. I must not go on in a youthful Style; however, I am upon the mending hand to-day, & hope soon to look as I did, for I have been yellow, accompanied by all the old Symptoms.

I am, dear Sir,
Yours Sincerely,
William Blake

3 July 1827

150. MRS. BLAKE TO JOHN LINNELL

18 MAY 1829

May 18th 1829

Received of Mr. J. Linnell
one pound Eleven shillings & sixpence for Homers Illiad & Oddisy[3]

for Mʳˢ Blake
Frederick Tatham

[1] A tempera on a panel of "Ugolino with his Sons and Grandsons in Prison", now in my collection.

[2] "The Devils mauling each other" (*Inferno*, canto xxii, l. 136), one of the seven Dante engravings.

[3] This was, no doubt, Blake's copy of Chapman's *Homer*, folio, 1606, which A. T. Story (*Life of Linnell*, i. 78) states was bought by Linnell after Blake's death. The present ownership of the volume is not known.

15 AUGUST 1827

Wednesday Even ᵍ
My Dear Friend,
  Lest you should not have heard of the Death of M ʳ Blake I have
Written this to inform you—He died on Sunday night [12 August]
at 6 Oclock in a most glorious manner. He said He was going to that
Country he had all His life wished to see & expressed Himself Happy,
hoping for Salvation through Jesus Christ—Just before he died His
Countenance became fair. His eyes Brighten'd and He burst out
into Singing of the things he saw in Heaven. In truth He Died like a
Saint as a person who was standing by Him Observed—He is to be
Buryed on Fridayay [sic] at 12 in morn ᵍ.¹ Should you like to go to
the Funeral—If you should there there [sic] will be Room in the
Coach.

Yrs affection ʸ
G. Richmond
Excuse this wretched scrawl

END OF LETTERS

¹ On 17 August in the cemetery at Bunhill Fields, "25 feet from the north wall
No. 80", as recorded by Cumberland on the letter from Blake of 12 April 1827.

REGISTER OF DOCUMENTS

REGISTER

1, 2. WILLEY REVELEY to BLAKE, AND HIS REPLY
[October 1791]

ADDRESSED ON THE OUTSIDE TO: Mr. Blake, Engraver, Hercules Buildings, Westminster Bridge.

A small folded sheet, bearing a note in the third person from Reveley addressed to Blake, with his reply on the other side.

Formerly in the Linnell collection. Sold at Christie's, 15 March 1918, with twelve others (lot 214, G. D. Smith, 80 gns.). Now in the H. E. Huntington Library, California.

PRINTED: Keynes, *Bibliography of Blake*, 1921, p. 454, *Writings*, 1925, ii, 17, *Poetry and Prose*, 1939, p. 831, *Complete Writings*, 1957, 1966, p. 790.

SOURCE OF TEXT: Photostat.

3. To GEORGE CUMBERLAND   6 December 1795

ADDRESSED TO: G. Cumberland Esq., Bishopsgate, near Egham, Surrey.

DATED: Lambeth 6 December 1795.

A single leaf, written on one side. No watermark.
Size 37·5 × 23 cm.

Now in the BM among the Cumberland Correspondence, Add. MSS 36498, f. 51.

PRINTED, *Hampstead Annual*, 1903; Russell, *Letters*, 1906, p. 53; Keynes, *Writings*, 1925, i, 344, *Poetry and Prose*, 1939, p. 831, *Complete Writings*, 1957, 1966, p. 790.

SOURCE OF TEXT: Original MS.

4. To GEORGE CUMBERLAND   23 December 1796

Not addressed.

DATED: Lambeth 23 Decemb^r, 1796.

A single leaf written on one side. No dated watermark.
Size 31 × 19 cm.

Now in the BM among the Cumberland Correspondence, Add. MSS 36498, f. 155.

PRINTED: *Hampstead Annual*, 1903; Russell, *Letters*, 1906, p. 56; Keynes, *Writings*, 1925, i, 355, *Poetry and Prose*, 1939, p. 832, *Complete Writings*, 1957, 1966, p. 791.

SOURCE OF TEXT: Original MS.

5. To DR. TRUSLER   16 August 1799

HEADED: To the Rev^d· D^r· Trusler.

DATED: Hercules Buildg^s, Lambeth, Aug^st 16, 1799.

A double leaf written on three sides. No dated watermark.
Size 19×19·5 cm.

Now in the BM among the Cumberland Correspondence, Add. MSS 36498, f. 324.

PRINTED: *Hampstead Annual*, 1903; Russell, *Letters*, 1906, p. 57; Keynes, *Writings*, 1925, ii, 173, *Poetry and Prose*, 1939, p. 833, *Complete Writings*, 1957, 1966, p. 791.

SOURCE OF TEXT: Original MS.

6. To DR. TRUSLER   23 August 1799

ADDRESSED TO: Rev^d Dr. Trusler, Englefield Green, Egham, Surrey.

DATED: 13 Hercules Buildings, Lambeth, August 23, 1799.

A double leaf written on three sides. Watermark dated 1795.
Size 19×15·5 cm.

Now in the BM among the Cumberland Correspondence, Add. MSS 36498, f. 328.

PRINTED: *Hampstead Annual*, 1903; Russell, *Letters*, 1906, p. 60; Keynes, *Writings*, 1925, ii, 174, *Poetry and Prose*, 1939, p. 834, *Complete Writings*, 1957, 1966, p. 793; Erdman, *Poetry and Prose*, 1965, p. 676.

SOURCE OF TEXT: Original MS.

7. To GEORGE CUMBERLAND   27 August 1799

ADDRESSED TO: Mr Cumberland, Bishopsgate, Windsor Great Park.

DATED: Hercules Buildings, Lambeth, Augst 26, 1799.

A double leaf, written on three sides. Watermark dated 1795.
Size 19 × 15·5 cm.

Now in the BM among the Cumberland Correspondence, Add. MSS
36498, f. 330.

PRINTED: *Hampstead Annual*, 1903; Russell, *Letters*, 1906, p. 64; Keynes,
Writings, 1925, ii, 177, *Poetry and Prose*, 1939, p. 836, *Complete Writings*, 1957,
1966, p. 794.

SOURCE OF TEXT: Original MS.

8. To JOHN FLAXMAN   14 December 1799

RECEIPT ADDRESSED TO: Mr Flaxman.

DATED: Decr. 14 1799.

An oblong slip of paper, 8 × 19 cm.

Now in the Roberts Collection, Haverford College, Haverford, Pa.

PRINTED: Printed for the first time 1956.

SOURCE OF TEXT: Photostat.

9. To WILLIAM HAYLEY   18 February 1800

PRINTED, EXTRACTS ONLY: Gilchrist, *Life*, 1880, i, 143. (Not otherwise
known.) Keynes, *Complete Writings*, 1957, 1966, p. 796.

SOURCE OF TEXT: Gilchrist's *Life*, 1880.

10. To WILLIAM HAYLEY   1 April 1800

ADDRESSED TO: William Hayley Esqr., Eartham, near Chichester, Sussex.

DATED: Hercules Buildings, Lambeth, 1 April, 1800.

A double leaf, 4°, written on the first leaf; with a part of the seal.

Sold at Sotheby's, 20 May 1878 (lot 2, Naylor, 25s.). Sold at Sotheby's 5
July 1909 (lot 106, Quaritch, £3 18s.).

Offered for sale in several catalogues of the stock of Mr. James Tregaskis
about 1910. Sold at the Anderson Galleries, New York, 10 Jan. 1908
($50.00), and at Sotheby's, 2 June 1919 (lot 113, Campbell, £18), 2 June
1932 (lot 492), and 31 July 1934 (lot 428).

PRINTED: Tregaskis's catalogues, in facsimile, c. 1910; Keynes, *Bibliography of Blake*, 1921, p. 447, *Writings*, 1925, ii, 179, *Poetry and Prose*, 1939, p. 838, *Complete Writings*, 1957, 1966, p. 796.

SOURCE OF TEXT: Photographic facsimile.

11. WILLIAM HAYLEY to BLAKE   17 April 1800

ADDRESSED: To Mr Blake, Engraver, Hercules Buildings, Lambeth, London.

DATED: Thursday, April 17, 1800. Postmarked Chichester, with seal.
A double leaf, 4°, written on three sides. Endorsed: "Letter from Hayley the Poet to Blake, found among the papers of the latter. F. Tatham."

Offered by Tregaskis & Son in June 1928 for £85. Sold at Sotheby's, 17 Feb. 1932 (King, £3 10s.). Now in my collection.

PRINTED by Tregaskis & Son in their catalogue. Otherwise unpublished.

SOURCE OF TEXT: Original MS.

12. To WILLIAM HAYLEY   6 May 1800

ADDRESSED TO: William Hayley Es^{qr,} Eartham, near Chichester, Sussex.

DATED: Lambeth, May 6, 1800.

A single leaf, 4°.

Sold at Sotheby's, 20 May 1878 (lot 1, Naylor, 3 gns.). In the Rowfant Library in 1886 in an album of ALS. Bought by Dodd Mead & Co., New York. Acquired in 1953 by Harvard University Library.

PRINTED: Gilchrist, *Life*, 1880, i, 144; Russell, *Letters*, 1906, p. 68; Keynes, *Writings*, 1925 ii, 179, *Poetry and Prose*, 1939, p. 838, *Complete Writings*, 1957, 1966, p. 797; Erdman, *Poetry and Prose*, 1965, p. 678.

SOURCE OF TEXT: Photostat.

13. WILLIAM HAYLEY to BLAKE   July 1800

HEADED: From Thomas Hayley to Wm. Blake.

UNDATED.

A single leaf written on one side.

Now in the library of Trinity College, Hartford, Conn.

PRINTED: In a slightly different form in Smith's *Nollekens and his Times*, 1828, ii, 465–6. Reprinted in Gilchrist's *Life*, 1880, i, 147.

SOURCE OF TEXT: Photostat.

14. To GEORGE CUMBERLAND   2 July 1800

ADDRESSED TO: Mr Cumberland, Bishopsgate, Windsor Great Park.

DATED: 13 Hercules Buildings, Lambeth. 2 July, 1800.

A double leaf, 4°, written on three sides.

Sold at Sotheby's, 11 April 1893. Afterwards in the collection of Charles Fairfax Murray, sold at Sotheby's, 5 February 1920 (lot 18). Offered by Messrs. Maggs in their catalogue no. 433, Dec. 1922, for £78, and again in no. 449, April 1924. Sold by the American Art Association, Anderson Galleries, 25 May 1938 (lot 73). Now in the Lessing J. Rosenwald Collection, Library of Congress, Washington, D.C.

PRINTED: Extracts were given in the sale catalogue of 1893, and these were reprinted in Russell, *Letters*, 1906, pp. 69–70. Printed in full by Ellis in *The Real Blake*, 1907, p. 206. Copied by me from the original MS in 1912 and printed in my *Bibliography of Blake*, 1921, p. 447; also in *Writings*, 1925, ii, 180, *Poetry and Prose*, 1939, p. 839, *Complete Writings*, 1957, 1966, p. 797; Erdman, *Poetry and Prose*, 1965, p. 678.

SOURCE OF TEXT: Photostat.

15. To JOHN FLAXMAN   12 September 1800

ADDRESSED TO: Mr. Flaxman, Buckingham Street, Fitzroy Square.

Postmark: 12 o'clock 12 Sp. 1800.

A double leaf, 4°, written on both sides of the first leaf.

Formerly in the collection of B. B. Macgeorge of Glasgow, sold at Sotheby's, 1 July 1924 (lot 134, Sawyer, £55). Acquired by Miss Tessie Jones. Bequeathed to The Pierpont Morgan Library in 1968.

PRINTED: Russell, *Letters*, 1906, p. 70; Keynes, *Writings*, 1925, ii. 182; Keynes, *Poetry and Prose*, 1939, p. 840, *Complete Writings*, 1957, 1966, p. 799; Erdman, *Poetry and Prose*, 1965, p. 679.

SOURCE OF TEXT: Original MS (transcribed in 1924) and recent photostat.

16. To MRS. ANNA FLAXMAN   14 September 1800

From Mrs Blake to Mrs Flaxman, in Blake's hand.

DATED: H. B., Lambeth, 14 Sept^r· 1800; with Blake's poem, "To my dear Friend, Mrs Anna Flaxman".

Formerly in the possession of Mrs. Flaxman's sister, Maria Denman, from whom Gilchrist obtained a copy. Now in The Pierpont Morgan Library.

PRINTED: Gilchrist, *Life*, 1880, i, 147; Russell, *Letters*, 1906, p. 72; E. V. Lucas, *The Second Post*, [1910], p. 97; Keynes, *Writings*, 1925, ii, 184; Keynes, *Poetry and Prose*, 1939, p. 841, *Complete Writings*, 1957, 1966, p. 800.

SOURCE OF TEXT: Photostat.

17. To WILLIAM HAYLEY   16 September 1800

A single leaf, 4°, with portrait, both inlaid.

Sold at Sotheby's, 20 May 1878 (lot 3, Webster, £2 17s.). Sold again with the collection of Louis J. Haber, Part III, at the Anderson Galleries, New York, 9 Dec. 1909 (lot 47, G. H. Richmond, $55.00). Now in the H. E. Huntington Library, California.

PRINTED, EXTRACTS ONLY: Sale catalogue, 1878; Gilchrist, *Life*, 1880, i, 148 (two sentences only); Keynes, *Writings*, 1925, ii, 185, *Poetry and Prose*, 1939, p. 843, *Complete Writings*, 1957, 1966, p. 801; Erdman, *Poetry and Prose*, 1965, p. 681.

IN FULL: *William Blake* by Mark Schorer, New York, 1946, p. 18.

SOURCE OF TEXT: Photostat. Reproduced here, facing p. 40.

18. To JOHN FLAXMAN   21 September 1800

ADDRESSED TO: Mr Flaxman, Buckingham Street, Fitzroy Square, London.

DATED: Felpham, Septr 21, 1800, Sunday Morning.

A double leaf, 4°, written on three sides.

Given by Flaxman to John Thomas Smith (see *Nollekens and his Times*, 1828, ii, 463). Afterwards in the collection of Charles Fairfax Murray, sold *en bloc* at Sotheby's, 5 Feb. 1920 (lot 19). Offered by Messrs. Maggs Bros. in cat. 425, June 1922 (£85). Bequeathed by the late Chauncey Brewster Tinker to Yale University.

PRINTED: *Nollekens and his Times*, 1828, ii, 464; Gilchrist's *Life*, 1880, i, 149; Russell, *Letters*, 1906, p. 74; Keynes, *Writings*, 1925, ii, 186, *Poetry and Prose*, 1939, p. 843, *Complete Writings*, 1957, 1966, p. 801.

SOURCE OF TEXT: Original MS, and photographic facsimile of third page.

19. To THOMAS BUTTS   23 September 1800

ADDRESSED TO: Mr Butts, G^t. Marlborough Street near Oxford Street London. ENDORSED: Mr Blake. His Account & Correspondence.

Postmark DATED: Sep. 23, 1800.

A double leaf, 4°, written on three sides. Wmk.: a shield surmounted by a crown.

From the Butts collection. Acquired from Captain Butts about 1906 by the late W. Graham Robertson and bequeathed by him to his executor, Mr. Kerrison Preston, who gave it with his Blake Collection to the City of Westminster Central Reference Library in 1967.

PRINTED: Gilchrist, *Life*, 1880, i, 151 (second half only); Russell, *Letters*, 1906, p. 77; Keynes, *Writings*, 1925, ii, 187, *Letters to Butts*, 1926, facsimile, *Poetry and Prose*, 1939, p. 844, *Complete Writings*, 1957, 1966, p. 803; Erdman, *Poetry and Prose*, 1965, p. 681.

SOURCE OF TEXT: Original MS, and photographic facsimile.

20. THOMAS BUTTS to BLAKE   end of September 1800

Rough draft of letter with erasures and alterations.

HEADED: Marlborough Street (no date).

On a double leaf, 4°, written on three sides. Wmk.: a fleur-de-lys, 1796. History as for no. 19.

PRINTED: Russell, *Letters*, 1906, p. 79 (extracts); Keynes, *Letters to Butts*, 1926; Mona Wilson, *Life*, 1927, p. 128.

SOURCE OF TEXT: Original MS.

21. To THOMAS BUTTS   2 October 1800

ADDRESSED TO: Mr Butts, Great Marlborough Street.

DATED: Felpham Octr 2^d 1800.

A double leaf, 4°, written on three sides. Wmk.: 1798.

History as for no. 19.

PRINTED: Gilchrist, *Life*, 1880, 1, 152; Russell, *Letters*, 1906, p. 81; Keynes, *Writings*, 1925, ii, 189, *Letters to Butts*, 1926, facsimile, *Poetry and Prose*, 1939, p. 845, *Complete Writings*, 1957, 1966, p. 804; Erdman, *Poetry and Prose*, 1965, p. 682.

SOURCE OF TEXT: Original MS and photographic facsimile.

22. To WILLIAM HAYLEY   26 November 1800

DATED: Felpham, 26 November, 1800.

Sold at Sotheby's, 20 May 1878 (lot 33, Quaritch, £3 14s.). Not traced.

PRINTED: Gilchrist, *Life*, 1880, i, 163; *Century Guild Hobby Horse*, 1886, i, 159;
Russell, *Letters*, 1906, p. 85; Keynes, *Writings*, 1925, ii, 192, *Poetry and Prose*,
1939, p. 848, *Complete Writings*, 1957, 1966, p. 806.

SOURCE OF TEXT: Gilchrist's *Life*, 1880.

23. [? To WILLIAM HAYLEY]   [c. 1800]

Probably not dated or addressed. A single leaf, 8°.

Sold anonymously at Sotheby's, 3 December 1888 (lot 13). Sold again with
the collection of H. V. Morten at Sotheby's, 5 May 1890 (lot 22, Ellis, 2
gns.). Not traced.

PRINTED, EXTRACT ONLY: Sale catalogue, 1888; sale catalogue, another
version, 1890; Keynes, *Writings*, 1925, ii, 193; Keynes, *Poetry and Prose*,
1939, p. 849; Keynes, *Complete Writings*, 1957, p. 807.

SOURCE OF TEXT: Sale catalogue, 1888, now first reprinted.

24. To THOMAS BUTTS   10 May 1801

DATED: Felpham, May 10, 1801.

A single leaf, 4°, written on both sides. The other half missing. Wmk.:
maker's device and monogram.

History as for no. 19.

PRINTED: Gilchrist, *Life*, 1880, i, 164; Russell, *Letters*, 1906, p. 88; Keynes,
Writings, 1925, ii, 195, *Letters to Butts*, 1926, facsimile, *Poetry and Prose*, 1939,
p. 850, *Complete Writings*, 1957, 1966, p. 808.

SOURCE OF TEXT: Original MS and photographic facsimile.

25. To THOMAS BUTTS   11 September 1801

ADDRESSED TO: Mr. Butts, Great Marlborough Street, London.

DATED: Felpham Cottage of Cottages the prettiest September 11, 1801.

A double leaf, f°, written on three sides. Wmk., first leaf: shield surmounted
by a crown; second leaf: F HAYES/1798.

History as for no. 19.

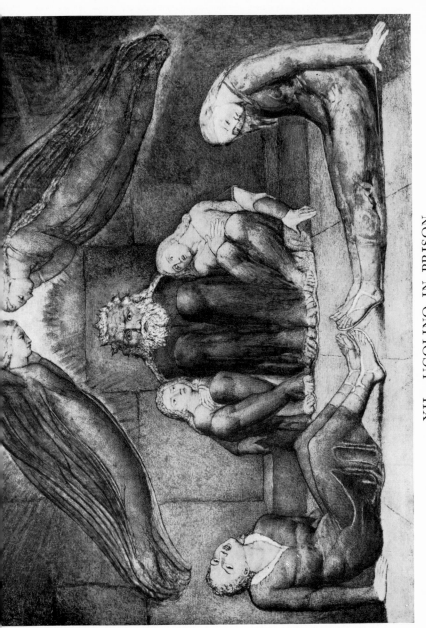

XII. UGOLINO IN PRISON

tempera on panel 1827

PRINTED: Gilchrist, *Life*, 1880, i, 167; Russell, *Letters*, 1906, p. 90 (printed in error as two letters); Keynes, *Writings*, 1925, ii, 196, *Letters to Butts*, 1926, facsimile, *Poetry and Prose*, 1939, p. 850, *Complete Writings*, 1957, 1966, p. 808; Erdman, *Poetry and Prose*, 1965, p. 685.

SOURCE OF TEXT: Original MS and photographic facsimile.

26. JOHN FLAXMAN to BLAKE   7 October 1801

On the third page of a letter to William Hayley, dated 7 October 1801.

Sold at Sotheby's with a series of seventeen letters from Flaxman to Hayley, 8 Nov. 1927 (lot 289). Offered by Messrs. Maggs in their catalogue 544, June 1930, for £12 10s. Later in the possession of A. N. L. Munby, from whom it passed to the Fitzwilliam Museum, Cambridge, 1949.

PRINTED: by Messrs. Sotheby and Maggs in their catalogues, and in Thomas Wright's *Life of W. B.*, 1929, ii, 184.

SOURCE OF TEXT: Original MS.

27. To JOHN FLAXMAN   19 October 1801

ADDRESSED: To Mr Flaxman, Sculptor, Buckingham Street, Fitzroy Square, London.

DATED: Oct 19 1801

A single leaf, 4°. A postscript has been added by Hayley.

Formerly in the collection of William Harris Arnold, sold at the Anderson Galleries, New York, 1924 (lot 53). Formerly deposited in the Alice Bemis Taylor Collection, Taylor Museum of the Colorado Springs Fine Arts Centre, Colorado Springs, Colorado. Now the property of Mrs. Charles G. Thompson.

PRINTED: Russell, *Letters*, 1906, p. 95; Keynes, *Writings*, 1925, ii, 198, *Poetry and Prose*, 1939, p. 852, *Complete Writings*, 1957, 1966, p. 810; Erdman, *Poetry and Prose*, 1965, p. 686.

SOURCE OF TEXT: Photostat.

28. To THOMAS BUTTS   10 January 1802

ADDRESSED TO: Mr. Butts, Great Marlborough Street, Oxford Street, London.

DATED: Felpham, Jany 10, 1802.

A double leaf, 4°, written on four sides. Wmk.: A BLACKWELL/1798.

177

History as for no. 19.

PRINTED: Gilchrist, *Life*, 1880, i, 172; Russell, 1906, p. 96; Keynes, *Writings*, 1925, ii, 199, *Letters to Butts*, 1926, facsimile, *Poetry and Prose*, 1939, p. 853, *Complete Writings*, 1957, 1966, p. 811; Erdman, *Poetry and Prose*, 1965, p. 687; Erdman, *Poetry and Prose*, 1965, p. 689.

SOURCE OF TEXT: Original MS and photographic facsimile.

29. To THOMAS BUTTS   22 November 1802

ADDRESSED TO: Mr. Butts, Gr Marlborough Street.

DATED: Felpham, Novr 22, 1802.

A double leaf, 4°, written on four sides. Wmk.: F HAYES/1798.

History as for no. 19.

PRINTED: Gilchrist, *Life*, 1880, i, 178; Russell, *Letters*, 1906, p. 102; Keynes, *Writings*, 1925, ii, 202, *Letters to Butts*, 1926, facsimile, *Poetry and Prose*, 1939, p. 856, *Complete Writings*, 1957, 1966, p. 814.

SOURCE OF TEXT: Original MS and photographic facsimile.

30. To THOMAS BUTTS   [22 November 1802]

Not addressed or dated.

A single leaf, 4°, written on two sides, the other half missing. Wmk.: large maker's device.

History as for no. 19.

PRINTED: Gilchrist, *Life*, 1880, i, 181; Russell, *Letters*, 1906, p. 107; Keynes, *Writings*, 1925, ii, 206, *Letters to Butts*, 1926, facsimile, *Poetry and Prose*, 1939, p. 859, *Complete Writings*, 1957, 1966, p. 816; Erdman, *Poetry and Prose*, 1965, p. 691.

SOURCE OF TEXT: Original MS and photographic facsimile.

31. To JAMES BLAKE   30 January 1803

Not addressed.

DATED: Felpham, January 30, 1803.

A double leaf, f°, written on four sides. Each half of the leaf is now mounted separately on a guard and they are bound together in a morocco volume by Sangorski and Sutcliffe, with a manuscript title-page, and a typescript of the letter at the end.

From the Morrison collection. Sold at Hodgson's, 21 March 1917 (lot 168, Dobell, £31). Afterwards acquired by Messrs. Maggs and sold by them to Lt.-Col. W. E. Moss. Sold with the Moss collection at Sotheby's, 2 March 1937 (lot 281, Rosenbach, £150). Now in the Lessing J. Rosenwald Collection, Library of Congress, Washington, D.C.

PRINTED: Keynes, *Bibliography*, 1921, p. 449; Keynes, *Writings*, 1925, ii, 239; Mona Wilson, *Life*, 1927, p. 140; Keynes, *Poetry and Prose*, 1939, p. 862, *Complete Writings*, 1957, 1966, p. 819; Erdman, *Poetry and Prose*, 1965, p. 694.

SOURCE OF TEXT: Photostat.

32. To THOMAS BUTTS   25 April, 1803

ADDRESSED TO: Mr. Butts, Gr^t Marlborough Street.

DATED: Felpham, April 25, 1803.

A double leaf, 4°, written on four sides. Wmk.: A BLACKWELL/1798.

History as for no. 19.

PRINTED: Gilchrist, *Life*, 1880, i, 184; Russell, *Letters*, 1906, p. 113; Keynes, *Writings*, 1925, ii, 242, *Letters to Butts*, 1926, facsimile, *Poetry and Prose*, 1939, p. 865, *Complete Writings*, 1957, 1966, p. 822; Erdman, *Poetry and Prose*, 1965, p. 696.

SOURCE OF TEXT: Original MS and photographic facsimile.

33. To THOMAS BUTTS   6 July 1803

Not addressed.

DATED: Felpham, July 6, 1803.

A double leaf, 4°, written on four sides. Wmk.: A BLACKWELL/1798.

History as for no. 19.

PRINTED: Gilchrist, *Life*, 1880, i, 186; Russell, *Letters* , 1906, p. 117; Keynes, *Writings*, 1925, ii, 245, *Letters to Butts*, 1926, facsimile, *Poetry and Prose*, 1939, p. 867, *Complete Writings*, 1957, 1966, p. 823.

SOURCE OF TEXT: Original MS and photographic facsimile.

34. INFORMATION OF JOHN SCOFIELD   15 August 1803

A contemporary manuscript, presumably taken down at Scofield's dictation.

Preserved as a copy (so marked) on the first recto of a double folio sheet, with a copy of Blake's refutation.

Formerly in the possession of H. Buxton Forman. Sold with the second portion of the Buxton Forman Library, Anderson Galleries, New York, April 1920 (in lot 64, $17). Acquired by Alan R. Brown, and given by him to Trinity College, Hartford, Conn., in 1940.

PRINTED: Nicoll and Wise, *Literary Anecdotes of the Nineteenth Century*, 1895, i, 5. Mona Wilson, *Life*, 1927, p. 147.

SOURCE OF TEXT: Photostat.

35. To THOMAS BUTTS   16 August 1803

ADDRESSED TO: Mr Butts, Gr Marlborough S^t, London

DATED: Felpham, August 16, 1803.

A double leaf, 4°, written on three sides. Wmk.: F HAYES/1798.

History as for no. 19.

PRINTED: Gilchrist, *Life*, 1880, i, 190; Russell, *Letters*, 1906, p. 124; Keynes, *Writings*, 1925, ii, 248, *Letters to Butts*, 1926, facsimile; Keynes, *Poetry and Prose*, 1939, p. 870, *Complete Writings*, 1957, 1966, p. 826; Erdman, *Poetry and Prose*, 1965, p. 698.

SOURCE OF TEXT: Original MS and photographic facsimile.

36. To THOMAS BUTTS   July 8–August 20, 1803

An Account between Blake and Thomas Butts written in Blake's hand, amounting to £14 14s. for eleven drawings, including "The Three Maries", delivered on July 8 and August 20, 1803.

From the Butts collection. Sold at Sotheby's, 24 June 1903 (lot 23, J. Mason, £3 5s.). Not traced.

Not yet printed.

37. MEMORANDUM BY BLAKE   August 1803

Blake's memorandum in refutation of John Scofield, presumably in Blake's own hand, and intended for the use of his counsel, Samuel Rose.

Preserved as a copy on the second to fourth sides of a double folio sheet, with Scofield's "Information", *q.v.*

PRINTED: Nicoll and Wise, *Literary Anecdotes of the Nineteenth Century*, 1895, i, 7; Keynes, *Writings*, 1925, ii, 252, *Poetry and Prose*, 1939, p. 874, *Complete Writings*, 1957, 1966, p. 437; Erdman, *Poetry and Prose*, 1965, p. 700.

SOURCE OF TEXT: Photostat.

38. To WILLIAM HAYLEY   19 September 1803

Presumably addressed and dated as above.

Sold at Sotheby's, 20 May 1878 (lot 4, Naylor, £2 12s.). Not traced.

PRINTED, EXTRACTS ONLY: Sale catalogue, 1878; Keynes, *Writings*, 1925, ii, 255, *Poetry and Prose*, 1939, p. 876, *Complete Writings*, 1957, 1966, p. 829.

SOURCE OF TEXT: Sale Catalogue, 1878.

39. To WILLIAM HAYLEY   7 October 1803

ADDRESSED: To William Hayley Esqre, Flepham, near Chichester, Sussex.

DATED: London, October 7, 1803.

A double leaf, 4°, written on three sides.

Sold at Sotheby's, 20 May 1878 (lot 5, Webster, 4 gns.). Formerly in the R. B. Adam Collection, Buffalo. Now the property of Mrs. Donald Hyde.

PRINTED: R. B. Adam, Christmas, 1929, facsimile; Keynes, *Poetry and Prose*, 1939, p. 876, *Complete Writings*, 1957, 1966, p. 829.

SOURCE OF TEXT: Photographic facsimile.

40. To WILLIAM HAYLEY   26 October 1803

DATED: South Molton Street, 26 October, 1803. Signed: W. and C. Blake.

Sold at Sotheby's together with letter no. 58, 20 May 1878 (lot 32, Quaritch, £3). Not traced.

PRINTED: Gilchrist, *Life*, 1880, i, 194; Russell, *Letters*, 1906, p. 130; Keynes, *Writings*, 1925, ii, 256, *Poetry and Prose*, 1939, p. 878, *Complete Writings*, 1957, 1966, p. 831.

SOURCE OF TEXT: Gilchrist's *Life*, 1880.

41. To WILLIAM HAYLEY   13 December 1803

ADDRESSED TO: William Hayley Esqre, Felpham, near Bognor, Sussex.

DATED: Tuesday night, 13 Dec^r, 1803.

A double leaf, 4°, written on three sides.

Sold at Sotheby's, 20 May 1878 (lot 8, Naylor, £2 7s.). Now in the library of the Maine Historical Society, Portland, Maine, U.S.A.

PRINTED: Brief extracts in the sale catalogue, 1878; Keynes, *Writings*, 1925, ii, 257, *Poetry and Prose*, 1939, p. 879. Printed in full for the first time, 1956, and in *Complete Writings*, 1957, 1966, p. 832.

SOURCE OF TEXT: Photostat.

42. SPEECH OF COUNSELLOR ROSE 11 January 1804

Delivered by Samuel Rose in Blake's defence at his trial at Chichester Sessions.

Preserved as a copy on four quarto leaves, marked at the top "taken in short hand by the Revd Mr Youatt".

Formerly in the possession of H. Buxton Forman. Sold with the second portion of the Buxton Forman Library at the Anderson Galleries, New York, April 1920 (in lot 64, $17). Acquired by Alan R. Brown, and given by him to Trinity College, Hartford, Conn., in 1940.

PRINTED: Nicoll and Wise, *Literary Anecdotes of the Nineteenth Century*, 1895, i, 11.

SOURCE OF TEXT: Photostat.

43. To WILLIAM HAYLEY 14 January 1804

ADDRESSED: William Hayley Esqre, Felpham, near Chichester, Sussex.

DATED: London, Jany 14, 1804.

A double leaf, 4°, written on three sides.

Sold at Sotheby's, 20 May 1878 (lot 9, Naylor, £2 15s.). It was in the Rowfant Library in 1886 in an album of ALS. Bought by Dodd Mead & Co., New York. Acquired in 1953 by Harvard University Library.

PRINTED: Gilchrist, *Life*, 1880, i, 199; Russell, *Letters*, 1806, p. 137; Keynes, *Writings*, 1925, ii, 258, *Poetry and Prose*, 1939, p. 880, *Complete Writings*, 1957, 1966, p. 853.

SOURCE OF TEXT: Photostat.

44. To WILLIAM HAYLEY 27 January 1804

ADDRESSED TO: William Hayley Esqre, Felpham, near Chichester, Sussex.

DATED: Sth Molton Street, Friday Jany 27, 1804.

A double leaf, 4°, written on three sides.

Sold at Sotheby's, 20 May 1878 (lot 10, Naylor, £5). It was in the Rowfant Library in 1886, in an album of ALS. Bought by Dodd Mead & Co., New York. Acquired in 1953 by Harvard University Library.

PRINTED: Gilchrist, *Life*, 1880, i, 201; Russell, *Letters*, 1906, p. 139; Keynes, *Writings*, 1925, ii, 259, *Poetry and Prose*, 1939, p. 881, *Complete Writings*, 1957, 1966, p. 834.

SOURCE OF TEXT: Photostat.

45. To WILLIAM HAYLEY   23 February 1804

ADDRESSED: To William Hayley Esqre.

DATED: Sth Molton Street, 23 Feb^y, 1804.

A double leaf, 4°, written on three sides.

Sold at Sotheby's, 20 May 1878 (lot 11, Quaritch, 4 gns.). Purchased from Quaritch for the BM 15 June 1878. Add. MSS 30262, f. 86.

PRINTED: Gilchrist, *Life*, 1880, i, 203; Russell, *Letters*, 1906, p. 142; Keynes, *Writings*, 1925, ii, 261, *Poetry and Prose*, 1939, p. 882, *Complete Writings*, 1957, 1966, p. 835.

SOURCE OF TEXT: Original MS.

46. To WILLIAM HAYLEY   12 March 1804

ADDRESSED: To William Hayley Esqre, Felpham, near Chichester, Sussex.

DATED: March 12, 1804.

A single leaf, 4°.

Sold at Sotheby's, 20 May 1878 (lot 7, Waller, £2 15s.). Afterwards in the collection of Joseph Mayer of Liverpool. Sold at Sotheby's, 19 July 1887 (in lot 189, Robson, £10 5s.). Later in the collection of H. Buxton Forman, and sold with his library at the Anderson Galleries, New York, 15 March 1920 (lot 69). In 1925 in the possession of Arthur F. Egner, New Jersey, U.S.A. Now the property of Mrs. Mary E. Malone.

PRINTED: Gilchrist, *Life*, 1880, i, 205; Russell, *Letters*, 1906, p. 146; Keynes, *Writings*, 1925, ii, 263, *Poetry and Prose*, 1939, p. 884, *Complete Writings*, 1957, 1966, p. 837.

SOURCE OF TEXT: Photostat.

47. To WILLIAM HAYLEY   16 March 1804

ADDRESSED: To William Hayley Esqre

DATED: 16 March, 1804.

A double leaf, 4°, written on three sides.

Sold at Sotheby's, 20 May 1878 (lot 12, Naylor, 3 gns.). In 1886 in the possession of "Mr. Shepherd, 46 Pall Mall", by whom it was lent to Mr. William Muir. Afterwards in the collection of Charles Fairfax Murray, sold at Sotheby's, 5 Feb. 1920 (lot 20). Offered by Messrs. Maggs Bros. in their cat. no. 433, Dec. 1922, for £52. Now in The Pierpont Morgan Library.

PRINTED: Appended to Muir's *Milton*, 1886, in facsimile; Keynes, *Bibliography*, 1921, p. 451, *Writings*, 1925, ii, 264, *Poetry and Prose*, 1939, p. 885, *Complete Writings*, 1957, 1966, p. 838.

SOURCE OF TEXT: Photostat.

48. To WILLIAM HAYLEY
21 March 1804

ADDRESSED: To William Hayley Esqre, Felpham.

DATED: Sth Molton Street, March 21, 1804.

A double leaf, 4°, written on two sides.

Sold at Sotheby's, 20 May 1878 (lot 13, Naylor, £3 5s.). Naylor Collection. Sold at Sotheby's, 27 July 1885 (lot 97, Waller, £3 7s.). Now in the Library of the Historical Society of Pennsylvania, Philadelphia.

PRINTED: Printed in full for the first time 1956 and in *Complete Writings*, 1957, 1966, p. 839.

SOURCE OF TEXT: Photostat.

49. To WILLIAM HAYLEY
31 March 1804

ADDRESSED: To William Hayley Esqre, Felpham, near Chichester, Sussex.

DATED: Sth Molton St, March 31, 1804.

A single leaf, 4°.

Sold at Sotheby's, 20 May 1878, together with letter no. 50 (lot 14, Waller, £4). Sold again at Sotheby's in the collection of Joseph Mayer of Liverpool, 19 July 1887 (in lot 189, Robson, £10 5s.). Afterwards in the collection of H. Buxton Forman, and sold with his library at the Anderson Galleries, New York, 15 March 1920 (lot 70). Acquired by Alan R. Brown, and given by him to Trinity College, Hartford, Conn., in 1940.

PRINTED: Russell, *Letters*, 1906, p. 230; Keynes, *Writings*, 1925, ii, 266, *Poetry and Prose*, 1939, p. 886, *Complete Writings*, 1957, 1966, p. 840.

SOURCE OF TEXT: Photostat.

50. To WILLIAM HAYLEY
2 April 1804

Presumably addressed and dated as above.

Sold at Sotheby's, 20 May 1878, together with letter no. 49 (lot 14, Waller, £4). Not traced.

PRINTED, WITHOUT THE BEGINNING: Gilchrist, *Life*, 1880, i, 205; Russell, *Letters*, 1906, p. 147; Keynes, *Writings*, 1925, ii, 267, *Poetry and Prose*, 1939, p. 887, *Complete Writings*, 1957, 1966, p. 840.

SOURCE OF TEXT: Gilchrist's *Life*, 1880.

51. TO WILLIAM HAYLEY
7 April 1804

ADDRESSED TO: William Hayley Esqre, Felpham, near Chichester, Sussex.

A double leaf, 4°, written on three sides.

Sold at Sotheby's, 20 May 1878 (lot 15, Naylor, £2 19s.). It was in the Rowfant Library in 1886, in an album of ALS. Bought by Dodd Mead & Co., New York. Acquired in 1953 by Harvard University Library.

PRINTED: Gilchrist, *Life*, 1880, i, 207; Russell, *Letters*, 1906, p. 148; Keynes, *Writings*, 1925, ii, 268, *Poetry and Prose*, 1939, p. 888, *Complete Writings*, 1957, 1966, p. 841.

SOURCE OF TEXT: Photostat.

52. To WILLIAM HAYLEY 27 April 1804

ADDRESSED TO: William Hayley Esqre, Felpham, near Chichester, Sussex.

Sold at Sotheby's, 20 May 1878 (lot 16, Waller, £2 10s.). Sold again at Sotheby's in the collection of Joseph Mayer of Liverpool, 19 July 1887 (in lot 189, Robson, £10 5s.). Afterwards in the collection of H. Buxton Forman, and sold with his library at the Anderson Galleries, New York, 15 March 1920 (lot 71). Now in the Collection of Mrs. Landon K. Thorne.

PRINTED: Gilchrist, *Life*, 1880, i, 207; Russell, *Letters*, 1906, p. 150; Keynes, *Writings*, 1925, ii, 269, *Poetry and Prose*, 1939, p. 889, *Complete Writings*, 1957, 1966, p. 842.

SOURCE OF TEXT: Photostat.

53. To WILLIAM HAYLEY 4 May 1804

Presumably addressed and dated as above.

A double leaf, 4°, written on three sides.

Sold at Sotheby's, 20 May 1878 (lot 17, Quaritch, £4). Not traced.

PRINTED: Gilchrist, *Life*, 1880, i, 209; Russell, *Letters*, 1906, p. 152; Keynes, *Writings*, 1925, ii, 270, *Poetry and Prose*, 1939, p. 890, *Complete Writings*, 1957, 1966, p. 843.

SOURCE OF TEXT: Gilchrist's *Life*, 1880.

54. To WILLIAM HAYLEY 28 May 1804

Presumably addressed and dated as above.

A double leaf, 4°, written on four sides.

Sold at Sotheby's, 20 May 1878 (lot 18, Quaritch, £5 10s.). Not traced.

PRINTED: Gilchrist, *Life*, 1880, i, 210; Russell, *Letters*, 1906, p. 156; Keynes, *Writings*, 1925, ii, 273, *Poetry and Prose*, 1939, p. 892, *Complete Writings*, 1957, 1966, p. 845.

SOURCE OF TEXT: Gilchrist's *Life*, 1880. (Wrongly dated 24 May 1804.)

55. To WILLIAM HAYLEY   22 June 1804

ADDRESSED: To William Hayley Esq*re*, Felpham, near Chichester, Sussex.

DATED: Sth Molton Street, 22 June, 1804.

A double leaf, 4°, written on three sides.

Sold at Sotheby's, 20 May 1878 (lot 20, Weston, 4 gns.). Now in The Pierpont Morgan Library.

PRINTED: Russell, *Letters*, 1906, p. 162; Keynes, *Writings*, 1925, ii, 277, *Poetry and Prose*, 1939, p. 895, *Complete Writings*, 1957, 1966, p. 848.

SOURCE OF TEXT: Photostat.

56. To WILLIAM HAYLEY   16 July 1804

Addressed and dated as above.

A double leaf, 4°, written on three sides.

Sold at Sotheby's, 20 May 1878 (lot 21, Naylor, £3 1s.). Naylor Collection. Sold at Sotheby's 27 July 1885 (lot 98, Bennett, £3 9s.). Sold again at Sotheby's 2 May 1965 for B. L. Simpson (Goodspeed £380). Now in the collection of Prof. F. W. Hilles, Newhaven, Conn.

PRINTED, EXTRACT ONLY: Sale catalogue, 1878; Keynes, *Writings*, 1925, ii, 279, *Poetry and Prose*, 1939, p. 897. First printed in full, *Yale Review*, Autumn, 1967.

SOURCE OF TEXT: Photostat.

57. To WILLIAM HAYLEY   7 August 1804

Presumably addressed and dated as above.

A double leaf, 4°, written on three sides.

Sold at Sotheby's, 20 May 1878 (lot 22, Naylor, £3 10s.). Not traced.

PRINTED, EXTRACTS ONLY: Sale catalogue, 1878; Keynes, *Writings*, 1925, ii, 279, *Poetry and Prose*, 1939, p. 897, *Complete Writings*, 1957, 1966, p. 849.

SOURCE OF TEXT: Sale catalogue, 1878.

58. To WILLIAM HAYLEY   9 August 1804

Presumably addressed and dated as above.

Signed W. and C. Blake.

Sold at Sotheby's, 20 May 1878, together with letter no. 40 (lot 32, Quaritch, £3). Not traced.

Unpublished.

59. To WILLIAM HAYLEY   28 September 1804

ADDRESSED: To William Hayley Esqre, Felpham.

DATED: Sth Molton St, 28 Sept^r, 1804.

One and a quarter pp., 4°.

Sold at Sotheby's, 20 May 1878 (lot 24, Waller, £2 13s.). Sold again at Sotheby's in the collection of Joseph Mayer of Liverpool, 19 July 1887 (in lot 189, Robson, £10 5s.). Afterwards in the collection of H. Buxton Forman, and sold with his library at the Anderson Galleries, New York, 15 March 1920 (lot 72). In 1927 in the collection of the late George C. Smith, jr., and sold at the Parke-Bernet Galleries, New York, 2 Nov. 1938 (lot 6, Rosenbach, $325.00). Now in the Lessing J. Rosenwald Collection, Library of Congress, Washington, D.C.

PRINTED: Gilchrist, *Life*, 1880, i, 214; Russell, *Letters*, 1906, p. 166 (both under the erroneous date, September 20, 1804); Keynes, *Writings*, 1925, ii, 280, *Poetry and Prose*, 1939, p. 897, *Complete Writings*, 1957, 1966, p. 850.

SOURCE OF TEXT: Photostat.

60. To WILLIAM HAYLEY   23 October 1804

Presumably addressed and dated as above.

A double leaf, 4°, written on three sides.

Sold at Sotheby's, 20 May 1878 (lot 23, Quaritch, £6 14s.). Not traced.

PRINTED: Gilchrist, *Life*, 1880, i, 215; Russell, *Letters*, 1906, p. 168; Keynes, *Writings*, 1925, ii, 281, *Poetry and Prose*, 1939, p. 899, *Complete Writings*, 1957, 1966, p. 851; Erdman, *Poetry and Prose*, 1965, p. 702.

SOURCE OF TEXT: Gilchrist's *Life*, 1880.

61. To WILLIAM HAYLEY   4 December 1804

ADDRESSED: To William Hayley Esqre, Felpham, near Chichester, Sussex.

DATED: London, Dec. 4, 1804.

A double leaf, 4°, written on three sides.

Sold at Sotheby's, 20 May 1878 (lot 26, Naylor, £4). Sold again at Sotheby's in the Naylor collection, 27 July 1885 (lot 99, Molini, £3 12s.). Sold at the Anderson Galleries, New York, 16 April, 1914 ($275·00). Bought by Mrs. Long. Now in the Library of Congress, Washington, D.C.

PRINTED: *Studies in Philology* (1964) lxi, ed. G. M. Harper; Keynes, *Complete Writings*, 1966, p. 942; Erdman, *Poetry and Prose*, 1965, p. 703. Extracts only from sale catalogue printed previously.

SOURCE OF TEXT: Photostat.

62. To WILLIAM HAYLEY

18 December 1804

Presumably addressed and dated as above.

A double leaf, 4°, written on three sides.

Sold at Sotheby's, 20 May 1878 (lot 27, Quaritch, £5 10s.). Not traced.

PRINTED: Gilchrist, *Life*, 1880, i, 218; Russell, *Letters*, 1906, p. 172; Keynes, *Writings*, 1925, ii, 284, *Poetry and Prose*, 1939, p. 901, *Complete Writings*, 1957, 1966, p. 853.

SOURCE OF TEXT: Gilchrist's *Life*, 1880.

63. To WILLIAM HAYLEY

28 December 1804

ADDRESSED: To William Hayley, Esqre, Felpham, near Chichester, Sussex.

DATED: Sth Molton Street, 28 Decr 1804.

A double leaf, 4°, written on four sides.

Sold at Sotheby's, 20 May 1878 (lot 28, Naylor, £7 10s.). Naylor Collection. Sold at Sotheby's, 27 July 1885 (lot 100, Barker, £3 5s.). In 1891 in the possession of Ferdinand J. Dreer, Philadelphia. Now in the library of the Historical Society of Pennsylvania, Philadelphia.

PRINTED: Boston Museum Catalogue, 1891, p. 43; Russell, *Letters*, 1906, p. 174; Keynes, *Writings*, 1925, ii, 286, *Poetry and Prose*, 1939, p. 902, *Complete Writings*, 1957, 1966, p. 854.

SOURCE OF TEXT: Photostat.

64. To WILLIAM HAYLEY

19 January 1805

ADDRESSED: To William Hayley Esqre.

DATED: Sth Molton Street, 19 Jan^y, 1805.

A double leaf, 4°, written on three sides.

Sold at Sotheby's, 20 May 1878 (lot 29, Naylor, £3 16s.). Naylor Collection. Sold at Sotheby's, 27 July 1885 (lot 101, Thibaudeau, £3 5s.). Now in the Roberts Collection, Haverford College, Haverford, Pa.

PRINTED: Printed in full for the first time, 1956 and in *Complete Writings*, 1957, 1966, p. 856.

SOURCE OF TEXT: Photostat.

65. To WILLIAM HAYLEY   22 January 1805

Presumably addressed and dated as above.

A double leaf, 4°, written on three sides.

Sold at Sotheby's, 20 May 1878 (lot 30, Quaritch, £4 8s.). Not traced.

PRINTED: Gilchrist, *Life*, 1880, i, 219; Russell, *Letters*, 1906, p. 178; Keynes, *Writings*, 1925, ii, 288, *Poetry and Prose*, 1939, p. 904, *Complete Writings*, 1957, 1966, p. 857.

SOURCE OF TEXT: Gilchrist's *Life*, 1880.

66. To THOMAS BUTTS   22 January 1805

Receipt for £12–12–0 on further account in Butts' hand with Blake's signature. On a slip of paper 8×20 cm. with embossed revenue stamp for fourpence at one end.

DATED: As above.

History as for no. 19.

PRINTED: First printed in full, 1956.

SOURCE OF TEXT: Original MS.

67. To WILLIAM HAYLEY   [postmark: 25 April 1805]

ADDRESSED TO: William Hayley Esqre,   Felpham, near Bognor, Sussex.

DATED: Friday.

Sold at Sotheby's, 20 May 1878 (lot 6, Naylor, £3 5s.). It was in the Rowfant Library in 1886 in an album of ALS. Bought by Dodd Mead & Co., New York. Acquired in 1953 by Harvard University Library.

PRINTED: Gilchrist, *Life*, 1880, i, 220; Russell, *Letters*, 1906, p. 180; Keynes, *Writings*, 1925, ii, 290, *Poetry and Prose*, 1939, p. 905, *Complete Writings*, 1957, 1966, p. 859.

SOURCE OF TEXT: Photostat.

68. To THOMAS BUTTS   12 May–3 March 1806

Debtor and Creditor Account between Blake and Thomas Butts, partly in Blake's hand with his receipt.

One sheet, 4°, written on both sides, 15·6 × 18·9 cm. with the receipt on a slip of paper 17·8 × 20 cm., attached by a wafer.

History as for no. 19.

PRINTED: Gilchrist, *Life*, 1880, ii, 278; Keynes, *Writings*, 1925, ii, 298, *Letters to Butts*, 1926, facsimile.

SOURCE OF TEXT: Original MS.

69. To WILLIAM HAYLEY   17 May 1805

Presumably addressed and dated as above.

A double leaf, written on three sides.

Sold at Sotheby's, 20 May 1878 (lot 25, Quaritch, 5 gns.). Not traced.

PRINTED, EXTRACTS ONLY: Sale catalogue, 1878; Keynes, *Writings*, 1925, ii, 292, *Poetry and Prose*, 1939, p. 907, *Complete Writings*, 1957, 1966, p. 860.

SOURCE OF TEXT: Sale catalogue, 1878.

70. To WILLIAM HAYLEY   4 June 1805

Presumably addressed and dated as above.

A single leaf, f°, written on both sides.

Sold at Sotheby's, 20 May 1878 (lot 31, Quaritch, £3 15s.). Not traced.

PRINTED: Gilchrist, *Life*, 1880, i, 222; Russell, *Letters*, 1906, p. 184; Keynes, *Writings*, 1925, ii, 293, *Poetry and Prose*, 1939, p. 907, *Complete Writings*, 1957, 1966, p. 861.

SOURCE OF TEXT: Gilchrist's *Life*, 1880.

71. To THOMAS BUTTS   5 July 1805

Receipt for £5. 7. 0. in Butts' hand with Blake's signature.

DATED: July 5, 1805.

From the Butts collection, acquired from Captain Butts about 1906 by the late W. Graham Robertson. Given by Robertson at a date unknown to the late A. E. Newton who inserted it in his copy of Keynes's *Bibliography of Blake*, 1921. This book was sold with the Newton library at the Parke-Bernet Galleries, New York, 17 April 1941 (lot 173, $75·00).

PRINTED: The text given here is conjectural as I have not seen the original for some years, but it is no doubt approximately correct.

72. To THOMAS BUTTS   7 September 1805

Receipt for £4–4–0 on further account in Butts' hand with Blake's signature. On a slip of paper 7·5 × 19 cm. with embossed revenue stamp for fourpence at one end.

DATED: 7: Sep^t 1805

History as for no. 19.

PRINTED: First printed in full 1956.

SOURCE OF TEXT: Original MS.

73. To WILLIAM HAYLEY   27 November 1805

ADDRESSED: To Mr Hayley.

DATED: 27 Novr 1805.

A double leaf, 4°, written on three sides.

Formerly in the collection of Robert Hoe, and sold with his library at the Anderson Galleries, New York, 25 April 1911 (lot 397, $180·00). Afterwards in the collection of Miss Amy Lowell, and bequeathed by her to the Harvard University Library, Cambridge, Mass.

PRINTED: Keynes, *Bibliography*, 1921, p. 453, *Writings*, 1925, ii, 294, *Poetry and Prose*, 1939, p. 908, *Complete Writings*, 1957, 1966, p. 861.

SOURCE OF TEXT: Photostat.

74. To WILLIAM HAYLEY   11 December 1805

ADDRESSED: To William Hayley Esqre, Felpham near Chichester, Sussex.

DATED: Sth Molton Street, Decemb^r 11, 1805.

A double leaf, 4°, written on three sides.

In 1893 in the possession of Mr. Daniel. Sold at Sotheby's, anon. sale, 28 July 1899 (lot 262, Thomas, 5 gns.). Sold at Hodgson's 22 June 1922 (lot 272, Edwards, £20 10s.). Afterwards in the collection of A. E. Newton (but not sold with his library in 1940). Then in the possession of Caroline Newton, and given by her to Geoffrey Keynes, Dec. 1956.

PRINTED: Ellis and Yeats, *Works*, 1893, i, 172; Russell, *Letters*, 1906, p. 187; Keynes, *Writings*, 1925, ii, 295, *Poetry and Prose*, 1939, p. 909. First printed accurately, 1956 and in *Complete Writings*, 1957, 1966, p. 862.

SOURCE OF TEXT: Original MS.

75. To RICHARD PHILLIPS   June 1806

ADDRESSED: To the Editor of the Monthly Magazine.

Original MS not known to have survived.

PRINTED: The *Monthly Magazine*, pt. I, July 1806, xxi, 520; Swinburne, *Critical Essay*, 1868, p. 62; Gilchrist, *Life*, 1880, i, 258; Russell, *Letters*, 1906, p. 90; Keynes, *Writings*, 1925, ii, 300, *Poetry and Prose*, 1939, p. 911, *Complete Writings*, 1957, 1966, p. 863; Erdman, *Poetry and Prose*, 1965, p. 705.

SOURCE OF TEXT: *Monthly Magazine*, 1806.

76. To THOMAS BUTTS   30 June 1806

Receipt for £21–10–0 on account in Butts' hand with Blake's signature. On a slip of paper 7·5 × 18·5 cm., with embossed revenue stamp for eight-pence at one end.

DATED: As above.

History as for no. 19.

PRINTED: First printed in full 1956.

SOURCE OF TEXT: Original MS.

77. To THOMAS BUTTS   9 September 1806

Receipt for £6–6–0 in Butts' hand with Blake's signature.

DATED: Septr 1806

XIII. MR. CUMBERLAND'S CARD

engraving on copper 1827

From the Butts collection. Separated at some unknown date from the other similar receipts in this collection. In 1942 in the possession of Mr. Ruthven Todd.

PRINTED: Gilchrist's *Life of Blake*, ed. Todd, 1942, p. 376.

SOURCE OF TEXT: As above.

78. To THOMAS BUTTS   15 October 1806

Receipt for £5–5–0 on further account in Butts' hand with Blake's signature. On a slip of paper 7·7 × 18·6 cm., with embossed revenue stamp for twopence at one end.

DATED: 15: Octo^r 1806

History as for no. 19.

PRINTED: First printed in full 1956.

SOURCE OF TEXT: Original MS.

79. To THOMAS BUTTS   29 January 1807

Receipt for £21 on further account in Butts' hand with Blake's signature. On a slip of paper with embossed revenue stamp at one end.

DATED: 29 Janry 1807.

From the Butts collection. It was reproduced in an article in *The Connoisseur*, vol. XIX, 1907, pp. 92–96, by Ada E. Briggs, sister-in-law of Captain Butts, and was presumably then in her possession.

PRINTED: Reproduced in facsimile in *The Connoisseur* (see above).

SOURCE OF TEXT: As above.

80. To THOMAS BUTTS   3 March 1807

Receipt for £28–6–0 on account, wholly in Blake's hand with his signature. On a slip of paper 7·4 × 18·8 cm., with embossed revenue stamp for eightpence at one end.

DATED: March 3 1807.

History as for no. 19.

13—TLOWB

PRINTED: First printed in full 1956.

SOURCE OF TEXT: Original MS.

81. R. H. CROMEK to BLAKE   May 1807

DATED: 64 Newman Street, May, 1807

After Blake's death it came into the possession of Allan Cunningham, and from him passed to his son, Peter Cunningham, by whom it was published in 1852.

PRINTED: *Gentleman's Magazine*, Feb. 1852; Gilchrist. *Life*, 1880, i, 252; Russell, *Letters*, 1906, p. 193; Mona Wilson, *Life*, 1927, p. 190.

SOURCE OF TEXT: *Gentleman's Magazine*, 1852.

82. To THOMAS BUTTS   2 June 1807

Receipt for £12–1–6 on further account in Butts' hand with Blake's signature. On a slip of paper 7·8 × 18·7 cm., with an embossed revenue stamp for twopence at one end.

DATED: As above.

History as for no. 19.

PRINTED: First printed in full 1956.

SOURCE OF TEXT: Original MS.

83. To THOMAS BUTTS   13 July 1807

Receipt for £15–15–0 on further account in Butts' hand with Blake's signature. On a slip of paper 8·5 × 21 cm., with embossed revenue stamp for fourpence at one end.

DATED: As above.

History as for no. 19.

PRINTED: First printed in full 1956.

SOURCE OF TEXT: Original MS.

84. To THOMAS BUTTS   6 October 1807

Receipt for £10–10–0 on further account, in Butts' hand with Blake's signature. On a slip of paper $8\cdot4 \times 21$ cm., with embossed revenue stamp for fourpence at one end.

DATED: 6: Octo^r 1807.

History as for no. 19.

PRINTED: First printed in full 1956.

SOURCE OF TEXT: Original MS.

85. To RICHARD PHILLIPS   15 October 1807

ADDRESSED TO: Richard Phillips Esqr N 6 Bridge Street, Black Friars.

DATED: Oct 14, 17 Sth Molton S^t.

A double leaf, 4°, written on two sides. Endorsed by the recipient: W. B. Rec^d Octr 27th 1807. With Mr P.'s Comps.

Now in the Boston Public Library.

PRINTED: Russell, *Letters*, 1906, p. 197; Keynes, *Writings*, 1925, ii, 304, *Poetry and Prose*, 1939, p. 912, *Complete Writings*, 1957, 1966, p. 865; Erdman, *Poetry and Prose*, 1965, p. 706.

SOURCE OF TEXT: Photostat.

86. To THOMAS BUTTS   14 January 1808

Receipt for £26–5–0 on further account, in Butts' hand with Mrs. Blake's signature. On a slip of paper $7\cdot7 \times 19\cdot5$ cm., with embossed revenue stamp for twopence at one end.

DATED: As above.

History as for no. 19.

PRINTED: First printed in full 1956.

SOURCE OF TEXT: Original MS.

87. To OZIAS HUMPHRY [first draft A]   18 January 1808

HEADED: To Ozias Humphry Esq$^{re\cdot}$

DATED: 18 January 1808.

A double leaf, 4°, gilt edges, written on four sides. Size $22 \times 18\cdot5$ cm. Wmk.: IVY MILL 1806.

This manifesto was quoted by J. R. Smith in 1828 in *Nollekens and his Times*, Smith probably having obtained it from William Upcott, the recipient's son. An inscription on the second version shows that Humphry possessed them both. There is nothing to show who owned this one after 1829 until it was offered for sale by Thomas Thorp in 1837 for 15s. It was afterwards in the collection of Major C. H. Simpson of Bath, sold at Sotheby's, 15 March 1916 (lot 33, G. D. Smith, £51). Acquired by Mr. Oliver R. Barrett, Chicago, and now in the possession of his son, Mr. Roger W. Barrett, Kenilworth, Illinois.

PRINTED: J. R. Smith, *Nollekens and his Times*, 1828, ii, 482. First accurately printed 1956 and *Complete Writings*, 1957, 1966, p. 442.

SOURCE OF TEXT: Photostat.

88. To OZIAS HUMPHRY [first draft B]   18 January 1808

HEADED: [To Ozias Humphry Esqr *del.*] To Ozias Humphrey Esq. R.A. [*in another hand*].

DATED: 18 January 1808.

A double leaf, 4°, remargined and mounted on gauze, written on four sides. Size 22 × 18·5 cm. Wmk.: IVY MILL 1806.

This document is a duplicate of no. 87 with a few changes and bears the same date. The chief variations are printed in italic in square brackets in the text printed on pp. 128–30. It is difficult to say which version was written first, but probably this draft was sent with the picture to Petworth House. It was unknown until it was discovered there in a cupboard by Mr. John Wyndham (now Lord Egremont) and Miss Beatrice Harris in 1952. It is now described by courtesy of the discoverers.

PRINTED: First printed 1956.

SOURCE OF TEXT: Original MS.

89. To OZIAS HUMPHRY [second draft]   February 1808

HEADED: To Ozias Humphry Esq$^{re.}$

DATED: Feby 1808

A double leaf, 4°, gilt edges, written on four sides. Size 22 × 18·5 cm. Wmk.: IVY MILL 1806.

This second version of the description of *The Last Judgment* was given to the Earl of Buchan by Humphry after he became blind. Humphry inscribed it below Blake's signature: "The Earl of Buchan—Of this duplicate paper wch I have the Honor to inclose I have not been able to read a single line. O. H." Some of the Earl of Buchan's papers came into the possession of William Upcott, whose collection, sold at Sotheby's in June 1846, included (lot 28) a "large parcel" of the Earl's miscellaneous correspondence. This letter may well have been among them. At the bottom of the second page it is inscribed "Dec 1862". This probably refers to its sale at Puttick's on 19 Dec. 1862. In 1863, when it was quoted by Gilchrist,[1] it was "in the possession of Mr. (J. H.) Anderdon". The next dated inscription is at the bottom of the fourth page: "Waller 5/5/– 1880". This probably indicates its purchase from Waller by Henry Cunliffe, after whose death it passed to his great-nephew, Lord Cunliffe, whose son is the present owner.

PRINTED: Gilchrist, *Life*, 1880, i, 260; Russell, *Letters*, 1906, p. 198; Keynes, *Writings*, 1925, iii, 2; Keynes, *Poetry and Prose*, 1939, p. 913. First accurately printed 1956. *Complete Writings*, 1957, 1966, p. 442. Erdman, *Poetry and Prose*, 1965, p. 542.

SOURCE OF TEXT: Photostat.

90. To THOMAS BUTTS   29 February 1808

Receipt for £10 on further account in Butts' hand with Blake's signature. On a slip of paper 7·8 × 17·9 cm. No revenue stamp.

DATED: 29 Febry 1808

History as for no. 19.

PRINTED: First printed in full 1956.

SOURCE OF TEXT: Original MS.

91. To THOMAS BUTTS   29 July 1808

Receipt for £10 on further account in Butts' hand with Blake's signature. On a slip of paper 8 × 19·7 cm., with embossed revenue stamp for twopence at one end.

DATED: As above.

History as for no. 19.

PRINTED: First printed in full 1956.

SOURCE OF TEXT: Original MS.

---

[1] Gilchrist mentions that it was obtained by J. R. Smith from Upcott, but this was assumed by Gilchrist, not stated by Smith. Gilchrist did not notice that Smith had quoted a different version.

92. To THOMAS BUTTS 3 November 1808

Receipt for £5–5–0 on further account in Butts' hand with Blake's signature. On a slip of paper 7·7 × 19 cm., with embossed revenue stamp for twopence at one end.

DATED: 3 Novem^r 1808

History as for no. 19.

PRINTED: First printed in full 1956.

SOURCE OF TEXT: Original MS.

93. To THOMAS BUTTS 7 December 1808

Receipt for £5–5–0 on further account in Butts' hand with Blake's signature. On a slip of paper 7·6 × 18·5 cm., with embossed revenue stamp for two-pence at one end.

DATED: 7 Decr 1808.

History as for no. 19.

PRINTED: First printed in full 1956.

SOURCE OF TEXT: Original MS.

94. GEORGE CUMBERLAND to BLAKE 18 December 1808

ADDRESSED: G. Cumberland Esqr Junr, N.64 Newman Street, Oxford Street, London.

DATED: Culworth, 18th December, 1808.

Now in the British Museum, Add MSS 36501, f. 312, among the Cumberland Correspondence.

PRINTED: Russell, *Letters*, 1906, p. 203.

Cumberland wrote this letter with a message to his son: "Dear George, Go on receit of this to Black Friars & when you have been to Sir R. Phillips to know if he got my 24 Pages of Biography sent by Fromonts Coach carriage Paid & booked on Wednesday last—take the above to Mr Blake and get him to answer it *directly* on the sheet of Paper on which you write your answer as to the receit of the Biography of Grignon . . . G. C."

SOURCE OF TEXT: Original MS.

95. To GEORGE CUMBERLAND 19 December 1808

ADDRESSED TO: George Cumberland.

DATED: 19th December, 1808.

A single leaf, 4°, written on both sides.

Now in the British Museum, Add. MSS 36501, f. 314, among the Cumberland Correspondence.

PRINTED: *Hampstead Annual*, 1903, pp. 54–69; Russell, *Letters*, 1906, p. 205; Keynes, *Writings*, 1925, iii, 87, *Poetry and Prose*, 1939, p. 915, *Complete Writings*, 1957, 1966, p. 865; Erdman, *Poetry and Prose*, 1965, p. 706.

SOURCE OF TEXT: Original MS.

96. To OZIAS HUMPHRY [c. 1809]

ADDRESSED TO: Ozias Humphry Esqre.

Not dated. A double leaf, 4°, written on two sides.

From the collection of C. J. Toovey. Sold at Sotheby's, 25 April 1912 (lot 10). Offered for sale by Messrs. Maggs Bros. in July 1912 (cat. 293, £35). Sold by the American Art Association, New York, on 16 April 1923 (lot 128, $125.00). Acquired by Alan R. Brown, and given by him to Trinity College, Hartford, Conn., in 1940.

PRINTED: An extract in Messrs. Magg's catalogue, with a facsimile. In full, Keynes, *Bibliography*, 1921, p. 454, *Writings*, 1925, iii, 123, *Poetry and Prose*, 1939, p. 915, *Complete Writings*, 1957, 1966, p. 866.

SOURCE OF TEXT: Photostat.

97. To THOMAS BUTTS 7 April 1809

Receipt for £21 on further account in Butts' hand with Blake's signature. On a slip of paper 8 × 20·4 cm. No revenue stamp.

DATED: As above.

History as for no. 19.

PRINTED: First printed in full 1956.

SOURCE OF TEXT: Original MS.

98. To THOMAS BUTTS 29 June 1809

Receipt for £10–10 on further account presumably similar to no. 97.

DATED: As above.

Sold at Sotheby's 19 Dec. 1932 with the property of Anthony Butts (lot 127, Spencer, £6). Seen by me but not recorded.

99. To THOMAS BUTTS   10 July 1809

Receipt for £10–10–0 on further account, in Butts' hand with Blake's signature. On a slip of paper 17·8 × 19·3 cm. No revenue stamp.

DATED: As above.

History as for no. 19.

PRINTED: First printed in full 1956.

SOURCE OF TEXT: Original MS.

100. To THOMAS BUTTS   10 August 1809

Receipt for £10–10–0 on further account in Butts' hand with Blake's signature. On a slip of paper 7·5 × 17·8 cm. No revenue stamp.

DATED: As above.

History as for no. 19.

PRINTED: First printed in full 1956.

SOURCE OF TEXT: Original MS.

101. To THOMAS BUTTS   4 October 1809

Receipt for £10–10–0 on further account in Butts' hand with Blake's signature. On a slip of paper 7·6 × 18·6 cm. No revenue stamp.

DATED: 4 Octo^r 1809.

History as for no. 19.

PRINTED: First printed in full 1956.

SOURCE OF TEXT: Original MS.

102. To THOMAS BUTTS   25 November 1809

Receipt for £20 on further account, in Butts' hand with Blake's signature. No revenue stamp. On a slip of paper 8 × 18·5 cm.

DATED: 25 Novr 1809.

History as for no. 19.

PRINTED: First printed in full 1956.

SOURCE OF TEXT: Original MS.

103. To THOMAS BUTTS   16 January 1810

Receipt for £21 on further account in Butts' hand with Blake's signature. No revenue stamp. On a slip of paper 7·5 × 2·1 cm.

DATED: 16 Janry 1810.

History as for no. 19.

PRINTED: Now first printed in full.

SOURCE OF TEXT: Original MS.

104. To THOMAS BUTTS   3 March 1810

Receipt for £10–10 on further account in Butts' hand with Blake's signature. No revenue stamp. On a slip of paper 8 × 19·8 cm.

DATED: 3 March 1810.

History as in no. 19.

PRINTED: First printed in full 1956.

SOURCE OF TEXT: Original MS.

105. To THOMAS BUTTS   14 April 1810

Receipt for £21 on further account in Butts' hand with Blake's signature. No revenue stamp. On a slip of paper 7·6 × 18·3 cm.

DATED: As above.

History as for no. 19.

PRINTED: First printed in full 1956.

SOURCE OF TEXT: Original MS.

106. To THOMAS BUTTS
30 June 1810

Receipt for £5–5–0 on further account in Butts' hand with Blake's signature. No revenue stamp. On a slip of paper 7·6 × 18·5 cm.

DATED: As above.

History as for no. 19.

PRINTED: First printed in full 1956.

SOURCE OF TEXT: Original MS.

107. To THOMAS BUTTS
14 July 1810

Receipt for £15–15–0 on further account in Butts' hand with Blake's signature. No revenue stamp. On a slip of paper 6·6 × 18·5 cm.

DATED: As above.

History as for no. 19.

PRINTED: First printed in full 1956.

SOURCE OF TEXT: Original MS.

108. To THOMAS BUTTS
20 September 1810

Receipt for £10–10–0 on further account in Butts' hand with Blake's signature. No revenue stamp. On a slip of paper 7·4 × 19·5 cm.

DATED: 20 Septr 1810.

History as for no. 19.

PRINTED: First printed in full 1956.

SOURCE OF TEXT: Original MS.

109. To THOMAS BUTTS
18 December 1810

Receipt for £10–10–0 on further account in Butts' hand, with Blake's signature. No revenue stamp. On a slip of paper 7·8 × 16 cm.

DATED: 18 Decr 1810.

History as for no. 19.

PRINTED: First printed in full 1956.

SOURCE OF TEXT: Original MS.

110. JOSIAH WEDGWOOD to BLAKE   29 July 1815

ADDRESSED TO: Mr Blake, 17 South Molton St.

DATED: Etruria, 29 July, 1815.

A copy is in the Wedgwood Museum at Barlaston, Stoke-on-Trent.

PRINTED: Keynes, *Times Literary Supplement*, 9 Dec. 1926; Keynes, *Blake Studies*, London, 1949, p. 71.

SOURCE OF TEXT: Original MS and photostat.

111. TO JOSIAH WEDGWOOD   8 September 1815

ADDRESSED: To Josiah Wedgwood Esqre.

DATED: 17 South Molton Street, 8 Septemb^r, 1815

A single leaf, 4°, written on one side.

Now in the Wedgwood Museum at Barlaston, Stoke-on-Trent.

PRINTED: Keynes, *Times Literary Supplement*, 9 December, 1926, *Poetry and Prose*, 1939, p. 916, *Complete Writings*, 1957, 1966, p. 866.

SOURCE OF TEXT: Original MS and photostat.

112. To DAWSON TURNER   9 June, 1818

ADDRESSED: To Dawson Turner Esqre, Yarmouth, Norfolk.

DATED: 9 June, 1818, 17 South Molton Street.

A double leaf, 4°, written on three sides.

Sold with the Dawson Turner collection of MSS at Puttick and Simpson's, 6 June 1859. Later offered by S. J. Davey for £6. 6. o. It was in the collection of W. A. White in 1921. Now in the A. S. W. Rosenbach Collection, Philadelphia.

PRINTED: Grolier Club Catalogue, 1905, p. 136; Russell, *Letters*, 1906, p. 207; Keynes, *Writings*, 1925, iii, 321, *Poetry and Prose*, 1939, p. 916, *Complete Writings*, 1957, 1966, p. 867.

SOURCE OF TEXT: Photostat.

113. INDEX TO SONGS OF INNOCENCE AND OF
       EXPERIENCE   c. 1818

Two leaves, 4°, headed as on p. 179.

Not dated, but the order of the plates as in this Index was followed only in one copy of the *Songs*, which is printed on paper with a watermark dated 1818 (see Keynes, *Bibliography*, 1921, p. 126).

Formerly bound with a MS copy of Cunningham's *Life of Blake*. Afterwards in the possession of William Muir. Now in the Lessing J. Rosenwald collection, Library of Congress, Washington, D.C.

PRINTED: In facsimile, with Muir's edition of *The Marriage of Heaven and Hell*, 1885.

SOURCE OF TEXT: Muir's facsimile. Photostat.

114. To JOHN LINNELL   12 August 1818

Receipt for £2 on account in Blake's hand with his signature. On a slip of paper 4 × 17 cm.

Formerly in the Linnell collection. Sold at Christie's 2 Dec. 1938 (in lot 62, Robinson, £78 15s.). Presented to Yale University Library by Mr. Otis T. Bradley in 1942.

PRINTED: First printed 1956.

SOURCE OF TEXT: Photostat.

114a. To JOHN LINNELL   11 September 1818

Receipt for £5 on account in Blake's hand with his signature. On a slip of paper 7·5 × 18·5 cm. with an embossed revenue stamp. Formerly in the possession of Samuel Palmer and of his son and grandson, Bryan Palmer, from whom I obtained it in 1957.

PRINTED: Now first printed.

SOURCE OF TEXT: Original MS.

115–117. To JOHN LINNELL   19 September–31 December 1818

Three receipts for laying in the engraving of Mr. Upton's portrait, all in Blake's hand, two with signatures. On three slips of paper 8·5 × 14, 7·5 × 18·5, 6·5 × 16·5 cm.

History as for no. 114.

PRINTED: First printed 1956.

SOURCE OF TEXT: Photostat.

118. To JOHN LINNELL   27 August 1819

Receipt for Songs of Innocence and Experience in Blake's hand with
signature. On a slip of paper 11 × 18·5 cm.

History as for no. 114.

PRINTED: First printed 1956.

SOURCE OF TEXT: Photostat.

119. To JOHN LINNELL [?]   11 October 1819

Not addressed.

DATED: Oct. 11, 1819, Monday Evening.

A single leaf, 8°, written on one side.

In the possession of Goodspeed, bookseller, of Boston in 1925. After-
wards in the collection of the late George C. Smith, jr., and sold at the
Parke-Bernet Galleries, New York, 2 Nov. 1938 (lot 7, Sessler, $45.00).
Afterwards in the collection of Moncure Biddle, and sold by him at the
Parke-Bernet Galleries, 29 April 1952 (lot 117, Schwartz, $100.00). Later
in the collection of Dr. E. Hanley, Bradford, Penn., U.S.A. Now at the
University of Texas.

PRINTED: Russell, Letters, 1906, p. 208; Keynes, Writings, 1925, iii, 353,
Poetry and Prose, 1939, p. 918, Complete Writings, 1957, 1966, p. 868.

SOURCE OF TEXT: Original MS and photostat.

120. To JOHN LINNELL   30 December 1819

Receipt for Jerusalem Chap. 2, in Blake's hand with signature. On a slip
of paper 11 × 18·5 cm. With a pencil note in the corner "2£ to Father/Paid
by Mr. Varley/lent 1/6".

History as for no. 114.

PRINTED: First printed 1956.

SOURCE OF TEXT: Photostat.

121. To JOHN LINNELL   30 April 1821

Receipt for [Marriage of] Heaven and Hell. In Blake's hand with signature.
On a slip of paper 7·5 × 18·5 cm.

History as for no. 114.

SOURCE: First printed 1956.

SOURCE OF TEXT: Photostat.

122. To JOHN LINNELL   1 March 1822

Receipt for £3 on account. In Blake's hand with signature. On a slip of paper 7 × 18·5 cm.

History as for no. 114.

PRINTED: First printed 1956.

SOURCE OF TEXT: Photostat.

122a. LINNELL'S CASH ACCOUNT BOOK   March 3 1822–Dec. 1836

These entries have been extracted from the Cash Account Book found among the Linnell family papers formerly borrowed by A. H. Palmer and now in the custody of Miss Joan Ivimy. One of them is signed by Blake in pencil (8 May 1822).

PRINTED: Some of these entries were mentioned in my article, "William Blake and John Linnell", *Times Lit. Sup.* June 13 1958. Others are now first printed.

SOURCE OF TEXT: Original MS.

123. MEMORANDUM BETWEEN BLAKE and LINNELL
                                                      25 March 1823

Memorandum concerning the engraving of the set of plates of "Job's Captivity", with receipt for the first payment. In Linnell's hand with signatures of both parties, and the receipt initialled by Blake. On a double leaf 18 × 11 cm. The front of the first leaf endorsed: Blake/Mem. &c, the verso marked "Blake". The memorandum is on the front of the second leaf, and the receipt on the verso.

History as for no. 114.

PRINTED: Story's *Life of Linnell*, 1892, i, 169–70 (very inaccurately); Keynes, *Times Literary Supplement*, 9 January, 1943, in "New Blake–Linnell Documents"; Keynes, *Blake Studies*, 1949, p. 137, with facsimile.

SOURCE OF TEXT: Photostat.

124. ACCOUNTS BETWEEN BLAKE AND LINNELL

March 1823–November 1825

Accounts for various payments for the Book of Job and other works. In Linnell's hand with Blake's initials against each sum. On three loose leaves numbered 1–3 and written on both sides, each 17·5 × 11·5 cm.

History as for no. 114.

PRINTED: First printed 1956.

SOURCE OF TEXT: Photostat.

125. SUBSCRIBERS TO THE BOOK OF JOB   October 1823–1833

Linnell's account book giving the amounts paid by the subscribers to the Book of Job with their names, and at the end an "Account of Expenses". In marbled paper wrappers with label on the front. The verso of the first leaf is written by Blake, the rest of the book is in Linnell's hand. Each leaf measures about 15 × 9 cm.

History as for no. 114.

PRINTED: Keynes, *Times Literary Supplement*, 9 January, 1943, in "New Blake-Linnell Documents", extracts. Also in *Blake Studies*, 1949. First printed in full 1956.

SOURCE OF TEXT: Photostat.

126. To JOHN LINNELL   [1825]

ADDRESSED TO: J. Linnell Esqre, Cirencester Place, Fitzroy Square.

DATED: 12 o'clock Wednesday.

A single leaf, 4°, written on one side.

Formerly in the Linnell collection. Sold at Christie's, 15 March 1918, with twelve others (lot 214, G. D. Smith, 80 gns.). Now in the H. E. Huntington Library, California.

PRINTED: Keynes, *Bibliography*, 1921, p. 455; Keynes, *Writings*, 1925, iii, 367, *Poetry and Prose*, 1939, p. 918, *Complete Writings*, 1957, 1966, p. 869.

SOURCE OF TEXT: Photostat.

127. To JOHN LINNELL   [7 June 1825]

ADDRESSED TO: Mr Linnell, 6 Cirencester Place, Fitzroy Square.

DATED: Tuesday Night.

A single leaf, 8°, written on one side.

History as for no. 126 (lot 209 in the sale).

PRINTED: Story, *Life of Linnell*, 1892, i, 234; Russell, *Letters*, 1906, p. 213; Keynes, *Writings*, 1925, iii, 370, *Poetry and Prose*, 1939, p. 921, *Complete Writings*, 1957, 1966, p. 868.

SOURCE OF TEXT: Photostat.

128. To MRS. LINNELL   11 October, 1825

ADDRESSED TO: Mrs Linnell, Collin's Farm, North End, Hampstead.

DATED: Tuesday, 11 October, 1825.

A double leaf, 4°, written on one side.

History as for no. 126.

PRINTED: Gilchrist, *Life*, 1880, i, 337; Story, *Life of Linnell*, 1892, i, 171; Russell, *Letters*, 1906, p. 209; Keynes, *Writings*, 1925, iii, 367, *Poetry and Prose*, 1939, p. 918, *Complete Writings*, 1957, 1966, p. 869.

SOURCE OF TEXT: Photostat.

129. To JOHN LINNELL   10 November 1825

ADDRESSED TO: John Linnell Esqre, Cirencester Place, Fitzroy Square.

DATED: Thursday Evening, 10 Nov^{r}, 1825, Fountain Court, Strand.

A single leaf, 4°, written on one side.

History as for no. 126.

PRINTED: Gilchrist, *Life*, 1180, i, 378; Story, *Life of Linnell*, 1892, i, 232; Russell, *Letters*, 1906, p. 210; Keynes, *Writings*, 1925, iii, 368, *Poetry and Prose*, 1939, p. 918, *Complete Writings*, 1957, 1966, p. 870.

SOURCE OF TEXT: Photostat.

130. To JOHN LINNELL   1 February 1826

ADDRESSED: To John Linnell Esqre, N 6 Cirencester Place, Fitzroy Square.

DATED: Feby 1, 1826. Postmark dated: 31 January.

A double leaf, 4°, written on two sides. Wmk.: Ruse & Turner 1810.

History as for no. 126 (lot 208 in the sale).

PRINTED: Gilchrist, *Life*, 1880, i, 390; Story, *Life of Linnell*, 1892, i, 232; Russell, *Letters*, 1906, p. 211; Keynes, *Writings*, 1925, iii, 368, *Poetry and Prose*, 1939, p. 919, *Complete Writings*, 1957, 1966, p. 871.

SOURCE OF TEXT: Photostat.

131. To MRS. LINNELL [? February 1826]

ADDRESS missing.

DATED: London, Sunday Morning.

A double leaf, 4°, written on one side. The leaf carrying the address has been torn off.

History as for no. 126.

PRINTED: Keynes. *Bibliography*, 1921, p. 455, *Writings*, 1925, iii, 370, *Poetry and Prose*, 1939, p. 920.

SOURCE OF TEXT: Photostat.

132. To JOHN LINNELL 31 March 1826

ADDRESSED TO: John Linnell Esqre, Cirencester Place.

DATED: Friday Evening, March 31, 1826.

A single leaf, 8°, written on one side.

Given by John Linnell to Mr. Cooper R.A. Feb. 1830. (Linnell papers, copied by A. H. Palmer).

Emma W. Bucknell collection, sold by the American Art Association, New York, 2 April 1928 (lot 73, Gabriel Wells, $390). David M. Newbold Collection, sold by Henkel's, Philadelphia, 9 Oct. 1928 (lot 339, $350). Offered with the estate of Gabriel Wells for $350.00 by Boesen, N.Y., March 1948. Now in the collection of Mrs. Landon K. Thorne.

PRINTED: Keynes, *Poetry and Prose*, 1939, p. 920, *Complete Writings*, 1957, 1966, p. 871.

SOURCE OF TEXT: Photostat.

133. To JOHN LINNELL 19 May 1826

ADDRESSED: To John Linnell Esqre, N 6 Cirencester Place, Fitzroy Square.

DATED: Friday Evening, May 19, 1826.

A single leaf, 4°, written on one side.

History as for no. 126.

PRINTED: Gilchrist, *Life*, 1880, i, 392; Russell, *Letters*, 1906, p. 214; Keynes, *Writings*, 1925, iii, 371, *Poetry and Prose*, 1939, p. 921, *Complete Writings*, 1957, 1966, p. 872.

SOURCE OF TEXT: Photostat.

134. To JOHN LINNELL   2 July 1826

ADDRESSED: To John Linnell Esqre, N 6 Cirencester Place, Fitzroy Square.

Postmark DATED: 2 July 1826. A single leaf, 4°, written on one side.

Formerly in the Linnell collection. Sold at Christie's, 15 March 1918 (lot 210, Dobell, 29 gns.). Now in the possession of Mrs. Edward L. Doheny.

PRINTED: Gilchrist, *Life*, 1880, i, 393; Story, *Life of Linnell*, 1892, i, 235; Russell, *Letters*, 1906, p. 215; Keynes, *Writings*, 1925, iii, 372, *Poetry and Prose*, 1939, p. 922, *Complete Writings*, 1957, 1966, p. 872.

SOURCE OF TEXT: Original MS.

135. To JOHN LINNELL   5 July 1826

ADDRESSED TO: John Linnell Esqre, Cirencester Place.

DATED: 5 July 1826.

A single leaf, 4°, written on one side.

History as for no. 126.

PRINTED: Gilchrist, *Life*, 1880, i, 394; Story, *Life of Linnell*, 1892, i, 236; Russell, *Letters*, 1906, p. 216; Keynes, *Writings*, 1925, iii, 373, *Poetry and Prose*, 1939, p. 922, *Complete Writings*, 1957, 1966, p. 873.

SOURCE OF TEXT: Photostat.

136. To JOHN LINNELL   14 July 1826

ADDRESSED: To Mr John Linnell, Cirencester Place, Fitz Roy Square.

DATED: July 14 1826.

Written on four leaves, 4°.

Formerly among the Linnell papers lent to A. H. Palmer and taken to Vancouver, B.C. Found by his son Bryan Palmer in 1959 and sold to the Pierpont Morgan Library. Printed in 1957 from a copy made by A. H. Palmer.

PRINTED: Keynes, *Complete Writings*, 1957, 1966, p. 873.

136a. To JOHN LINNELL   14 July 1826

Receipt for the copyright and plates of "the Book of Job". In Blake's hand, with signature of witness, Edw$^{d.}$ Jno. Chance. On a slip of paper 7·5 × 18·5 cm.

History as for no. 114.

PRINTED: Keynes, *Times Literary Supplement*, 9 Jan. 1943, in "New Blake–Linnell Documents"; Keynes, *Blake Studies*, 1949, p. 139, with facsimile. (Mentioned, but not printed in full, in Story's *Life of Linnell*, 1892, i, 170.)

SOURCE OF TEXT: Photostat.

137. To JOHN LINNELL   16 July 1826

ADDRESSED: To John Linnell Esqre, Cirencester Place, Fitzroy Square.

DATED: Sunday afternoon, July 16, 1826.

A single leaf, 4°, written on one side.

History as for no. 126.

PRINTED: Gilchrist, *Life*, 1880, i, 394; Story *Life of Linnell* 1892 1, 236; Russell, *Letters*, 1906, p. 217; Keynes, *Writings*, 1925, iii, 373, *Poetry and Prose*, 1939, p. 923, *Complete Writings*, 1957, 1966, p. 874.

SOURCE OF TEXT: Photostat.

138. To JOHN LINNELL   29 July 1826

ADDRESSED TO: Mr Linnell, 6 Cirencester Place, Fitzroy Square.

DATED: 29 July 1826.

A single leaf, 4°, written on one side.

History for as no. 126.

PRINTED: Keynes, *Bibliography*, 1921, p. 456, *Writings*, 1925, iii, 374, *Poetry and Prose*, 1939, p. 923, *Complete Writings*, 1957, 1966, p. 874.

SOURCE OF TEXT: Photostat.

139. To MRS. ADERS   29 July 1826

Receipt for Songs of Innocence [and of Experience], in Blake's hand with signature. On a slip of paper 8 × 18·5 cm.

History as for no. 114.

PRINTED: First printed 1956.

SOURCE OF TEXT: Photostat.

140. To JOHN LINNELL   1 August 1826

ADDRESSED: To Mr Linnell, Cirencester Place, Fitzroy Square.

DATED: Aug^st 1. 1826.

A single leaf, 4°, written on one side.

History as for no. 126.

PRINTED: Gilchrist, *Life*, 1880, i, 395; Story, *Life of Linnell*, 1892, i, 237; Russell, *Letters*, 1906, p. 218; Keynes, *Writings*, 1925, iii, 375, *Poetry and Prose*, 1939, p. 924, *Complete Writings*, 1957, 1966, p. 875.

SOURCE OF TEXT: Photostat.

140a. To MRS. CHARLES ADERS   29 December 1826

DATED: 3 Fountain Court Strand 29 Decr 1826.

A single leaf, 4°, written on one side only.

Formerly in an album formed by Mrs. Aders. Later the property of the Hon. Audrey Pauncefote. Sold at Sotheby's, 16 Dec. 1958 (lot 483, J. Schwartz, £24). Now in the library of the University of Texas.

PRINTED: Keynes, *Complete Writings*, 1966, p. 944.

SOURCE OF TEXT: Photostat.

141. To JOHN LINNELL   27 January 1827

ADDRESSED TO: Mr Linnell, 6 Cirencester Place, Fitzroy Square.

DATED: Saturday Night, Jany 27 1827.

A single leaf, 4°, written on one side.

History as for no. 126.

PRINTED: Keynes, *Bibliography*, 1921, p. 456; Keynes, *Writings*, 1925, iii, 389, *Poetry and Prose*, 1939, p. 924, *Complete Writings*, 1957, 1966, p. 875.

SOURCE OF TEXT: Photostat.

142. To JOHN LINNELL   February 1827

ADDRESSED TO: Mr Linnell, Cirencester Place, Fitzroy Square.

Not dated.

A single leaf, 4°, written on one side.

Formerly in the Linnell collection. Sold at Christie's, 15 March 1918 (lot 211, Swayne, 29 gns.). Resold by the American Art Association, Anderson Galleries, 25 May 1938 (lot 74). Now in the Lessing J. Rosenwald Collection, Library of Congress, Washington, D.C.

PRINTED: Gilchrist, *Life*, 1880, i, 398; Story, *Life of Linnell*, 1892, i, 238; Russell, *Letters*, 1906, p. 218; Keynes, *Writings*, 1925, iii, 389, *Poetry and Prose*, 1939, p. 925, *Complete Writings*, 1957, 1966, p. 876.

SOURCE OF TEXT: Photostat.

143. To JOHN LINNELL   ? February 1827

ADDRESSED TO: J Linnell Esqre.

Not dated. Written on a long slip of paper, which was evidently left by Blake at Linnell's house.

History as for no. 126.

PRINTED: Keynes, *Bibliography*, 1921, p. 457, *Writings*, 1925, iii, 390, *Poetry and Prose*, 1939, p. 925, *Complete Writings*, 1957, 1966, p. 876.

SOURCE OF TEXT: Photostat.

144. To JOHN LINNELL   15 March 1827

ADDRESSED TO: Mr Linnell, Cirencester Place, Fitzroy Square.

DATED: 15 March, 1827.

A single leaf, 4°, written on one side.

Formerly in the Linnell collection. Sold at Christie's, 15 March 1918 (lot 212, Carfax, 30 gns.). Then in the collection of T. H. Riches, and now in the Fitzwilliam Museum, Cambridge.

PRINTED: Gilchrist, *Life*, 1880, i, 398; Russell, *Letters*, 1906, p. 220; Keynes,

Writings, 1925, iii, 390, *Poetry and Prose*, 1939, p. 925, *Complete Writings*, 1957, 1966, p. 876.

SOURCE OF TEXT: Original MS.

145. To MARIA DENMAN   14 March 1827

ADDRESSED: To Miss Denman, Buckingham Street, Fitzroy Square.

DATED: Wednesday Morning, 18 [14] March 1827 3 Fountain Court Strand. A single leaf, 4°, 21·5 × 16·5 cm.

Sold at Henckel's Auction Rooms, New York, in 1912 (lot 554, $30.00). Afterwards in the possession of Mr. W. T. Spencer, London, until about 1930. Now in the New York Public Library, Berg Collection.

PRINTED: Wright's *Life of Blake*, 1929, ii, 114 (correctly dated 14 March, 1827), *Complete Writings*, 1957, 1966, p. 877.

SOURCE OF TEXT: Photostat.

146. To JOHN LINNELL   [1827]

ADDRESSED TO: John Linnell Esqre, Cirencester Place, Fitzroy Square. Not dated. A single leaf, 8°.

Formerly in the collection of W. A. White, New York, and had been inserted in copy Q of the *Songs of Innocence*. Now at Yale University.

PRINTED: Grolier Club Catalogue, 1905, p. 138; Russell, *Letters*, 1906, p. 221; Keynes, *Writings*, 1925, iii, 391, *Poetry and Prose*, 1939, p. 926, *Complete Writings*, 1957, 1966, p. 877.

SOURCE OF TEXT: Photostat.

147. To GEORGE CUMBERLAND   12 April 1827

ADDRESSED TO: George Cumberland Esqre, Culver Street, Bristol.

DATED: 12 April 1827, N 3 Fountain Court Strand.

A double leaf, 4°, written on two sides. On the recto of the second leaf are notes by Cumberland on Blake's death and burial and his card plate, a print from which is pasted on below.

Formerly in the Fairfax Murray collection, sold at Sotheby's, 5 Feb. 1920 (lot 21). Afterwards in the possession of Messrs. Maggs, and offered by them in several catalogues. Now in the Fitzwilliam Museum, Cambridge (purchased 1936).

PRINTED: Ellis and Yeats, *Works*, 1893, i, 162; Ellis, *The Real Blake*, 1906, p. 433; Russell, *Letters*, 1906, p. 221; Keynes, *Writings*, 1925, iii, 392, *Poetry and Prose*, 1939, p. 926. First printed accurately and in full, 1956. *Complete Writings*, 1957, 1966, p. 878; Erdman, *Poetry and Prose*, 1965, p. 707.

SOURCE OF TEXT: Original MS.

148. To JOHN LINNELL   25 April 1827

ADDRESSED TO: Mr Linnell, 6 Cirencester Place, Fitzroy Square.

DATED: 25 April 1827.

A single leaf, 4°, written on one side.

History as for no. 126 (lot 213 in the sale).

PRINTED: Gilchrist, *Life*, 1880, i, 400; Story, *Life of Linnell*, 1892, i, 239; Russell, *Letters*, 1906, p. 224; Keynes, *Writings*, 1925, iii, 393, *Poetry and Prose*, 1939, p. 928, *Complete Writings*, 1957, 1966, p. 879.

SOURCE OF TEXT: Photostat.

149. To JOHN LINNELL   3 July 1827

ADDRESSED TO: Mr Linnell, 6 Cirencester Place, Fitzroy Square.

DATED: 3 July 1827.

A single leaf, 8°, written on one side.

History as for no. 126.

PRINTED: Gilchrist, *Life*, 1880, i, 403; Story, *Life of Linnell*, 1892, i, 240; Russell, *Letters*, 1906, p. 225; Keynes, *Writings*, 1925, iii, 394, *Poetry and Prose*, 1939, p. 928, *Complete Writings*, 1957, 1966, p. 880.

SOURCE OF TEXT: Photostat.

150. MRS BLAKE to JOHN LINNELL   18 May 1829

DATED: May 18th 1829.

Receipt for Homer from Mrs. Blake. In Frederick Tatham's hand with his signature. On a slip of paper 8·5 × 18 cm.

History as for no. 114.

PRINTED: First printed 1956.

SOURCE OF TEXT: Photostat.

151. GEORGE RICHMOND to SAMUEL PALMER   15 August 1827

DATED: Wednesday Even ᵍ, i.e. three days after Blake's death, which took place on Sunday, 12 August 1827.

Formerly in the possession of A. H. Palmer and exhibited at the Palmer Exhibition, Victoria and Albert Museum, 1926 (no. 11 in the catalogue). Sold with the Palmer Collection at Christie's, 20 Feb. 1928 (lot 34, Stevens and Brown, 18 gns.). Afterwards in the possession of Sessler of Philadelphia.

PRINTED: Gilchrist, *Life*, 1880, i, 406; Palmer Exhibition Catalogue, 1926, p. 22.

SOURCE OF TEXT: Photostat.

INDEX